Introduction to UNIVERSITY COMMUNITY

SC STATE UNIVERSITY
1896

Kendall Hunt
publishing company

Cover images © South Carolina State University

www.kendallhunt.com
Send all inquiries to:
4050 Westmark Drive
Dubuque, IA 52004-1840

Copyright © 2015 by Kendall Hunt Publishing Company

ISBN 978-1-4652-7832-6

Printed in the United States of America

Brief Contents

Contents

Chapter 6: Learning Style and Intelligence
83

Chapter 7: Taking Notes, Writing and Speaking
113

Chapter 8: Fiscal Literacy
Managing Money and Minimizing Debt   143

SC State University History

CAMPUS

South Carolina State University, located in the city of Orangeburg, which is 40 miles east of the state capital at Columbia, is only a five minute walk from the heart of the city.

The University owns 160 acres of land. An additional 286 acres are located at Camp Harry E. Daniels in Elloree, South Carolina. This property, however, is not included in the total amount of land owned by South Carolina State University.

HISTORY

The Constitutional Convention of 1895 enacted provisions authorizing the South Carolina Legislature to create the College by a severance of the state's interest from Claflin College. In pursuance of such authorization, the General Assembly in 1896 enacted statutes providing for the establishment of a normal, industrial, agricultural and mechanical college. The same Legislature provided for the appointment of a Board of Trustees, an administration, a faculty, and for the adoption of rules and regulations to govern the operation of the College.

Pursuant to this organization, a faculty composed of 13 South Carolinians was chosen by Dr. Thomas E. Miller, a former Congressman from South Carolina, who had been appointed as the first President of the College; and on March 4, 1896, the doors of the institution were opened as a land-grant college. The College plant consisted of 135 acres, eight small buildings, a small dairy herd, and a few farm animals. Because of the meager facilities, academic instruction was mostly given on logs hewn from the campus wilderness, in the tradition of the Mark Hopkins ideal college. These logs were later made into lumber for the first dormitory and classroom buildings.

In 1911 Robert Shaw Wilkinson, a native of Charleston and a former Professor of Physics at the College, was elected President. Under his administration, the income of the College was increased from both federal and state sources, and a federal appropriation for extension work was added.

After 21 years of sincere service, Dr. Wilkinson passed; and on March 15, 1932, the presidency of the College was undertaken by Miller F. Whittaker, who at that time was Director of the Mechanical Department. Some of the outstanding activities that marked President Whittaker's administration were the establishment of a Law School, Extension School units in 15 South Carolina communities, and a Reserve Officers' Training Corps Infantry Unit.

Reprinted by permission of South Caroline State University.

President Whittaker gave 18 years of dynamic service to the College, and in 1949 he died with a firm faith that: "The College is serving the people of this state as never before. The worth of the institution is best expressed in the community relationship, which it maintains, and the improvement of rural and civic life, which it promotes through its graduates, its faculty, and its extension agencies. The College has exhibited its economic, civic, and social worth to the Commonwealth of South Carolina."

In 1950 Benner C. Turner, Dean of the School of Law, was elected President of the College. He retired in 1967 after 17 years of service.

Under President Turner's administration, the College's growth was tremendous, both in academic activities as well as in physical and human resources. Outstanding changes included the rapid growth of both undergraduate and graduate enrollments; increases in the number of faculty and staff; increases in the number holding doctoral degrees, the reorganization of the administrative and instructional areas of the College; major improvements in the physical plant which included the renovation of buildings and the construction of many new buildings, among which were a new academic building, dormitories for both men and women, a cafeteria, walkways, drives, roads and attractive landscaping. All added to the comfort and beauty of the campus.

The legal and official name of the institution was changed to South Carolina State College, by the act of the General Assembly of 1954.

Upon the retirement of Dr. Turner, the Board of Trustees appointed Dr. M. Maceo Nance, Jr., Vice President of Business and Finance, as Acting President of the College to serve until a successor to the former president could be chosen. The appointment became effective June 24, 1967. Dr. Nance was elected President by the Board on June 23, 1968, and was inaugurated November 27, 1968. Under President Nance's administration, the College experienced unprecedented growth in academics, students, faculty, staff and physical facilities. Twenty degree programs were established including the doctorate in Educational Administration. The majority of the qualified faculty held doctoral degrees. Many academic programs received professional accreditation, while the College maintained its regional accreditation. Scholarship programs and faculty chairs were enhanced and initiated to promote the pursuit of knowledge. In keeping with the land-grant mission of the College, the 1890 Research and Extension program (United States Department of Agriculture), through its services and research, assisted in improving the quality of life for the citizens of South Carolina. In recognition of the need for additional school-community interaction, an Adult and Continuing Education unit and a comprehensive college- community relations program were established and promoted. National and international awards were bestowed on many academic programs and extracurricular activities. Dr. M. Maceo Nance, Jr., retired June 30, 1986 after serving as President for 19 years.

The Board of Trustees appointed Dr. Albert E. Smith, the sixth President of South Carolina State College, effective July 1, 1986. Dr. Smith, with a theme of "New Directions," immediately advanced a set of institutional goals which included the development of a strategic plan, renewed emphasis on academics, and the improvement of student life, the strengthening of enrollment, fiscal management efficiency and improved relations with all college constituencies.

In five-and-one-half years, the Smith administration increased student enrollment to more than 5,000; established an Office of Research and Grants Administration which resulted in a dramatic increase in research-related funding; initiated a division of Development and Institutional Relations which stimulated significant growth in alumni support; implemented a computerized integrated online system in the library; instituted a new Honors Program and Student Exchange Program; brought on board a Master of Arts degree in teaching and expanded the post RN completion program for beginning students; created a School of Freshman Studies; initiated plans for the funding and construction of a Fine Arts Center, a new dormitory on campus, and a Convention Center at Camp Harry E. Daniels; secured initial accreditation and reaccreditation for all programs submitted to accrediting agencies between August 1986 and January 1992. One of the most profound changes of the Smith administration was the development of plans and strategy, which resulted in the Institution's name designation being changed from College to University in 1992. Dr. Smith served as President of South Carolina State University from July 1, 1986, to January 5. 1992.

On January 6, 1992, the Board of Trustees named Dr. Carl A. Carpenter, a professor in the School of Education and former Vice President for Academic Affairs, as Interim President. Dr. Carpenter served in this capacity until a new president was named in September 1992.

On September 30, 1992, the Board of Trustees elected Dr. Barbara R. Hatton as the first woman to assume the presidency of South Carolina State University. Beginning her duties on January 4, 1993, Dr. Hatton was inaugurated seventh President of the University on November 13, 1993. As a result of her vision and leadership, significant steps were taken to move the institution toward becoming the inclusive university of the twenty-first century. Among the steps were: restructuring to reduce the number of administrative positions and increase the number of faculty positions; aligning and renaming academic departments and schools; achieving full accreditation status for programs in music, nursing, social work, speech pathology and audiology in addition to reaccreditation of teacher education programs; initiating legislation which allowed engineering technology graduates to sit for the engineering licensure examination in South Carolina, and opening an Office of State and Community Relations in Columbia. Capital improvement projects included the Oliver C. Dawson Bulldog Stadium, the Student Center Plaza and acquisition of the Dawn Center.

On June 13, 1995, the Board of Trustees named Dr. Leroy Davis, Vice President for Student Services, as interim President. Immediately following his appointment, Dr. Davis initiated a number of changes which resulted in significantly improved constituent support and confidence in the University's management of its resources. These changes included new management policies and procedures, increased faculty hiring, and increased faculty participation in University governance. On April 10, 1996, after a national search, the Board of Trustees elected Dr. Leroy Davis as the eighth President of South Carolina State University. Prior to serving as Interim President and being elected President, Dr. Davis served the University in several capacities including Professor of Biology, Vice Provost for Academic Administration, and Vice President for Student Services. After his appointment to the presidency, Dr. Davis initiated plans to establish Centers of Excellence in each of the five academic schools; increased scholarship support to recruit more academically talented freshmen, designated tuition and fee revenues for program accreditation, improvement of information technology services, faculty salary equity increases, and increased student activities support: implemented a new tenure and promotion policy; established the first University Staff Senate; increased University partnerships and collaborations; and implemented new community service programs in the areas of healthcare and economic development and construction of a Fine Arts Building; restructured academic and administrative support programs; reaffirmed the accreditation of several academic programs; reorganized the President's Cabinet and established the University Council and the President's Advisory Board. Dr. Davis retired from the University on June 30, 2002 after serving as president for six years.

On July 1, 2002, following the retirement of Dr. Davis, the Board of Trustees appointed Ernest A. Finney, Jr., former South Carolina Supreme Court Justice, as Interim President of the University to serve until a successor to the former president could be chosen. During his tenure, the only undergraduate Nuclear Engineering program at an HBCU was developed in conjunction with the University of Wisconsin. The University received funding in the amount of $9 million to construct a state of-the-art transportation research facility and became the lead institution to provide statewide coordination for the South Carolina Alliance for Minority Participation (SCAMP), as well as a $5 million grant to increase the number of minority students participating in mathematics, science, engineering and technology.

On May 16, 2003, the Board of Trustees named Dr. Andrew Hugine, Jr., the ninth President of South Carolina State University. President Hugine developed an Alumni Heritage Endowment, a perpetual fund for scholarships, capital improvements, and endowed chairs. Faculty, Staff, and Student Cabinets were established. The front entrance to the campus was renovated and upgraded; a security booth was constructed; and a new, enormous Bulldog mascot was unveiled to adorn the front entrance. Major renovations and improvements were made to selected dormitories, academic buildings, and the Smith-Hammond-Middleton Memorial Center.

Under President Hugine's leadership, an agreement with the University of South Carolina launched a faculty/student exchange program in nuclear engineering; the University Transportation Center was named the James E. Clyburn Transportation Center, and the Walnut Room was named the Robert S. Evans Walnut Room. In addition, the Real Estate Foundation 501(c) 3, the Research and Development Foundation and the Advancement Foundation were established. Also, the 1890 Extension Office Complex was completed. The Student Success and Retention Programs were developed, and the five undergraduate schools within Academic Affairs were reorganized and elevated into three colleges.

Other university accomplishments during Dr. Hugine's presidency include: the Computer Science program received its initial accreditation by the Computing Accreditation Commission of ABET, and a Master of Business Administration degree with concentrations in Agribusiness and Entrepreneurship was approved. The 1890 Research and Extension Division purchased a mobile technology unit and the University Board of Visitors was established. Additionally, the nursing program received accreditation from the Commission for Collegiate Nursing Education.

In 2005, the University began work on a $42 million apartment-style residence hall. The new 772-bed living facility (Hugine Suites) was the largest construction project in the history of the University. The University completed multi-million dollar renovations to the Pitt and Washington Dining Hall facilities; alumni giving reached a record $1 million; the Master's in Transportation degree program was established; and the Thomas E. Miller Society was established to recognize $100,000 lifetime givers.

In addition, through the United States Agency for International Development (USAID) Africa initiative, SC State partnered with the country of Tanzania to provide textbooks and other learning materials to the students in Africa. The University also was ranked by *Washington Monthly* magazine, as number nine as a national university and number one in the area of social mobility. In 2007, South Carolina State hosted the first debate of the 2008 Presidential cycle on Thursday, April 26.

It was produced by NBC News and hosted by SC State. MSNBC's signature political program, "Hardball with Chris Matthews," aired live from South Carolina State University.

On December 13, 2007, Dr. Leonard A. McIntyre was named Interim President. During his tenure, Interim President McIntyre and a delegation from the University delivered the first set of textbooks (165,000) to the students of Zanzibar. In addition, His Excellency Amani Karume, President of Zanzibar served as the Commencement speaker in spring 2008. South Carolina State University and Francis Marion University announced the launch of the new I-95 Corridor Initiative seeking innovative ways to address long-running development challenges in eastern South Carolina. Renovations also began on Lowman Hall.

On June 6, 2008, the Board of Trustees named Dr. George E. Cooper the 10th President of South Carolina State University. Under his leadership, Orangeburg-Calhoun Technical College and South Carolina State University signed an agreement creating "The Gateway Program" between the two-year college and the four-year university. In addition, the Dr. Clemmie Embly Webber Educational Resource Center was named and dedicated at the I.P. Stanback Museum and Planetarium. Construction began on the Hodge Hall Annex. Other notable achievements include capturing the 2008 MEAC championship and a berth in the prestigious Football Championship Subdivision (FCS) playoff, and the 2009 world premiere of the documentary, "Scarred Justice: The Orangeburg Massacre 1968." Outstanding collections acquired and exhibited at the University included: The Miller F. Whittaker Library named and dedicated The Cecil Williams Collection: "A Visual Chronicle of African American History," and the I.P. Stanback Museum and Planetarium exhibited "James Brown: Preserving the Legacy" collection.

In 2010 Coach Willie E. Jeffries was given the designation Head Football Coach Emeritus; and the Willie E. Jeffries Field was named at the Oliver C. Dawson Bulldog Stadium. The University was reaccredited by the Southern Association of Colleges and Schools (SACS) through 2020. The Leroy Davis, Sr. Hall, which houses the Department of Physical Sciences, was dedicated.

Dr. Rita Jackson Teal assumed the responsibilities as Acting President on March 31, 2012.

On July 5, 2012, Dr. Cynthia A. Warrick was appointed Interim President. In 2013, the Dedication and Open House for the Engineering and Computer Science Complex was held; the University was named one of the newest associate members of Oak Ridge Associated Universities (ORAU) university consortium; the University's College of Education, Humanities and Social Sciences received continuing accreditation from the Council for the Accreditation of Educator Preparation (CAEP).; and the SC State tennis teams captured the 2013 Mid-Eastern Athletic Conference Men's and Women's Tennis Championship titles.

Dr. W. Franklin Evans assumed the responsibilities as Acting President on June 1, 2013.

On April 18, 2013, the Board of Trustees named Thomas J. Elzey President of South Carolina State University. On June 15th, he assumed the responsibilities as the eleventh president. Under the guidance of President Elzey, two new Master of Science Degree Programs, Energy and Environmental Science and Bio-Engineering Sciences, were developed and subsequently approved by the South Carolina Commission on Higher Education (SCCHE). Other accomplishments include: the restoration of the clock tower at Miller F. Whittaker Library; the development of a new organizational structure, which more effectively manages the academic, fiscal and operational divisions of the university; improvement of campus grounds; and increased giving of scholarship funds from the University Foundation, alumni and individual supporters.

PRESIDENTS OF THE INSTITUTION

Thomas E. Miller, B.A., M.A., LL.D.	1896-1911
Robert Shaw Wilkinson, B.A., M.A., Ph.D.	1911-1932
Miller F. Whittaker, B.S., M.S., LL.D.	1932-1949
Benner C. Turner, B.A., LL.B., LL.D.	1950-1967
M. Maceo Nance, Jr., A.B., M.A., LL.D., L.H.D.	1968-1986
Albert E. Smith, B.S., M.S., Ph.D.	1986-1992
Barbara R. Hatton, B.S., M.A., M.E.A., Ph.D.	1993-1995
Leroy Davis, Sr., B.S., M.S., Ph.D.	1996-2002
Andrew Hugine, Jr., B.S. M.Ed., PhD.	2003-2007
George E. Cooper, B.S., M.S., Ph.D.	2008-2012
Thomas J. Elzey, B.S., M.S., P.M.P.	2013-2015

MISSION STATEMENT

South Carolina State University is a historically Black public 1890 land-grant senior comprehensive institution of approximately 4,500-6,000 students. Located in Orangeburg, South Carolina, SC State is committed to providing affordable and accessible quality baccalaureate programs in the areas of business, applied professional sciences, mathematics, natural sciences, engineering, engineering technology, education, arts, and humanities. A number of programs are offered at the master's level in teaching, human services and agribusiness, and the educational specialist and doctorate programs are offered in educational administration.

SC State University prepares highly skilled, competent and socially aware graduates to enable them to work and live productively in a dynamic, global society. Through technology and traditional methods of teaching and learning, research and service, the University enhances the quality of life of citizens and contributes to the economic development of the state and nation.

(This mission statement was approved by the SC State University Board of Trustees on March 30, 2010).

ADMINISTRATIVE ORGANIZATION

The authority and responsibility for the governance of South Carolina State University is vested in the Board of Trustees. The Board of Trustees, directly or through its authorized committees, establishes general policies of the University and formulates its broad program of educational activities. The Board elects the president of the University to whom it delegates full authority and responsibility for the detailed administration of the institution.

The faculty, subject to the review by the President and Board of Trustees, has legislative powers in all matters pertaining to the standards of admissions, registration, requirements for and the granting of degrees earned in courses, the curriculum, instruction, research, extracurricular activities, the educational policies and the standards of the University, and all other matters pertaining to the conduct of faculty affairs, including the discipline of its own member

The Orangeburg Massacre

2

On the night of February 8, 1968, nine (9) South Carolina Highway Patrolmen fired shotguns into a crowd of black students demonstrating on the front of the campus of South Carolina State College. Three students were killed, and twenty-eight were injured. Virtually all of the students hit by shotgun pellets were hit in the back. The shootings were the culmination of lengthy protests against the vestiges of segregation and racial discrimination in Orangeburg, especially the "white only" policy of the All-Star Bowling Lanes.

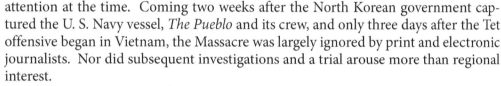

This tragedy that became known locally and across South Carolina as the Orangeburg Massacre received little national attention at the time. Coming two weeks after the North Korean government captured the U. S. Navy vessel, *The Pueblo* and its crew, and only three days after the Tet offensive began in Vietnam, the Massacre was largely ignored by print and electronic journalists. Nor did subsequent investigations and a trial arouse more than regional interest.

The traumatic events of 1968—President Lyndon Johnson's abdication, Dr. Martin Luther King's assassination, Robert F. Kennedy's murder, the tumultuous Democratic National Convention in Chicago, and Richard Nixon's political resurrection in the November election—largely relegated the events in Orangeburg to obscurity. Only the publication of *the Orangeburg Massacre* by Jack Bass and Jack Nelson helped to keep the story alive. But FBI Director J. Edgar Hoover managed, with some success, to suppress circulation of the book because he believed it was too critical of his agency.

In the past four decades, historians have—with few exceptions—ignored Orangeburg while rarely failing to devote attention to the student uprisings at Berkeley and Columbia in 1968 and the killings at Kent State and Jackson State in May 1970. The events in South Carolina do not fit neatly into the antiwar protests of the late sixties nor do they find a place in the bloody confrontations over civil rights that occurred in Alabama and Mississippi earlier in the decade. But those events do fit into a tradition of student activism on the campuses of South Carolina State and Claflin, and in the Orangeburg black community.

A dozen years before the Massacre, students at S.C. State went on strike, refusing to attend classes, in protest against

Reprinted by permission of William C. Hine.

both the actions of the White Citizens Council in Orangeburg and the authoritarian policies of the college president, Benner C. Turner. In February 1960, just days after the sit-ins began at the Woolworth store in Greensboro, North Carolina, South Carolina State and Claflin students were launching their own sit-in at the local Kress lunch counter.

On March 15, 1960, students peacefully marched to challenge segregation in Orangeburg only to be met by law enforcement officers and then fire hoses. Nearly 400 were arrested. Nonviolent protests and demonstrations continued through the early 1960s. in 1967 students went on strike in "the Cause," staying out of class in opposition to the autocratic policies of long-time college President Benner C. Turner. Turner subsequently retired.

Therefore the events on February 8th can be meaningfully comprehended only as part of the larger and longer tradition of student activism on the Claflin and South Carolina State campuses.

For decades after the Massacre, the black and white communities in Orangeburg remained deeply divided over the meaning and memory of what happened on February 8, 1968. For many people in Orangeburg, the Massacre was a divisive issue and a source of persistent racial animosity.

Then in 1999 on the eve of the 31st anniversary of the Massacre, more than 250 black and white residents of the Orangeburg community called for racial reconciliation in a plea published in the *Times and Democrat* on February 7. "Orangeburg Let us Heal Ourselves…" that call has had a dramatic and positive impact. In 2001 Gov. Jim Hodges expressed deep regret on behalf of the state at that year's ceremony. Then Gov. Mark Sanford issued an apology in 2003.

While racial divisions have not been eliminated, they have been significantly reduced. The Orangeburg of 2008 is a far more harmonious community than the Orangeburg of 1968.

For that we can be grateful.

Wounded on the campus of SC State University on February 8, 1968

Herman Boller	Albert Dawson	Nathaniel Jenkins	Ernest Schuler
Johnny Bookhart	Bobby Eaddy	Thomas Kennerly	Jordan Simmons, III
Thompson Braddy	Herbert Gadson	Joseph Lambright	Ronald Smith
Bobby K. Burton	Sam Grant	Richard McPherson	Frankie Thomas
Ernest Carson	Sam Grate	Harvey Lee Miller	Robert Watson
John H. Elliott	Joseph Hampton	Harold Riley	Robert Lee Williams
Robert Lee Davis	Charles Hildebrand	Cleveland Sellers	Savannah Williams

The Student Nonviolent Coordinating Committee
Statement of Purpose (1960)

We affirm the philosophical or religious ideal of nonviolence as the foundation of our purpose, the presupposition of our faith, and the manner of our action. Nonviolence as it grows from Judaeo-Christian tradition seeks a social order of justice permeated by love. Integration of human endeavor represents the crucial first step toward such a society.

Through nonviolence, courage displaces fear; love transforms hate. Acceptance dissipates prejudice; hope ends despair. Peace dominates war; faith reconciles doubt. Mutual regard cancels enmity. Justice for all over throws injustice. The redemptive community supersedes systems of gross social immorality.

Love is the central motif of nonviolence. Love is the force by which God binds man to Himself and man to man. Such love goes to the extreme; it remains loving and forgiving even in the midst of hostility. It matches the capacity of evil to inflict suffering with an even more enduring capacity to absorb evil, all the while persisting in love.

By appealing to conscience and standing on the moral nature of human existence, nonviolence nurtures the atmosphere in which reconciliation and justice become actual possibilities.

Touching All the Bases

Using Powerful Student Success Principles and Key Campus Resources

3

ACTIVATE YOUR THINKING | *Reflection* **3.1** | **LEARNING GOAL**

1. How do you think college will be different from high school?

2. What do you think it will take to be successful in college? (What personal characteristics, qualities, or strategies do you feel are most important for college success?)

> **LEARNING GOAL**
>
> To equip you with a set of powerful success strategies that you can use immediately to get off to a fast start in college and that you can use continually throughout your college experience to achieve success.

The Most Powerful Research-Based Principles of College Success

Research on human learning and student development indicates four powerful principles of college success:

1. Active involvement
2. Use of campus resources
3. Interpersonal interaction and collaboration
4. Personal reflection and self-awareness (Astin, 1993; Kuh et al., 2005; Light, 2001; Pascarella & Terenzini, 1991, 2005; Tinto, 1993).

The four principles of success can be remembered by visualizing them as the four bases of a baseball diamond—as depicted in Figure 3.1.

FIGURE 3.1

The Diamond of College Success

Touching the First Base of College Success: Active Involvement

The bottom line is this: To maximize your success in college, you cannot be a passive spectator; you need to be an active player.

The principle of active involvement includes the following key components:

- The amount of personal time devoted to learning in college.
- The degree of personal effort or energy (mental and physical) put into the learning process.

Think of something you do with intensity, passion, and commitment. If you were to approach academic work in the same way, you would be faithfully implementing the principle of active involvement.

One way to ensure that you're actively involved in the learning process and putting forth high levels of energy or effort is to take action on what you're learning. You can engage in any of the following actions to ensure that you are investing a high level of effort and energy:

- **Writing.** Write in response to what you're trying to learn.
  Example: Write notes when reading rather than passively underlining sentences.
- **Speaking.** Say aloud what you're trying to learn.
  Example: Explain course concepts to a study-group partner rather than studying them silently.
- **Organizing.** Connect or integrate the ideas you're trying to learn.
  Example: Create an outline, diagram, or concept map to visually connect ideas, as illustrated in Figure 3.1.

The following section explains how you can apply both key components of active involvement—spending time and expending energy—to the major learning challenges that you will encounter in college.

Time Spent in Class

The total amount of time you spend on learning is associated with how much you learn and how successfully you learn. This association leads to a straightforward recommendation: Attend all class sessions in all your courses. It may be tempting to skip or cut classes because college professors are less likely to monitor your attendance or take roll than your high school teachers. However, don't let this new freedom fool you into thinking that missing classes has no impact on your college grades. Over the past 75 years, many research studies in many types of courses have shown a direct relationship between class attendance and course grades—as one goes up or down, so does the other (Anderson & Gates, 2002; Credé, Roch, & Kieszczynka, 2010; Grandpre, 2000; Kowalewski, Holstein, & Schneider, 1989; Launius, 1997; Shimoff & Catania, 2001). Figure 3.2 represents the results of a study conducted at the City Colleges of Chicago, which shows the relationship between students' class attendance during the first five weeks of the term and their final course grades.

FIGURE 3.2

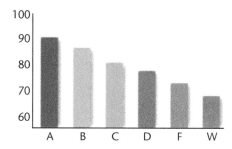

Relationship between Class Attendance Rate and Course Final Grades

Time Spent on Coursework outside the Classroom

In college, you will spend fewer hours per week sitting in class than you did in high school; however, you'll be expected to spend more of your own time on academic work outside of class. Studies clearly show that when college students spend more time on academic work outside of class, they learn more and earn higher grades (National Survey of Student Engagement, 2009).

Reflection 3.2

During your senior year of high school, how many hours per week did you spend on schoolwork outside of class?

Active Listening and Note Taking

You'll find that college professors rely heavily on the lecture method—they profess their knowledge by speaking for long stretches of time, and the students' job is to listen and take notes on the knowledge they dispense. This method of instruction places great demands on your ability to listen carefully and take notes that are both accurate and complete.

The best way to apply the principle of active involvement during a class lecture is to engage in the physical action of writing notes. Writing down what your instructor is saying in class "forces" you to pay closer attention to what is being said and reinforces your retention of what was said. By taking notes, you not only hear the information (auditory memory), you also see it on paper (visual memory) and feel it in the muscles of your hand as you write it (motor memory).

Remember

Your role in the college classroom is not to be a passive spectator or an absorbent sponge that sits back and simply soaks up information through osmosis. Instead, your role is more like that of an aggressive detective or investigative reporter who's on a search-and-record mission. You need to actively search for information by picking your instructor's brain, picking out your instructor's key points, and recording your "pickings" in your notebook.

See Do It Now! 3.1 for top strategies on classroom listening and note taking that you can put into action right now.

Finish class with a rush of attention, not a rush out the door!

3.1

Listening and Note-Taking Strategies

One task that you'll be expected to perform at the start of your first term in college is taking notes in class. Studies show that professors' lecture notes are the number one source of test questions (and test answers) on college exams. Get off to a fast start by using the following strategies to improve the quality of your note taking:

1. **Get to every class.** Whether or not your instructors take roll, you're responsible for all material covered in class. Remember that a full load of college courses (15 units) only requires that you be in class about 13 hours per week. If you consider your class work to be a full-time job, any job that requires you to show up for about 13 hours a week is a pretty sweet deal. It's a deal that supplies you with much more educational freedom than you had in high school. To miss a class session in college when you're required to spend so little time in class per week is an abuse of this educational freedom. It's also an abuse of the money you, your family, or taxpaying American citizens pay to support your college education.

2. **Get to every class on time.** During the first few minutes of a class session, instructors often share valuable information, such as reminders, reviews, and previews.

3. **Get organized.** Bring the right equipment to class. Get a separate notebook for each class, write your name on it, date each class session, and store all class handouts in it.

4. **Get in the right position.**
   - The ideal place to sit is in the front and center of the room, where you're in the best position to hear and see what's going on.
   - The ideal posture is upright and leaning forward, because your body influences your mind. If your body is in an alert and ready position, your mind is likely to follow.
   - The ideal social position is to be near people who will not distract you or detract from the quality of your note taking.

5. **Get in the right frame of mind.** Get psyched up; come to class with attitude—an attitude that you're going to pick your instructor's brain, pick up answers to test questions, and build up your course grade.

6. **Get it down (in writing).** Actively look, listen, and record important points at all times in class. Pay special attention to whatever information instructors put in writing, whether it is on the board, on a slide, or in a handout.

7. **Don't let go of your pen.** When in doubt, write it out; it's better to have it and not need it than to need it and not have it.

> **Remember**
> Most college professors do not write all important information on the board for you; instead, they expect you to listen carefully to what they're saying and write it down for yourself.

8. **Finish strong.** During the last few minutes of class, instructors often share valuable information, such as reminders, reviews, and previews.

9. **Stick around.** When class ends, don't immediately bolt; instead, hang out for a few moments and quickly review your notes (by yourself or with a classmate). If you find any gaps, check them out with your instructor before the instructor leaves the classroom. This quick end-of-class review will help your brain retain the information it just received.

Note: For more detailed information on listening and note taking, see Chapter 5.

Active Class Participation

> **Remember**
> Research shows that, in all subject areas, most test questions on college exams come from the professor's lectures, and that students who take better class notes get better course grades.

You can become actively involved in the college classroom by arriving at class prepared (e.g., having done the assigned reading), by asking relevant questions, and by contributing thoughtful comments during class discussions. When you communicate orally, you elevate your level of active involvement in the learning process because speaking requires you to exert both mental energy (thinking about what you are going to say) and physical energy (moving your lips to say it). Thus, class participation will increase your ability to stay alert and attentive in class. It also sends a clear message to the instructor that you are a motivated student who takes the course seriously and wants to learn. Since class participation accounts for a portion of your final grade in many courses, your attentiveness and involvement in class can have a direct, positive effect on your final grade.

Reflection **3.3**

When you enter a classroom, where do you usually sit?

Why do you sit there? Is it a conscious choice or more like an automatic habit?

Do you think that your usual seat places you in the best possible position for listening and learning in the classroom?

Active Reading

Writing not only promotes active listening in class but also can promote active reading out of class. Taking notes on information that you're reading (or on information you've highlighted while reading) keeps you actively involved in the reading process because it requires more mental and physical energy than merely reading the material or passively highlighting sentences. (See Do It Now! 3.2 for top tips on reading college textbooks that you can put into practice immediately.)

3.2   DO IT **NOW**

Top Strategies: Improving Textbook Reading Comprehension and Retention

If you haven't already acquired textbooks for your courses, get them immediately and get ahead on your reading assignments. Information from reading assignments ranks right behind lecture notes as a source of test questions on college exams. Your professors are likely to deliver class lectures with the expectation that you have done the assigned reading and can build on that knowledge when they're lecturing. If you haven't done the reading, you'll have more difficulty following and taking notes on what your instructor is saying in class. Thus, by not doing the reading you pay a double penalty: You miss information that will appear directly on course exams, and you miss information delivered by your instructor in class because you don't have the background knowledge to make sense of it. College professors also expect you to

relate or connect what they talk about in class to the reading they have assigned. Thus, it's important to start developing good reading habits now. You can do so by using the following strategies to improve your reading comprehension and retention.

Student *Perspective*

"I recommend that you read the first chapters right away because college professors get started promptly with assigning certain readings. Classes in college move very fast because, unlike high school, you do not attend class five times a week but two or three times a week."

—Advice to new college students from a first-year student

(continued)

1. **Read with the right equipment.**
   - Bring tools to record and store information. Always bring a writing tool (pen, pencil or paper) to record important information and a storage space (notebook or computer) in which you can save and retrieve information acquired from your reading for later use on tests and assignments.
   - Have a dictionary nearby to quickly find the meaning of unfamiliar words that may interfere with your ability to comprehend what you're reading. Looking up definitions of unfamiliar words does more than help you understand what you're reading: it's also an effective way to build your vocabulary. A strong vocabulary will improve your reading comprehension in all college courses, as well as your performance on standardized tests, such as those required for admission to graduate and professional schools.
   - Check the back of your textbook for a glossary of terms which lists key terms included in the book. Each academic subject or discipline has its own vocabulary, and knowing the meaning of these terms is often the key to understanding the concepts covered in the text. Don't ignore the glossary; it's more than an ancillary or afterthought to the textbook. Use it regularly to increase your comprehension of course concepts. Consider making a photocopy of the glossary of terms at the back of your textbook so that you can have a copy of it in front of you while you're reading, rather than having to repeatedly stop, hold your place, and go to the back of the text to find the glossary.

2. **Get in the right position.** Sit upright and have light coming from behind you, over the side of your body opposite your writing hand. This will reduce the distracting and fatiguing effects of glare and shadows.

3. **Get a sneak preview.** Approach the chapter by first reading its boldface headings and any chapter outline, summary, or end-of-chapter questions that may be provided. This will supply you with a mental map of the chapter's important ideas before you start your reading trip and provide an overview that will help you keep track of the chapter's major ideas (the "big picture"), reducing the risk that you'll get lost among the smaller details you encounter along the way.

4. **Use boldface headings and subheadings.** Headings are cues for important information. Turn them into questions, and then read to find their answers. This will launch you on an answer-finding mission that will keep you mentally active while reading and enable you to read with a purpose. Turning headings into questions is also a good way to prepare for tests because you're practicing exactly what you'll be expected to do on tests—answer questions.

5. **Pay attention to the first and last sentences.** Absorb opening and closing sentences in sections beneath the chapter's major headings and subheadings. These sentences often contain an important introduction and conclusion to the material covered in that section of the text.

6. **Finish each of your reading sessions with a short review.** Recall what you have highlighted or noted as important information (rather than trying to cover a few more pages). It's best to use the last few minutes of reading time to "lock in" the most important information you've just read because most forgetting takes place immediately after you stop processing (taking in) information and start doing something else.

Remember

Your goal while reading should be to discover or uncover the most important information, and the final step in the reading process is to review (and lock in) the most important information you discovered.

Note: More detailed information on reading comprehension and retention is provided in Chapter 5.

Touching the Second Base of College Success: Use of Campus Resources

Your campus environment contains multiple resources designed to support your quest for educational and personal success. Studies show that students who take advantage of campus resources report higher levels of satisfaction with college and get more out of the college experience (Pascarella & Terenzini, 1991, 2005).

"Do not be a PCP (Parking Lot→ Classroom→ Parking Lot) student. The time you spend on campus will be a sound investment in your academic and professional success."

—Drew Appleby, professor of psychology

Remember

Involvement with campus services is not just valuable, it's also "free"—the cost of these services has already been covered by your college tuition. By investing time and energy in campus resources, you not only increase your prospects for personal success but also maximize the return on your financial investment in college—you get a bigger bang for your buck.

Successful students are actively involved inside and outside the classroom, and involvement outside of class includes making use of campus resources. An essential first step in making effective use of campus resources is to become aware of what they are and what they're designed to do. The following sections describe what key campus services are offered on most college campuses and why they should be utilized.

Learning Center (a.k.a. Academic Support or Academic Success Center)

Remember

The Learning Center or Academic Support Center is a place where all learners benefit.

This is your campus resource for strengthening your academic performance. The individual and group tutoring provided by this campus service can help you master difficult course concepts and assignments, and the people working here are professionally trained to help you learn how to learn. While your professors may have expert knowledge of the subject matter they teach, learning resource specialists are experts on the process of learning. These specialists can equip you with effective learning strategies and show you how you can adjust or modify your learning strategies to meet the unique demands of different courses and teaching styles you encounter in college.

Writing Center

Many college campuses offer specialized support for students who would like to improve their writing skills. Typically referred to as the Writing Center, this is the place where you can receive assistance at any stage of the writing process, whether it be collecting and organizing your ideas, composing your first draft, or proofreading your final draft. Since writing is an academic skill that you will use in many of your courses, if you improve your writing, you're likely to improve your overall academic performance.

Disability Services

If you have a physical or learning disability that is interfering with your performance in college, or think you may have such a disability, Disability Services is the campus resource to consult for assistance and support. Programs and services typically provided by this office include:

- Assessment for learning disabilities;
- Verification of eligibility for disability support services;
- Authorization of academic accommodations for students with disabilities; and
- Specialized counseling, advising, and tutoring.

College Library

"The next best thing to knowing something is knowing where to find it."

—Dr. Samuel Johnson, English literary figure and original author of the *Dictionary of the English Language* (1747)

The library is your campus resource for finding information and completing research assignments (e.g., term papers and group projects). Librarians are professional educators who provide instruction outside the classroom. You can learn from them just as you can learn from faculty inside the classroom. Furthermore, the library is a place where you can acquire skills for locating, retrieving, and evaluating information that you may apply to any course you are taking or will ever take.

Your college library is your campus resource for developing research skills that let you access, retrieve, and evaluate information, which are skills for achieving both educational and occupational success.

Academic Advising Center

Whether or not you have an assigned academic advisor, the Academic Advising Center is a campus resource for help with course selection, educational planning, and choosing or changing a major. Studies show that college students who have developed clear educational and career goals are more likely to persist in college until they complete their college degree (Willingham, 1985; Wyckoff, 1999). As a first-year college student, being undecided or uncertain about your educational and career goals is nothing to be embarrassed about. However, you should start thinking about your future now. Connect early and often with an academic advisor to help you clarify your educational goals and find a field of study that best complements your interests, talents, and values.

Office of Student Life (a.k.a. Office of Student Development)

The Office of Student Life is your campus resource for student development opportunities outside the classroom, including student clubs and organizations, recreational programs, leadership activities, and volunteer experiences. Research consistently shows that experiential learning that takes place outside the classroom is as important to college students' personal development and future success as learning from their course work (Kuh, 1995; Kuh, Douglas, Lund, & Ramin-Gyurnek, 1994; Pascarella & Terenzini, 2005). (This is why they are referred to as "co-curricular experiences" rather than "extracurricular activities.")

Devoting some out-of-class time to these co-curricular experiences should not interfere with your academic performance. Keep in mind that in college you'll be spending much less time in the classroom than you did in high school. As mentioned previously, a full load of college courses (15 units) only requires that you be in class about 13 hours per week. This should leave you with enough time to become involved in learning experiences on campus. Evidence indicates that college students who become involved in co-curricular, volunteer, and part-time work experiences that total *no more than 15 hours per week* earn higher grades than students who do not get involved in any out-of-class activities.

Although it's important to get involved in co-curricular experiences on your campus, try to limit your involvement to no more than two or three major campus organizations at any one time. Restricting the number of your out-of-class activities should enable you to keep up with your studies; it will be more impressive to future schools or employers because a long list of involvement in numerous activities may suggest you're padding your resume with things you did superficially (or never really did at all).

"Just a [long] list of club memberships is meaningless; it's a fake front. Remember that quality, not quantity, is what counts."

—Lauren Pope, director of the National Bureau for College Placement

Remember

Co-curricular experiences are also resume-building experiences, and campus professionals with whom you interact regularly while participating in co-curricular activities (e.g., the director of student activities or dean of students) are valuable resources for personal references and letters of recommendation to future schools or employers.

Financial Aid Office

This campus resource is designed to help you finance your college education. If you have questions concerning how to obtain assistance in paying for college, the staff of this office is there to guide you through the application process. The paperwork needed to apply for and secure financial aid can sometimes be confusing or overwhelming. Don't let this intimidate you enough to prevent you from seeking financial aid; assistance is available to you from the knowledgeable staff in the Financial Aid Office. You can also seek help from this office to find:

- Part-time employment on campus through a work-study program;
- Low-interest student loans;
- Grants; and
- Scholarships.

If you have any doubt about whether you are using the most effective plan for financing your college education, make an appointment to see a professional in your Financial Aid Office.

Counseling Center

Counseling services can provide you with a valuable source of support in college, not only for helping you cope with the stress associated with the transition to college, but also by helping you gain self-awareness and reach your full potential. Personal counseling can promote your self-awareness and self-development in social and emotional areas of your life that are important for mental health, wellness, and personal growth.

Remember
College counseling is not just for students who are experiencing emotional problems. It's for all students who want to enrich their overall quality of life.

Health Center

Making the transition from high school to college often involves adjustments and decisions affecting your health and wellness. Good health habits help you cope with stress and reach peak levels of performance. The Health Center on your campus is the resource for information on how to manage your physical health and maintain wellness. It is also the place to go for help with illnesses, sexually transmitted infections or diseases, and eating or nutritional disorders.

Career Development Center (a.k.a. Career Center)

Research on college students indicates that they are more likely to stay in school and graduate when they have some sense of how their present academic experience relates to their future career goals (Levitz & Noel, 1989; Tinto, 1993; Wyckoff, 1999). Studies also show that most new students are uncertain about what career they would like to pursue (Gordon & Steele, 2003). So, if you're uncertain about your future career, you're a member of a club that includes a very large number of other first-year students. This uncertainty is normal because you haven't had the opportunity for hands-on work experience in the real world of careers.

The Career Development Center is the place to go for help in finding a meaningful answer to the important question of how to connect your current college experience with your future career goals. This campus resource typically provides such services as personal career counseling, workshops on career exploration and development, and career fairs where you're able to meet professionals working in different fields. Although it may seem like the beginning of your career is light-years away because you're just beginning college, the process of exploring, planning, and preparing for career success starts in the first year of college.

Touching the Third Base of College Success: Interpersonal Interaction and Collaboration

Learning is strengthened when it takes place in a social context that involves interpersonal interaction. As some scholars put it, human knowledge is "socially constructed" or built up through interpersonal interaction and dialogue. According to these scholars, your conversations with others become internalized as ideas in your mind and influence your way of thinking. Thus, by having frequent, intelligent conversations with others, you broaden your knowledge and deepen your thinking.

Reflection **3.4**

Look back at the major campus resources that have been mentioned in this section. Which two or three of them do you think you should use *immediately*?

Why have you identified these resources as your top priorities right now?

Ask your course instructor for recommendations about what campus resources you should consult during your first term on campus. Compare their recommendations with your selections.

Four particular forms of interpersonal interaction have been found to be strongly associated with student learning and motivation in college:

1. Student-faculty interaction
2. Student-advisor interaction
3. Student-mentor interaction
4. Student-student (peer) interaction

Interacting with Faculty Members

Studies repeatedly show that college success is strongly influenced by the quality and quantity of student-faculty interaction *outside the classroom*. Such contact is associated with the following positive outcomes for college students:

- Improved academic performance;
- Increased critical thinking skills;
- Greater satisfaction with the college experience;

- Increased likelihood of completing a college degree; and
- Stronger desire to seek education beyond college (Astin, 1993; Pascarella & Terenzini, 1991, 2005).

These positive outcomes are so strong and widespread that we encourage you to immediately begin seeking interaction with college faculty outside of class time. Here are some of the easiest ways to do so.

1. **Seek contact with your instructors immediately after class.** If you are interested in talking about something that was discussed in class, approach your instructor as soon as the class session ends. Interaction with instructors immediately after class can help them get to know you as an individual, which should increase your confidence and willingness to seek subsequent contact in other settings.

2. **Seek interaction with your course instructors during their office hours.** One of the most important pieces of information on a course syllabus is your instructor's office hours. Make note of them and make an earnest attempt to capitalize on them. College professors specifically reserve out-of-class time for office hours during which they are expected to be available to students. Try to make at least one visit to the office of each of your instructors, preferably early in the term, when quality time is easier to find, rather than at midterm, when major exams and assignments begin to pile up. Even if your early contact with instructors is only for a few minutes, it can be a valuable icebreaker that helps your instructors get to know you as a person and helps you feel more comfortable interacting with them in the future.

3. **Connect with your instructors through e-mail.** Electronic communication is another effective way to interact with an instructor, particularly if that professor's office hours conflict with your class schedule, work responsibilities, or family commitments. If you are a commuter student who does not live on campus, or if you are an adult student juggling family and work commitments along with your academic schedule, e-mail communication may be an especially effective and ef-

ficient mode of student-faculty interaction. If you're shy or hesitant about "invading" your professor's office space, e-mail can provide a less threatening way to interact and may give you the self-confidence to eventually seek face-to-face contact with an instructor.

However, you should never email faculty with the following questions after missing class:

- Did I miss anything in class today?
- Could you send me your teaching notes or PowerPoint from the class I missed?

Also, when you're in class with faculty, use personal technology respectfully by following the guidelines in Snapshot Summary 3.1.

Snapshot Summary

3.1 Guidelines for Civil and Responsible Use of Personal Technology in the College Classroom

- Turn your cell phone completely off, or leave it out of the classroom. In the rare case of an emergency when you think you need to leave it on, inform your instructor.
- Don't check your cell phone during the class period by turning it off and on.
- Don't text message during class.
- Don't surf the Web during class.
- Don't touch your cell phone during any exam because this may be viewed by the instructor as a form of cheating.

Interaction with Academic Advisors

An academic advisor may serve as a very effective referral agent who can direct you to, and connect you with, campus support services that can promote your success. An advisor can also help you understand college procedures and navigate the bureaucratic maze of university policies and politics.

Your academic advisor should be someone whom you feel comfortable speaking with, someone who knows your name, and someone who's familiar with your personal interests and abilities. Give your advisor the opportunity to get to know you personally, and seek your advisor's input on courses, majors, and personal issues that may be affecting your academic performance.

Reflection 3.5

Do you have a personally assigned advisor?

If yes, do you know who this person is and where he or she can be found?

If no, do you know where to go if you have questions about your class schedule or academic plans?

If you have been assigned an advisor and cannot develop a good relationship with this person, ask the director of advising or academic dean if you could be assigned to someone else. Ask other students about their advising experience and whether they know an advisor they can recommend to you.

If your college does not assign you a personal advisor, but offers advising services in an Advising Center on a drop-by or drop-in basis, you may see a different advisor each time you visit the center. If you are not satisfied with this system of multiple advisors, find one advisor with whom you feel most comfortable and make that person your personal advisor by scheduling your appointments in advance. This will enable you to consistently connect with the same advisor and help you develop a close, ongoing relationship with that person.

Remember

An academic advisor is not someone you see just once per term when you need to get a signature for class scheduling and course registration. Advisors can be much more than course schedulers: they can be mentors. Unlike your course instructors, who will change from term to term, your academic advisor may be the one professional on campus with whom you have regular contact and a stable, ongoing relationship throughout your college experience.

Interaction with a Mentor

A mentor may be described as an experienced guide who takes personal interest in you and the progress you're making toward your goals. (For example, in the movie *Star Wars*, Yoda served as a mentor for Luke Skywalker.) A mentor can assist you in troubleshooting difficult or complicated issues that you may not be able to resolve on your own and is someone with whom you can share good news, such as your success stories and personal accomplishments. Look for someone on campus with whom you can develop this type of trusting relationship. Many people on campus have the potential to be outstanding mentors, including the following:

- Your academic advisor
- Your instructor in a first-year seminar or experience course
- Faculty in your intended major
- Juniors, seniors, or graduate students in your intended field of study
- Working professionals in careers that interest you
- Academic support professionals (e.g., professional tutors in the Learning Center)
- Career counselors
- Personal counselors
- Learning assistance professionals (e.g., from the Learning Center)
- Student development professionals (e.g., the director of student life or residential life)
- Campus minister or chaplain
- Financial aid counselors

Interaction with Peers (Student-Student Interaction)

Studies repeatedly point to the power of the peer group as a source of social and academic support during the college years (Pascarella & Terenzini, 2005). Peer support is especially important during the first term of college. At this stage of the college experience, new students have a strong need for belonging and social acceptance because many of them have just left the lifelong security of family and hometown

FIGURE 3.3

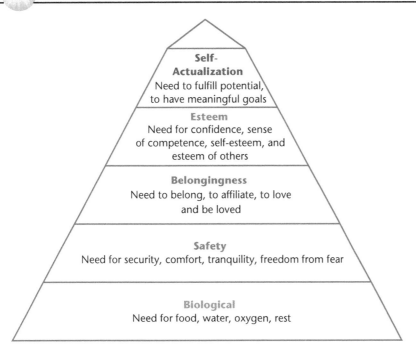

Abraham Maslow's Hierarchy of Needs

friends. As a new student, it may be useful to view the early stage of your college experience through the lens of psychologist Abraham Maslow's hierarchy of human needs (see Figure 3.3). According to Maslow's hierarchy of needs, humans cannot reach their full potential and achieve peak performance until their more basic emotional and social needs have been met (e.g., their needs for personal safety, social acceptance, and self-esteem). Making early connections with your peers helps you meet these basic human needs, provides you with a base of social support to ease your integration into the college community, and prepares you to move up to higher levels of the need hierarchy (e.g., achieving educational excellence and fulfilling your potential).

Getting involved with campus organizations or activities is one way to connect you with other students. Also, try to interact with students who have spent more time at college than you. Sophomores, juniors, and seniors can be valuable social resources for a new student. You're likely to find that they are willing to share their experiences with you because you have shown an interest in hearing what they have to say. You may be the first person who has ever asked them what their experiences have been like on your campus. You can learn from their experiences by asking them which courses and instructors they would recommend or what advisors they found to be most well informed and personable.

Remember

Your peers can be more than competitors or a source of negative peer pressure: they can also be collaborators, a source of positive social influence, and a resource for college success. Be on the lookout for classmates who are motivated to learn and willing to learn with you, and keep an eye out for advanced students who are willing to assist you. Start building your social support network by surrounding yourself with success-seeking and success-achieving students. They can be a stimulating source of positive peer power that can drive you to higher levels of academic performance and heighten your drive to complete college.

Reflection **3.6**

Think about the students in your classes this term. (1) Are there any students who might be good members to connect with and form learning teams? (2) Do you have any classmates who are currently in more than one class with you and who might be good peer partners to team up with and work together on the courses you have in common?

Collaboration with Peers

Simply defined, collaboration is the process of two or more people working interdependently toward a common goal, rather than working independently or competitively. Collaboration involves true teamwork, in which teammates support each other's success and take equal responsibility for helping the team move toward its shared goal.

To maximize the power of collaboration, use the following guidelines to make wise choices about teammates who will contribute positively to the quality and productivity of your learning team:

1. Observe your classmates with an eye toward identifying potentially good teammates. Look for fellow students who are motivated and who will likely contribute to your team's success, rather than those whom you suspect may just be hitchhikers looking for a free ride.

2. Don't team up exclusively with peers who are similar to you in terms of their personal characteristics, backgrounds, and experiences. Instead, include teammates who differ from you in age; gender; ethnic, racial, cultural, or geographical background; learning style; and personality characteristics. Such variety brings different life experiences, styles of thinking, and learning strategies to your team, which enrich not only its diversity but its quality as well. Simply stated, studies show that we learn more from people who are different from us than we do from people who are similar to us.

   Furthermore, if your team consists only of friends or classmates whose interests and lifestyles are similar to your own, this familiarity can interfere with your team's focus and performance because your common experiences can get you off track and on to topics that have nothing to do with the learning task (e.g., what you did last weekend or what you are planning to do next weekend).

Remember

Keep in mind that learning teams are not simply study groups formed the night before an exam. Effective learning teams collaborate more regularly and work on more varied academic tasks than late-night study groups. Following are various types of learning teams that you may join or form to improve your performance on key academic tasks in college.

Note-Taking Teams

Immediately after a class session ends, take a couple of minutes to team up with other students to compare and share notes. Since listening and note taking are demanding tasks, it's likely that a student may pick up an important point that the others overlooked and vice versa. Also, by teaming up immediately after class to review your notes together, your team has the opportunity to consult with the instructor about any missing or confusing information before your instructor leaves the room.

Reading Teams

After completing your reading assignments, team up with classmates to compare your highlighting and margin notes. Compare notes on what you identified as the most important points in the reading that should be studied for upcoming exams.

Writing Teams

Students can provide each other with feedback that they can use to revise and improve the quality of their own writing. Studies show that when peers assess each other's writing, the quality of their writing and their attitudes toward writing improve (Topping, 1998). You can form peer-writing teams to help at any or all of the following stages in the writing process:

1. **Topic selection and refinement.** To help each other come up with a list of possible topics and subtopics to write about;
2. **Pre-writing.** To clarify your writing purpose and audience;
3. **First draft.** To improve your general writing style and tone; and
4. **Final draft.** To proofread and correct mechanical errors before submitting your written work.

Library Research Teams

Many first-year students are unfamiliar with the process of conducting academic research at a college or university library. Some students experience "library anxiety" and will try to avoid even setting foot in the library, particularly if it's large and intimidating (Malvasi, Rudowsky, & Valencia, 2009). Forming library research teams is an effective way for you to develop a social support group that can make trips to the library less intimidating and transform library research from a solitary experience into a collaborative venture that's done as a team.

> **Remember**
> *It's perfectly acceptable and ethical to team up with others to search for and share resources. This isn't cheating or plagiarizing—as long as your final product is completed individually and what you turn in to the instructor represents your own work.*

Team-Instructor Conferences

Visiting instructors in their office with other classmates is an effective way to get additional assistance in preparing for exams and completing assignments for the following reasons:

- You're likely to feel more comfortable about venturing onto your instructors' "turf" in the company of peers, rather than entering this unfamiliar territory on your own. As the old expression goes, "There's safety in numbers."
- When you make an office visit as a team, the information shared by the instructor is heard by more than one person, so your teammates may pick up some useful information that you may have missed, misinterpreted, or forgotten to write down (and vice versa).

- You save your instructors time by allowing them to help multiple students at the same time, which reduces the likelihood that they'll have to engage in "repeat performances" for individual students making separate visits at different times.
- You send a message to instructors that you're serious about the course and are a motivated student because you've taken the time—ahead of time—to connect with your peers and prepare for the office visit.

Study Teams

Research clearly demonstrates that college students learn as much from peers as they do from their instructors and textbooks (Astin, 1993; Pascarella & Terenzini, 2005). Research on study groups, in particular, indicates that they are effective only if each member has done required course work in advance of the team meeting—for example, if each group member has done the required readings and other course assignments. Thus, to fully capitalize and maximize the power of study teams, each team member should study individually *before* studying with the group. Each member should come prepared with specific information or answers to share with teammates and specific questions or points of confusion about which they hope to receive help from the team. This ensures that all team members are individually accountable and equally responsible for doing their own learning and contributing to the learning of their teammates.

Test Results-Review and Assignment-Review Teams

After receiving the results of course examinations and assignments, you can collaborate with peers to review your results as a team. When you compare your answers to the answers of other students, you're better able to identify the sources of your mistakes; by seeing the answers of teammates who received maximum credit on certain questions, you get a clearer picture of where you went wrong and what you should do to get it right next time. Teaming up after tests and assignments *early in the term* is especially effective because it enables you to get a better idea of what the instructor expects from students throughout the remainder of the course. You can use this information as early feedback to diagnose your mistakes, improve your next performance, and raise your course grade while there's still plenty of time left in the term to do so.

Learning Communities

Your college may offer you the opportunity to participate in a learning community program, in which the same group of students registers for the same block of courses during the same term. If this opportunity is available to you, try to take advantage of it because research suggests that students who participate in learning community programs are more likely to:

- Become actively involved in classroom learning,
- Form their own learning groups outside of class,
- Report greater intellectual gains, and
- Continue their college education (Tinto, 1997, 2000).

If learning community programs are not offered on your campus, consider creating smaller, more informal learning communities on your own by finding other first-year students who are likely to be taking the same courses as you (e.g., the same general education or pre-major courses). Team up with these students during registration to see if you can enroll in the same two or three courses together. This will allow you to reap the benefits of a learning community, even though your college may not offer a formal learning-community program.

Studies repeatedly show that students who become socially integrated or connected with other members of the college community are more likely to complete their first year of college and continue on to complete their college degrees (Tinto, 1993; Pascarella & Terenzini, 2005). For effective ways to make these interpersonal connections, see Do It Now! 3.3.)

3.3   DO IT NOW

Making Connections with Members of Your College Community

Consider these top 10 tips for making important interpersonal connections in college. Start making these connections now so that you can begin constructing a base of social support that will strengthen your performance during your first term and, perhaps, throughout your college experience.

1. Connect with a peer or student development professional whom you may have met during orientation.
2. Connect with peers who live near you or who commute to school from the same community in which you live. If your schedules are similar, consider carpooling together.
3. Join a college club, student organization, campus committee, intramural team, or volunteer service group whose members may share the same personal or career interests as you. If you can't find a club or organization you were hoping to join, consider starting it on your own. For example, if you're an English major, consider starting a writing club or a book club.
4. Connect with a peer leader who has been trained to assist new students (e.g., peer tutor, peer mentor, or peer counselor) or with a peer who has more college experience than you (e.g., sophomore, junior, or senior).
5. Connect with classmates and team up with them to take notes, complete reading assignments, and study for exams. (Look especially to team up with a peer who may be in more than one class with you.)
6. Connect with faculty members, particularly in a field that you're considering as a major, by visiting them during office hours, conversing briefly with them after class, or communicating with them via e-mail.
7. Connect with an academic support professional in your college's Learning Center for personalized academic assistance or tutoring related to any course in which you'd like to improve your performance.
8. Connect with an academic advisor to discuss and develop your educational plans.
9. Connect with a college librarian to get early assistance and a head start on any research project that you've been assigned.
10. Connect with a personal counselor or campus minister to discuss any college adjustment or personal life issues that you may be experiencing.

Note: For more information on meeting people and forming friendships, see Chapter 9.

Reflection 3.7

Four categories of people have the potential to serve as mentors for you in college:

1. Experienced peers

2. Faculty (instructors)

3. Administrators (e.g., office and program directors)

4. Staff (e.g., student support professionals and administrative assistants)

Think about your first interactions with faculty, staff, and administrators on campus. Do you recall anyone who impressed you as being approachable, personable, and helpful? If you did, make a note of the person's name in case you'd like to seek out that person again. (If you haven't met such a person yet, when you do, be sure you remember who it is, because that person may be someone who can serve as a mentor for you.)

Touching the Fourth (Home) Base of College Success: Personal Reflection and Self-Awareness

The final step in the learning process, whether it be learning in the classroom or learning from experience, is to step back from the process, thoughtfully review it, and connect it to what you already know. Reflection may be defined as the flip side of active involvement; both processes are necessary for learning to be complete. Learning requires not only effortful action but also thoughtful reflection. Active involvement gets and holds your focus of *attention*, which enables information to reach your brain, and personal reflection promotes *consolidation*, which locks that information into your brain's long-term memory (Bligh, 2000; Roediger, Dudai, & Fitzpatrick, 2007).

Brain research reveals that different brain wave patterns are associated with the mental states of involvement and reflection (Bradshaw, 1995). In Figure 3.4, the pattern on the left shows the brain waves of someone who is actively involved in the learning task and attending to it. The pattern on the right shows the brain waves of someone who is thinking deeply about information that has been attended to and taken in, which will help consolidate or lock that information into the person's long-term memory. Thus, effective learning combines active mental involvement (characterized by high-amplitude "beta" brain waves) with thoughtful reflection (characterized by high-frequency "alpha" brain waves—similar to someone in a meditative state).

Reflection 3.8

Think about the students in your classes this term. Are there any students whom you might want to join with to form learning teams?

Do you have any classmates who are in more than one class with you and who might be good peer partners for the courses you have in common?

FIGURE 3.4

High-Amplitude Brain Waves Associated with a Mental State of *Active Involvement.*

High-Frequency Brain Waves Associated with a Mental State of *Reflective Thinking.*

© Kendall Hunt

Personal reflection also involves introspection—turning inward and inspecting yourself to gain deeper *self-awareness* of what you've done, what you're doing, or what you intend to do. Two forms of self-awareness are particularly important for success in college:

1. Self-assessment
2. Self-monitoring

> "We learn to do neither by thinking nor by doing; we learn to do by thinking about what we are doing."
>
> —George Stoddard, Professor Emeritus, University of Iowa

Self-Assessment

Simply defined, self-assessment is the process of reflecting on and evaluating characteristics of your "self," such as your personality traits, learning habits, personal strengths, and personal weaknesses that need improvement. Self-assessment is the critical first step in the process of self-improvement, personal planning, and effective decision making. The following are important target areas for self-assessment because they reflect personal characteristics that play a pivotal role in promoting success in college and beyond:

- **Personal interests.** What you like to do or enjoy doing.
- **Personal values.** What is important to you and what you care about doing.
- **Personal abilities or aptitudes.** What you do well or have the potential to do well.
- **Learning habits.** How you go about learning and the usual approaches, methods, or techniques you use to learn.
- **Learning styles.** How you prefer to learn—the way you like to:
  - Receive information—the learning format you prefer (e.g., learning by reading, listening, or experiencing);
  - Perceive information—what sensory modality you prefer to use (e.g., vision, sound, or touch);

- Process information—how you prefer to deal with or think about information you've taken in (e.g., whether you like to think about it on your own or discuss it with others).
- **Personality traits.** Your temperament, emotional characteristics, and social tendencies (e.g., whether you lean toward being outgoing or reserved);
- **Academic self-concept.** What kind of student you think you are and how you perceive yourself as a learner (e.g., your level of self-confidence and whether you believe academic success is within your control or depends on factors beyond your control).

Reflection **3.9**

How would you rate your academic self-confidence at this point in your college experience? (Circle one.)

very confident   somewhat confident
somewhat unconfident   very unconfident

Why did you make this choice?

Self-Monitoring

Research indicates that one characteristic of successful learners is that they monitor or watch themselves and maintain self-awareness of:

"Successful students know a lot about themselves."

—Claire Weinstein and Debra Meyer, professors of educational psychology at the University of Texas

- Whether they're using effective learning strategies (e.g., they are aware of their level of attention or concentration in class);
- Whether they're comprehending what they are attempting to learn (e.g., if they're understanding it at a deep level or merely memorizing it at a surface level); and
- How to regulate or adjust their learning strategies to meet the demands of different academic tasks and subjects.

You can begin to establish good self-monitoring habits by creating a routine of periodically pausing to reflect on the strategies you're using to learn and "do" college. For instance, you can ask yourself the following questions:

- Am I listening attentively to what my instructor is saying in class?
- Do I comprehend what I am reading outside of class?
- Am I effectively using campus resources that are designed to support my success?
- Am I interacting with campus professionals who can contribute to my current success and future development?
- Am I interacting and collaborating with peers who can contribute to my learning and increase my level of involvement in the college experience?
- Am I effectively implementing the success strategies identified in this book?

Remember

Successful students and successful people are mindful—*they watch what they're doing and remain aware of whether they're doing it effectively and to the best of their ability.*

Summary and Conclusion

Research reviewed in this chapter points to the conclusion that successful students are:

1. **Involved.** They invest time and effort in the college experience;
2. **Resourceful.** They capitalize on their surrounding resources;
3. **Interactive.** They interact and collaborate with others; and
4. **Reflective.** They are self-aware learners who assess and monitor their own performance.

Successful students are students who could honestly check almost every box in the following self-assessment checklist of success-promoting principles and practices.

A Checklist of Success-Promoting Principles and Practices

1. **Active Involvement**
   Inside the classroom, I:

   ☑ **Get to class.** Treat it like a job; if you cut, your pay (grade) will be cut.
   ☑ **Get involved in class.** Come prepared, listen actively, take notes, and participate.

   Outside the classroom, I:

   ☑ **Read actively.** Take notes while you read to increase attention and retention.
   ☑ **Double up.** Spend twice as much time on academic work outside the classroom than you spend in class—if you're a full-time student, that makes it a 40-hour academic workweek (with occasional "overtime").

2. **Use of Campus Resources**
   I capitalize on academic and student support services, such as the following:

   ☑ Learning Center
   ☑ Writing Center
   ☑ Disability Services
   ☑ College Library
   ☑ Academic Advising Center
   ☑ Office of Student Life
   ☑ Financial Aid Office
   ☑ Counseling Center
   ☑ Health Center
   ☑ Career Development Center
   ☑ Experiential Learning Resources

3. **Interpersonal Interaction and Collaboration**
   I interact with the following people:

   ☑ **Peers.** I join student clubs and participate in campus organizations.
   ☑ **Faculty members.** I connect with professors and other faculty members immediately after class, in their offices, or via e-mail.
   ☑ **Academic advisors.** I see an advisor for more than just a signature to register. I've found an advisor I can relate to and with whom I can develop an ongoing relationship.
   ☑ **Mentors.** I try to find experienced people on campus who can serve as trusted guides and role models.

I collaborate by doing the following:

- ☑ **Forming learning teams.** I join not only last-minute study groups but also teams that collaborate more regularly to work on such tasks as taking lecture notes, completing reading and writing assignments, conducting library research, and reviewing results of exams or course assignments.
- ☑ **Participating in learning communities.** I enroll in two or more classes with the same students during the same term.

4. **Personal Reflection and Self-Awareness**

I engage in:

- ☑ **Self-Assessment.** I reflect on and evaluate my personal traits, habits, strengths, and weaknesses.
- ☑ **Self-Monitoring.** I maintain self-awareness of how I'm learning in college and whether I'm using effective strategies that will enable me to do college well.

Reflection 3.10

Before exiting this chapter, look back at the Checklist of Success-Promoting Principles and Practices and see how these ideas compare with those you recorded at the start of this chapter, when we asked you how you thought college would be different from high school and what it would take to be successful in college.

What ideas from your list and our checklist tend to match?

Were there any ideas on your list that were not on ours, or vice versa?

Learning More through the World Wide Web

Internet-Based Resources for Further Information on Liberal Arts Education

For additional information related to promoting your success in college, we recommend the following Web sites:

www.cgcc.cc.or.us/StudentServices/TipsCollegeSuccess.cfm

www.dartmouth.edu/~acskills/success/

www.studygs.net

Chapter 3 Exercises

3.1 Birds of a Different Feather: High School versus College

Read the following list of differences between high school and college and rate each difference on a scale from 1 to 4 in terms of how aware you were of this difference when you began college (1 = totally unaware; 2 = not fully aware; 3 = somewhat aware, 4 = totally aware)

Class schedules are typically made for high school students.

College students make their own class schedules, either on their own or in consultation with an academic advisor.

Awareness Rating _____

High school classes are scheduled back-to-back at the same time every day with short breaks in between.

Larger time gaps can occur between college classes, and they are scheduled at various times throughout the day (and night).

Awareness Rating _____

Class attendance in high school is mandatory and checked daily.

Class attendance in college is not mandatory; in many classes, attendance is not even taken.

Awareness Rating _____

> "In college, if you don't go to class, that's you. Your professor doesn't care really if you pass or fail."
> —First-year student (Engle, Bermeo, & O'Brien, 2006).

High school teachers often write all important information they cover in class on the board.

College professors frequently expect students to write down important information contained in their lectures without explicitly writing it on the board or including it on PowerPoint slides.

Awareness Rating _____

High school teachers often re-teach material in class that students were assigned to read.

College professors often do not teach the same material covered in assigned reading and information from the assigned reading still appears on exams.

Awareness Rating _____

High school teachers often take class time to remind students of assignments and their due dates.

College professors list their assignments and due dates on the course syllabus and expect students to keep track of them on their own.

Awareness Rating _____

> "College teachers don't tell you what you're supposed to do. They just expect you to do it. High school teachers tell you about five times what you're supposed to do."
> —College sophomore (Appleby, 2008)

Homework assignments (e.g., math problems) in high school are typically turned in to the teacher, who checks and grades the students' work.

Assigned work in college often is not turned in to be checked or graded; students are expected to have the self-discipline to do the work on their own.

Awareness Rating _____

High school students spend most of their learning time in class; they spend much less time studying outside of class than they spend in class.

College students typically spend no more than 15 hours per week in class and are expected to spend at least two hours studying out of class for every hour they spend in class.

Awareness Rating _____

Tests in high school often take place frequently and cover limited amounts of material. College exams are given less frequently (e.g., midterm and final) and tend to cover large amounts of material.

Awareness Rating _____

Make-up tests and extra-credit opportunities are often available to students in high school.

In college, if an exam or assignment is missed, rarely do students have a chance to make it up or to recapture lost points through extra-credit work.

Awareness Rating _____

A grade of "D" in high school is still passing.

In college, a grade point average below "C" puts a student on academic probation, and if it doesn't improve to C or higher, the student may be academically dismissed.

Awareness Rating _____

In high school, students go to offices of campuses only if they have to or are required to (e.g., if they forgot to do something or did something wrong).

In college, students go to campus offices to enhance their success by taking advantage of the services and support they provide.

Awareness Rating _____

Name:_____   Due Date:_____

University 101 - Bulldog CAMPUS Resources

Build a list of support services available to you on campus. Identify the type of services available and how you could benefit from each of them. Identify one person in that office to list as your resource contact and ask for a telephone number to reach them or the main office. Include room numbers in your location and first and last names of your contact persons. This assignment will be included in your portfolio, so do your best work. **When entering each office**, provide a greeting (Good morning! or Good afternoon!), introduce yourself and let the person know the purpose for your visit. **You are required to record all the information for this assignment**.

1.   My Primary Academic Advisor

Advisor's Name_____ Telephone: (   )_____

Department of _____

Office Location:_____

How will I benefit?_____

2.   Student Success and Retention Programs

List two services this office provides and identify one staff person along with contact information.

Service 1:_____

Service 2:_____

How will I benefit?_____

Employee_____ Telephone: (   )_____

Office Location:_____

3.   Multipurpose Academic Computer Lab

List one service this office provides and identify one staff person along with contact information.

Service 1:_____

Name_____ Telephone: (   )_____

Office Location:_____

How will I benefit?_____

4.   Counseling and Self-Development Center

List two services this office provides and identify one staff person along with contact information.

Service 1:_____

Service 2:_____

Name_____ Telephone: (   )_____

Office Location:_____

How will I benefit?_____

5. **Financial Aid Office**

List one service this office provides and identify one staff person along with contact information.

Service 1:_____

How often must the **Free Application for Federal Student Aid** (FAFSA) be completed?_____

What is the SC State University deadline to complete the FAFSA?_____

Name_____ Telephone: (   )_____

Office Location:_____

How will I benefit?_____

6. **Accounts Receivables**

List one service this office provides and identify one staff person along with contact information.

Service 1:_____

Name_____ Telephone: (   )_____

Office Location:_____

How will I benefit?_____

7. **Brooks Health Center**

List two services this office provides and identify one staff person along with contact information.

Service 1:_____

Service 2:_____

Name_____ Telephone: (   )_____

Office Location:_____

How will I benefit?_____

8. **Career Center**

List two services this office provides and identify one staff person along with contact information.

Service 1:_____

Service 2:_____

How will I benefit?_____

Name_____ Telephone: (   )_____

Office Location:_____

9. **Museum and Planetarium**

List two services this office provides and identify one staff person along with contact information.

Service 1:_____

Service 2:_____

How will I benefit?_____

Name_____ Telephone: (   )_____

Office Location:_____

10. Moss Hall Computer Lab (1st floor)

List one service this office provides and identify one staff person along with contact information.

Service 1:_____

Name_____ Telephone: (_____)_____

Office Location:_____

How will I benefit?_____

11. Registrar's Office

List two services this office provides and identify one staff person along with contact information.

Service 1:_____

Service 2:_____

How will I benefit?_____

Name_____ Telephone: (_____)_____

Office Location:_____

12. Reserve Officers' Training Corps (ROTC)

List one service this office provides and identify one staff person along with contact information.

Service 1:_____

Name_____ Telephone: (_____)_____

Office Location:_____

How will I benefit?_____

13. Student Life and Leadership

List one service this office provides and identify one staff person along with contact information.

Service 1:_____

Name_____ Telephone: (_____)_____

Office Location:_____

How will I benefit?_____

14. Campus Police Department

List one service this office provides and identify one staff person along with contact information.

Service 1:_____

Name_____ Telephone: (_____)_____

Office Location:_____

How will I benefit?_____

Name two on-campus dining facilities for students

15.   1st on-campus facility_____

16.   2nd on-campus facility_____

Name:_____   Date:_____

Introduction to the University Community (UNIV 101)
Academic Advisement Assignment

Directions: *Faculty and student engagement is the foundation to fostering your academic, educational and career goals. This activity is designed to help you build on this relationship.* ***Read each question carefully and answer it fully.***

20 Points Each.

1. **What is your major?** *(Print the full name of the major; for ex. Management not Business Management - Use the sample change of major form to help you)*

   _____

2. **What is the FULL name of your academic department and where is it located? Identify the TITLE and Name of your department chairperson.**

   Department Name:_____

   Department Chairperson:_____

                                   Title   *First Name*   *Last Name*

   Location:_____

            Room Number   *Building Name*

3. **Completely CIRCLE the academic college that offers your major?**

   a. School of Business

   b. College of Graduate and Professional Studies (CGPS)

   c. Student Success and Retention Programs (SSRP – Undecided Students)

   d. College of Education, Humanities and Social Science (CEHSS)

   e. College of Science, Mathematics, Engineering, and Technology (CSMET)

4. **List the TITLE and FULL name of the person who is listed as your advisor in Bulldog Connection?** *If you need help, visit the Multipurpose Academic Computer (MAC) Lab in 314 Moss Hall.*

   Advisor's Title and Full Name: _____

   Advisor's Office Location_____

   Advisor's Office Telephone: (   ) __ __ __ - __ __ __ __

   Advisor's Email Address:_____

5. Attach a copy of your **Concise Student Class Schedule** for **next semester**.

Alone and Disconnected: Feeling Like Calling It Quits

Josephine is a first-year student in her second week of college. She doesn't feel like she's fitting in with other students on her campus. She also feels guilty about the time she's taking time away from her family and her old high school friends who are not attending college, and she fears that her ties with them will be weakened or broken if she continues spending so much time at school and on schoolwork. Josephine is feeling so torn between college and her family and former friends that she's beginning to have second thoughts about whether she should have gone to college.

Reflection and Discussion Questions

1. What would you say to Josephine that might persuade her to stay in college?

2. What could Josephine's college have done more during her first two weeks on campus to make her (and other students) feel more connected with college and less disconnected from family?

3. What could Josephine do for herself right now to minimize the conflict she's experiencing between her commitment to college and her commitment to family and high school friends?

Goal Setting, Motivation, and Character

Moving from Dreams to Plans to Action

ACTIVATE YOUR THINKING · *Reflection* · **4.1**

What does being "successful" mean to you?

LEARNING GOAL

To help you set and strive for meaningful goals and maintain your motivation to reach those goals.

Defining Success

"Achieving a desired outcome" is how *success* is commonly defined. The word *success* derives from the Latin root *successus*, meaning "to follow or come after" (as in the word *succession*). Thus, by definition, success involves an order or sequence of actions that lead to a desired outcome. The process starts with identifying an end (goal) and then finding a means (sequence of steps) to reach that goal (achieving success). Goal setting is the first step in the process of becoming successful because it gives you something specific to strive for and ensures that you start off in the right direction. Studies consistently show that setting goals is a more effective self-motivational strategy than simply telling yourself that you should try hard and do your best (Boekaerts, Pintrich, & Zeidner, 2000; Locke & Latham, 1990).

By setting goals, you show initiative—you initiate the process of gaining control of your future and taking charge of your life. When you take initiative, you demonstrate what psychologists call an *internal* locus of control: you believe that the locus (location or source) of control for events in your life is inside of you, rather than being *external*, or outside of you and beyond your control, determined by such factors as innate ability, luck, chance, or fate (Rotter, 1966; Carlson, Buskist, Heth, & Schmaltz, 2007). People with an internal locus of control believe that success is influenced more by attitude, effort, commitment, and preparation than by natural ability or inborn intelligence (Jernigan, 2004).

Research has revealed that individuals with a strong internal locus of control display the following characteristics:

1. Greater independence and self-direction (Van Overwalle, Mervielde, & De Schuyer, 1995);
2. Higher levels of learning and achievement (Wilhite, 1990); and
3. Better physical health (Maddi, 2002; Seligman, 1991).

> "I'm a great believer in luck, and I find the harder I work the more I have of it."
>
> —Thomas Jefferson, 3rd president of the United States

> "What lies behind us and what lies in front of us are small matters compared to what lies within us."
>
> —Ralph Waldo Emerson, 19th-century American essayist and lecturer

An internal locus of control also contributes to the development of another positive trait that psychologists call *self-efficacy*—the belief that you have the power to produce a positive effect on the outcomes of your life (Bandura, 1994). People with low self-efficacy tend to feel helpless, powerless, and passive; they allow things to happen to them rather than taking charge and making things happen for them. Individuals with a strong sense of self-efficacy initiate action, exert effort, and sustain that effort until they reach their goals. If they encounter setbacks or bad breaks along the way, they don't give up or give in; they persevere or push on (Bandura, 1986, 1997). They don't have a false sense of entitlement—that they're entitled to or owed anything; they believe success is something that's earned and the harder they work at it, the more likely they'll get it.

Students with a stronger sense of self-efficacy also possess a strong sense of personal responsibility. As the breakdown of the word *responsible* implies, they are "response" "able"—that is, they believe they are able to respond effectively to personal challenges, including academic challenges.

Students with a strong sense of *academic* self-efficacy have been found to:

1. Put considerable effort into their studies;
2. Use active-learning strategies;
3. Capitalize on campus resources;
4. Persist in the face of obstacles (Multon, Brown, & Lent, 1991; Zimmerman, 1995, 2000).

Reflection 4.2

You are not required by law or by others to attend college; you've made the decision to continue your education. Do you believe you are in charge of your educational destiny?

Why or why not?

Strategies for Effective Goal Setting

Motivation begins with goal setting. Goals may be classified into three general categories: long-range, mid-range, and short-range, depending on the length of time it takes to reach them and the order in which they are to be achieved. Short-range goals need to be completed before a mid-range goal can be reached, and mid-range goals must be reached before a long-range goal can be achieved. For example, if your long-range goal is a successful career, you must complete the courses required for a degree (mid-range goal) that will allow you entry into a career; to reach your mid-range goal of a college degree, you need to successfully complete the courses you're taking this term (short-range goal).

This planning process is called *means-end analysis*; it involves working backward from your long-range goal (the end) and identifying the order and timing of the mid-range and short-range subgoals (the means) that need to be taken to reach your long-range goal (Brooks, 2009; Newell & Simon, 1959).

Setting Long-Range Goals

Setting effective long-range goals involves a process that has two components: (1) self-awareness, or self-insight into who you are now, and (2) self-projection, or a vision of what you want to become. When you engage in both of these processes, you're able to see a connection between your short-range and long-range goals.

Long-range goal setting enables you to take an approach to your future that is proactive—acting beforehand to anticipate and control your future life rather than putting it off and being forced to react to it without a plan. Setting long-range goals and planning ahead also helps reduce feelings of anxiety about the future because when you give forethought to your future, you gain greater power to control it—i.e., you develop a stronger sense of self-efficacy. As the old saying goes, "To be forewarned is to be forearmed."

"To fail to plan is to plan to fail."

—Robert Wubbolding, internationally known author, psychologist, and teacher

Reflection **4.3**

In what area or areas of your life do you feel that you've been able to exert the most control and achieve the most positive results?

In what area or areas do you wish you had more control and were achieving better results?

What strategies have you used in those areas of your life where you've taken charge and gained control? Could you apply the same strategies to those areas in which you need to gain more control?

Remember that setting long-range goals and developing long-range plans doesn't mean you can't adjust or modify them. Your goals can undergo change as you change, develop skills, acquire knowledge, and discover new interests or talents. Finding yourself and discovering your path in life are among the primary purposes of a college education. Don't think that the process of setting long-range goals means you are locking yourself into a premature plan and reducing your options. Instead, long-range goal setting just gives you a map that provides you with some sense of direction about where you're going, which can also provide you with the ignition and motivation to get going.

"You've got to be careful if you don't know where you're going because you might not get there."

—Yogi Berra, Hall of Fame baseball player

Steps in the Goal-Setting Process

Effective goal setting involves a four-step sequence:

1. **Awareness of yourself.** Your personal interests, abilities and talents, and values;

↓

2. **Awareness of your options.** The range of choices available to you;

↓

3. **Awareness of the options that best fit you.** The goals that are most compatible with your personal abilities, interests, values, and needs;

↓

4. **Awareness of the process.** The steps you need to take to reach your chosen goal.

"You have brains in your head. You have feet in your shoes. You can steer yourself any direction you choose."

—Theodore Seuss Giesel, a.k.a. Dr. Seuss, author of children's books including *Oh, the Places You'll Go!*

Discussed below are strategies for taking each of these steps in the goal-setting process.

Step 1. Self-Awareness

The goals you choose to pursue say a lot about who you are and what you want from life. Thus, self-awareness is a critical first step in the process of goal setting. You must know yourself before you can choose the goals you want to achieve. While this may seem obvious, self-awareness and self-discovery are often overlooked aspects of the goal-setting process. Deepening your self-awareness puts you in a better position to select and choose goals and to pursue a personal path that's true to who you are and what you want to become.

"Know thyself, and to thine own self be true."

—Plato, ancient Greek philosopher

> **Remember**
> *Self-awareness is the first and most important step in the process of making any important life choice or decision. Good decisions are built on a deep understanding of one's self.*

No one is in a better position to know who you are, and what you want to be, than *you*. One effective way to get to know yourself more deeply is through self-questioning. You can increase self-awareness by asking yourself questions that can stimulate your thinking about your inner qualities and priorities. Effective self-questioning launches you on an inward quest or journey to self-insight and self-discovery, which is the essential first step to effective goal setting. For example, if your long-range goal is career success, you can launch your voyage toward achieving this goal by asking yourself thought-provoking questions related to your personal:

"In order to succeed, you must know what you are doing, like what you are doing, and believe in what you are doing."

—Will Rogers, Native American humorist and actor

1. **Interests.** What you like to do;
2. **Abilities and talents.** What you're good at doing; and
3. **Values.** What you believe is worth doing.

The following questions are designed to sharpen your self-awareness with respect to your interests, abilities, and values. As you read each question, briefly note what thought or thoughts come to mind about yourself.

Your Personal Interests

1. What tends to grab your attention and hold it for long periods of time?
2. What sorts of things are you naturally curious about and tend to intrigue you?
3. What do you enjoy and do as often as you possibly can?
4. What do you look forward to or get excited about?
5. What are your favorite hobbies or pastimes?
6. When you're with friends, what do you tend to talk most about or spend most of your time doing?
7. What has been your most stimulating or enjoyable learning experience?
8. If you've had previous work or volunteer experience, what jobs or tasks did you find most enjoyable or stimulating?
9. When time seems to fly by for you, what are you usually doing?
10. When you choose to read, what topics do you read about?
11. When you open a newspaper or log on to the Internet, where do you tend to go first?
12. When you find yourself daydreaming or fantasizing about your future life, what's going on or what are you doing?

Reflection 4.4

From your responses to the preceding questions, identify one long-range goal you could pursue that's compatible with your personal interests. In the space that follows, write down the goal and your interests that are compatible with it.

Your Personal Abilities and Talents

1. What seems to come easily or naturally to you?
2. What would you say is your greatest personal strength or talent?
3. What do you excel at when you apply yourself and put forth your best effort?
4. What are your most advanced or well-developed skills?
5. What would you say has been the greatest accomplishment or achievement in your life thus far?
6. What about yourself are you most proud of, or what do you take the most pride in doing?
7. When others come to you for advice or assistance, what is it usually for?
8. What would your best friend or friends say is your best quality, trait, or characteristic?
9. When you had a strong feeling of being successful after you had done something, what was it that you did?
10. If you've received awards or other forms of recognition, what did you do to earn them?
11. With which types of learning tasks or activities have you experienced the most success?
12. In what types of courses do you tend to earn the highest grades?

> "Never desert your line of talent. Be what nature intended you for and you will succeed."
>
> —Sydney Smith, 18th-century English writer and defender of the oppressed

Reflection 4.5

From your responses to the preceding questions, identify a long-range goal you could pursue that's compatible with your personal abilities and talents. In the space that follows, write down the goal and your abilities and talents that are compatible with it.

Your Personal Values

1. What matters most to you?
2. If you were to single out one thing you stand for or believe in, what would it be?
3. What would you say are your highest priorities in life?
4. What makes you feel good about what you're doing when you're doing it?
5. If there were one thing in the world you could change, improve, or make a difference in, what would it be?
6. When you have extra spending money, what do you usually spend it on?
7. When you have free time, what do you usually spend it on?
8. What does "making it big in life" mean to you?
9. How would you define success? (What would it take for you to feel that you were successful?)
10. How would you define happiness? (What would it take for you to feel happy?)
11. Do you have any heroes or anyone you admire, look up to, or believe has set an example worth following? If yes, who and why?

> "Do what you value; value what you do."
>
> —Sidney Simon, author of Values Clarification and In Search of Values

> "Success is getting what you want. Happiness is wanting what you get."
>
> —Dale Carnegie, author of the bestselling book How to Win Friends and Influence People (1936) and founder of the Dale Carnegie Course, a worldwide program for business based on his teachings

12. Which of the following four personal qualities would you want to be known for? Rank them in order of priority to you (1 = highest, 4 = lowest).

_____ Smart

_____ Wealthy

_____ Creative

_____ Caring

Reflection 4.6

From your responses to the preceding questions, identify a long-range goal you could pursue that's compatible with your personal values. In the space that follows, write down the goal and your values that are compatible with it.

Step 2. Awareness of Your Options

The second critical step in the goal-setting process is to become aware of your options for long-range goals. For example, to effectively choose a career goal, you need to be aware of the career options available to you and have a realistic understanding of the types of work performance required by these careers. To gain this knowledge, you'll need to capitalize on available resources by doing the following:

1. Reading books about different careers
2. Taking career development courses
3. Interviewing people in different career fields
4. Observing (shadowing) people working in different careers

Step 3. Awareness of Options That Best "Fit" You

A third key step in the goal-setting process is becoming aware of the full range of options available to you as potential goals. For instance, in college you have multiple courses and majors from which to choose. To deepen your awareness of whether a field may be a good fit for you, take a course in that field to test out how well it matches your interests, values, talents, and learning style. Ideally, you want to select a field that closely taps into, or builds on, your strongest skills and talents.

Choosing a field that's compatible with your strongest abilities will enable you to master the skills required by that field more deeply and efficiently. You are also more likely to succeed or excel in a field that draws on your talents, and the success you experience will, in turn, strengthen your self-esteem, self-confidence, and drive to continue with it. You've probably heard of the proverb "If there's a will, there's a way"— when you're motivated, you're more likely to succeed. It's also true that "If there's a way, there's a will"—when you know how to do something well, you're more motivated to do it.

Step 4. Awareness of the Key Steps Needed to Reach Your Goal

This is the fourth and final step in an effective goal-setting process. For example, if you've set the goal of achieving a college degree in a particular major, you need to be aware of the courses you need to complete to reach that major. Similarly, with a career goal, you need to know what major or majors lead to that career; some careers may require a specific major, but many careers may be reached through a variety of different majors. (See Chapter 11 for more details.)

Reflection 4.7

Think about a major you've chosen or are considering and answer the following questions:

1. Why are you considering this major? What led or caused you to become interested in this choice? Why or why not?

2. Would you say that your interest in this major is motivated primarily by intrinsic factors—i.e., factors "inside" of you, such as your personal abilities, interests, needs, and values? Or is your interest in the career motivated more heavily by extrinsic factors—i.e., factors "outside" of you, such as starting salary or meeting the expectations of parents?

Remember

The process of effective goal setting applies to more than just educational goals. It's a strategic process that could and should be applied to any goal you set for yourself in life, at any stage of your life.

The word *motivation* derives from the Latin *movere*, meaning "to move." Success comes to those who overcome inertia—they first initiate momentum to start moving them toward their goal; then they maintain motivation until their goal is reached. Goal setting only creates the potential for success; it takes motivation to turn this potential into reality by converting intention into action. You can have the best-planned goals and all the knowledge, strategies, and skills to be successful, but if you don't have the will to succeed, there's no way you will succeed. Studies show that without a strong personal commitment to achieve a goal, that goal will not be achieved, no matter how well designed the plan is to reach it (Locke, 2000; Locke & Latham, 1990).

"You can lead a horse to water, but you can't make him drink."

—Author unknown

Snapshot Summary

4.1 The SMART Method of Goal Setting

A popular mnemonic device for remembering the key components of a well-designed goal is the acronym "SMART" (Doran, 1981; Meyer, 2003).

A SMART goal is one that is:

Specific—it states exactly what the goal is and what will be done to achieve it.

Example: I'll achieve at least a "B" average this term by spending 25 hours per week on my course work outside of class and by using the effective learning strategies described in this book. (As opposed to the non-specific goal, "I'm really going to work hard.")

Meaningful (and Measurable)—it's a goal that really matters to the individual, for which progress can be steadily measured or tracked.

Example: I will achieve at least a "B" average this term because it will enable me to get into a field that I really want to pursue as a career, and I will measure my progress toward this goal by keeping track of the grades I'm earning in all my courses throughout the term.

Actionable—it identifies the concrete actions or behaviors that will be engaged in to reach the goal.

Example: I will achieve at least a "B" average this term by (1) attending all classes, (2) taking detailed notes in all my classes, (3) completing all reading assignments before their due dates, and (4) avoiding cramming by studying in advance of all my major exams.

Realistic—the goal capable of being achieved or attained.

Example: Achieving a "B" average this term will be a realistic goal for me because my course load is manageable and I will not be working at my part-time job for more than 15 hours per week.

Timed—the goal that is broken down into a timeline that includes short-range, mid-range, and long-range steps.

Example: To achieve at least a "B" average this term, first I'll acquire the information I need to learn by taking complete notes in class and on my assigned readings (short-range step). Second, I'll study the information I've acquired from my notes and readings in short study sessions held in advance of major exams (mid-range step). Third, I'll hold a final review session for all information previously studied on the day before my exams, and after exams I'll review my test results as feedback to determine what I did well and what I need to do better in order to maintain at least a "B" average (long-range step).

Note: The strategy for setting SMART goals is a transferable process that can be applied to reaching goals in any aspect or dimension of your life, including health-related goals such as losing weight, social goals such as meeting new people, and fiscal goals such as saving money. The SMART goal-setting strategy can help you achieve goals for any and all elements of holistic (whole-person) development described in Chapter 2 (p. 43).

Strategies for Maintaining Motivation and Progress toward Your Goals

Reaching your goals requires will and energy; it also requires skill and strategy. Listed here are strategies for maintaining your motivation and commitment to reaching your goals.

Visualize reaching your long-range goal. Create mental images of being successful. For example, if your goal is to achieve a college degree, imagine a crowd of cheering family, friends, and faculty at your graduation. Visualize how you'll be able to cherish and carry this proud memory with you for the rest of your life, and how the benefits of a college degree will last your entire lifetime. Imagine yourself in the career that your college degree enabled you to enter. Visualize your typical workday going something like this: You wake up in the morning and hop out of bed enthusiastically, looking forward to your day at work. When you're at work, time flies by, and before you know it, the day's over. When you return to bed that night and look back on your day, you feel good about what you did and how well you did it.

Put your goals in writing. When you put your goals in writing, you remain aware of them and remember them. This can stimulate your motivation to pursue your plan into action by serving almost like a written contract that holds you accountable to following through on your commitment. Place your written goals where you see them regularly. Consider writing them on sticky notes and posting them in multiple places that you encounter on a daily basis (e.g., your laptop, refrigerator, and bathroom mirror). If you keep them constantly in sight, you'll keep them constantly in mind.

Remember: The next best thing to accomplishing something immediately is immediately writing down your intention to do it!

Map out your goals. Lay out your goals in the form of a flowchart to show the steps you'll be taking to move from your short-range to mid-range to long-range goals. Visual diagrams can help you "see" where you want to go, enabling you to connect where you are now and where you want to be. Diagramming can also be energizing because it gives you a sneak preview of the finish line and a map-like overview of how to get there.

Keep a record of your progress. Research indicates that the act of monitoring and recording progress toward goals can increase motivation to continue pursuing them (Locke & Latham, 2005; Matsui, Okada, & Inoshita, 1983). The act of keeping records of your progress increases your motivation by giving you frequent feedback on your progress and positive reinforcement for staying on track and moving toward your target (long-range goal) (Bandura & Cervone, 1983; Schunk, 1995). For example, mark your accomplishments in red on your calendar, or keep a journal of the goals you've reached; your entries will keep you motivated by supplying you with concrete evidence of your progress and commitment. You can also chart or graph your progress, which provides a powerful visual display of your upward trends and patterns. Keep the chart where you can see it on a daily basis so you can use it as an ongoing source of inspiration and motivation. You can add musical inspiration by playing a motivational song in your head to keep you going (e.g., "We Are the Champions" by Queen).

Develop a skeletal resume of your career goals. Include your goals as separate sections or categories that will be fleshed out as you complete them. Your to-be-completed resume can provide a framework or blueprint for organizing, building, and tracking progress toward your goals. It can also serve as a visual reminder of the things you plan to accomplish and eventually showcase to potential employers. Furthermore, every time you look at your growing resume, you'll be reminded of your past accomplishments, which can energize and motivate you to reach your goals. As you fill in and build up your resume, you will see (literally) how much you have achieved, which boosts your self-confidence and motivation to continue achieving. (For a sample skeletal resume, see Chapter 12, p. 296.)

Reward yourself for making steady progress toward your long-range goal. Reward is already built into reaching your long-range goal because it represents the end of your trip: it lands you at your desired destination. However, short- and mid-range goals may not be desirable ends in themselves; often, they are merely the means to a desirable end (your long-range goal). Consequently, you need to intentionally reward yourself for landing on these smaller stepping stones up the path to your long-range goal. When you complete these short- and mid-range goals, record and reward your accomplishments (e.g., celebrate your successful completion of midterms or finals by treating yourself to something you enjoy).

Like any other habit, the habit of perseverance and persistence through all intermediate steps needed to reach a long-range goal is more likely to continue if it's followed by a reward (positive reinforcement). The process of setting small goals, moving steadily toward them, and rewarding yourself for reaching them is a simple but powerful strategy. It helps you maintain motivation over the extended period needed to reach your long-range goal.

Capitalize on available campus resources that can help you stay on track and moving toward your goal. Studies indicate that college success results from a combination of what students do for themselves (personal responsibility) and what students do to capitalize on resources available to them—i.e., their resourcefulness (Pascarella & Terenzini, 1991, 2005). Successful college students are resourceful students; they seek out and take advantage of college resources to help them reach their goals.

For example, a resourceful student who is having trouble deciding what field of study to pursue for a degree will seek assistance from an academic advisor on campus. A resourceful student who is interested in a particular career but is unclear about the best educational path to take toward that career will use the Career Development Center as a resource.

Use your social resources. Ask yourself, "Who can help me stick to my plan and complete the steps needed to reach my goal?" The power of social support groups for helping people achieve personal goals is well documented by research in various fields (Brissette, Cohen, & Seeman, 2000; Ewell, 1997). You can use the power of people by surrounding yourself with peers who are committed to successfully achieving their educational goals and by avoiding "toxic" people who are likely to poison your plans or dampen your dreams.

Find supportive, motivated friends and make a mutual pact to help each other reach your respective goals. This step could be taken to a more formal level by drawing up a "social contract" whereby you and your partner are "co-witnesses" or designated social-support agents whose role is to help each other stay on track and moving toward long-range goals.

Convert setbacks into comebacks. The type of thoughts you have after experiencing a setback can affect your emotional reaction to the setback and the action you take in response to it. What you think about a poor performance (e.g., a poor test grade) can affect your emotional reaction to that grade and what action, or lack of action, you take to improve it. You can react to the poor grade by knocking yourself down with a putdown ("I'm a loser") or by building yourself back up with a positive pep talk ("I'm going to learn from my mistakes on this test and rebound with a stronger performance on the next one").

It's noteworthy that the root of the word *failure* is *fallere*, which means to "trip or fall," while the root word for *success* is *successus*, which means "to follow or come after." Thus, when we fail at something, it doesn't mean we've been defeated: it just means we've stumbled and fallen. Success can still be achieved after the fall by getting up, not giving up, and continuing to take the succession of steps needed to successfully reach our goal.

> "Willpower is the personal strength and discipline, rooted in strong motivation, to carry out your plans. 'Waypower' is the exertion of willpower that helps you find resources and support."
>
> —Jerry Pattengale, history professor and author of *The Purpose-Guided Student: Dream to Succeed*

> "Develop an inner circle of close associations in which the mutual attraction is not sharing problems or needs. The mutual attraction should be values and goals."
>
> —Denis Waitley, former mental trainer for U.S. Olympic athletes and author of *Seeds of Greatness*

> "What happens is not as important as how you react to what happens."
>
> —Thaddeus Golas, *Lazy Man's Guide to Enlightenment*

Reflection **4.8**

What would you say is the biggest setback or obstacle you've overcome in your life thus far?

How did you overcome it? (What enabled you to get past it or prevented you from being blocked by it?)

Maintain positive expectations. Just as your thoughts in reaction to something that's already taken place can affect your motivation to keep striving for success, thoughts about what you expect to happen next can affect whether you maintain your motivation to succeed. Your expectations of things to come can be either positive or negative. For example, before a test you could think, "I'm poised, confident, and ready to do it." Or you could think, "I know I'm going to fail this test; I just know it."

Expectations can lead to what sociologists and psychologists have called a *self-fulfilling prophecy*—a positive or negative expectation leads you to act in a way that is consistent with your expectation, which, in turn, makes your expectation come true. For instance, if you expect you're going to fail an exam ("What's the use? I'm going to fail anyway."), you're less likely to put as much effort into studying for the test. During the test, your negative expectation is likely to reduce your test confidence and elevate you test anxiety; for example, if you experience difficulty with the first item on a test, you may get anxious and begin to think you're going to have difficulty with all remaining items and flunk the entire exam. All of this negative thinking is likely to increase the probability that your expectation of doing poorly on the exam will become a reality.

> "Whether you think you can or you can't, you're right."
>
> —Henry Ford, founder of Ford Motor Company

Reflection 4.9

Would you consider yourself to be an optimist or a pessimist?

In what situations are you more likely to think optimistically and pessimistically?

Why?

In contrast, positive expectations can lead to a positive self-fulfilling prophecy: If you expect to do well on an exam, you're more likely to demonstrate higher levels of effort, confidence, and concentration, all of which combine to increase the likelihood that you'll earn a higher test grade. Research shows that learning and practicing positive self-talk serves to promote hope—belief in one's ability to reach goals and the ability to actually reach them (Snyder, 1994).

Keep your eye on the prize. Don't lose sight of the long-term consequences of your short-term choices and decisions. Long-range thinking is the key to reaching long-range goals. Unfortunately, however, humans are often more motivated by short-range thinking because it produces quicker results and more immediate gratification. It's more convenient and tempting to think in the short term ("I like it. I want it. I want it now."). Studies show that the longer the delay between the time when a decision is made and the time when the negative consequences of that decision are experienced, the less likely we are to consider the consequences of our decisions (Ainslie, 1975; Elster & Lowenstein, 1992; Goldstein & Hogarth, 1997). For example, choosing to do what you feel like doing instead of doing work that needs to be done is why so many people procrastinate, and choosing to use a credit card to get something now instead of saving money to buy it later is why so many people pile up credit-card debt.

To be successful in the long run, you need to keep your focus on the big picture—your dream. At the same time, you need to focus on the details—the due dates, to-do lists, and day-to-day duties that require perspiration but keep you on track and going in the right direction.

> "A pessimist sees the difficulty in every opportunity; an optimist sees the opportunity in every difficulty."
>
> —Winston Churchill

> "You've got to think about 'big things' while you're doing small things, so that all the small things go in the right direction."
>
> —Alvin Toffler, American futurologist and author who predicted the future effects of technology on our society

The Importance of Personal Character

Reaching your goals depends on acquiring and using effective strategies, but it takes something more. Ultimately, success emerges from the inside out; it flows from positive qualities or attributes found within you, which, collectively, form your personal character.

We become effective and successful human beings when our actions and deeds become a natural extension of who we are and how we live. At first, developing the habits associated with achieving success and leading a productive life may require substantial effort and intense concentration because these behaviors may be new to us. However, if these actions occur consistently enough, they're transformed into natural habits.

When you engage in effective habits regularly, they become virtues. A virtue may be defined as a characteristic or trait that is valued as good or admirable, and someone who possesses a collection of important virtues is said to be a person of character. There are three key character traits or virtues that typify highly motivated people:

1. Drive
2. Discipline
3. Determination

Drive

Drive is the force within you that supplies you with the energy needed to initiate action. Much like shifting into the drive gear is necessary to move your car forward, it takes personal drive to move forward and toward your goals. People with drive are not just dreamers: they are also doers. They take the action needed to convert their dreams into reality; they hustle—they go all out and give it their all, all of the time, to achieve their goals. College students with drive approach college with passion and enthusiasm. They don't hold back and work halfheartedly; they give 100 percent by putting their whole heart and soul into it.

Discipline

Discipline includes such positive qualities as commitment, devotion, and dedication. These personal qualities enable us to keep going and moving toward our long-range goals over an extended period of time. Successful people think big but start small; they take all the small steps and diligently do all the little things that need to be done, which, in the long run, add up to a big accomplishment—achievement of their long-range goal.

People who are self-disciplined accept the day-to-day sweat, toil, and perspiration needed to attain their long-term aspirations. They're willing to tolerate short-term strain or pain for long-term gain. They have the self-control and self-restraint needed to resist the impulse for instant gratification or the temptation to do what they feel like doing instead of what they need to do. They're willing to sacrifice their immediate needs and desires in the short run to do what is necessary to put them where they want to be in the long run.

"If you do not find it within yourself, where will you go to get it?"

—Zen saying (Zen is a branch of Buddhism that emphasizes seeing deeply into the nature of things and ongoing self-awareness)

"We are what we repeatedly do. Excellence, then, is not an act, but a habit."

—Aristotle, ancient Greek philosopher

"Sow an act and you reap a habit; sow a habit and you reap a character; sow a character and you reap a destiny."

—Frances E. Willard, 19th-century American educator and women's rights activist

"Whoever wants to reach a distant goal must take many small steps."

—Helmut Schmidt, former chancellor of West Germany

Student
Perspective

"Why is it so hard when I *have* to do something and so easy when I *want* to do something?"

—First-year college student

> **Remember**
>
> *Sometimes you've got to do what you have to do in order to get to do what you want to do.*

Reflection 4.10

Think about something that you do with drive, effort, and intensity. What thoughts, attitudes, and behaviors do you display when you do it?

Do you see ways in which you could apply the same approach to achieving your goals in college?

> "Self-discipline is the ability to make yourself do the thing you have to do, when it ought to be done, whether you like it or not."
>
> —Thomas Henry Huxley, 19th-century English biologist

Remember

Sacrifices made for a short time can bring benefits that last a lifetime.

Determination

Individuals with the character trait of determination pursue their goals with a relentless tenacity. They have the fortitude to persist in the face of frustration and the resiliency to bounce back after setbacks. If they encounter something on the road to their goal that's hard to do, they work harder and longer to do it. When they encounter a major bump or barrier, they don't let it stand in their way by giving up or giving in; instead, they dig deeper and keep going.

People with determination are also more likely to seek out challenges. Rather than remaining stagnant and simply doing what's safe, secure, or easy, they stay hungry and display an ongoing commitment to personal growth and development; they keep striving and driving to be the best they can possibly be in all aspects of life.

> "SUCCESS is peace of mind which is a direct result of self-satisfaction in knowing you made the effort to become the best that you are capable of becoming."
>
> —John Wooden, college basketball coach and creator of the "Pyramid of Success"

Summary and Conclusion

Goal setting is the key to igniting motivation; maintaining motivation after it has been ignited requires use of effective self-motivational strategies, such as:

- Visualizing reaching your long-range goals;
- Putting goals in writing;
- Creating a visual map of your goals;
- Keeping a record of your progress;
- Rewarding yourself for progress toward long-range goals;
- Converting setbacks into comebacks by using positive self-talk and maintaining positive expectations; and
- Keeping your eye on the long-term consequences of your short-term choices and decisions.

Successfully setting and reaching goals also depends on personal character. The following character traits or virtues typify highly motivated and successful people:

Drive. The internal force that provides energy to overcome inertia and initiate action.

Discipline. Commitment, devotion, and dedication that enable you to sustain your effort over time.

Determination. The capacity to relentlessly pursue your goals, persist in the face of frustration, and bounce back after any setback.

Remember

Success isn't a short-range goal: it's not a sprint but a long-distance run that takes patience and perseverance to complete. What matters most is not how fast you start but where you finish. Goal setting will get you going and motivation will keep you going until you cross the finish line.

Learning More through the World Wide Web

Internet-Based Resources for Further Information on Goal Setting

For additional information related to the ideas discussed in this chapter, we recommend the following Web sites:

Goal Setting:

www.siue.edu/SPIN/activity.html

Self-Motivational Strategies:

www.selfmotivationstrategies.com

Developing Personal Character: Who's Watching? Character and Integrity in the 21st Century

www.calea.org/calea-update-magazine/issue-100/who-s-watching-character-and-integrity-21st-century

4.1 Prioritizing Important Life Goals

Consider the following life goals. Rank them in the order of their priority for you (1 = highest, 5 = lowest).

___ Emotional well-being

___ Spiritual growth

___ Physical health

___ Social relationships

___ Rewarding career

Self-Assessment Questions

1. What were the primary reasons behind your first- and last-ranked choices?
2. Have you established any short- or mid-range goals for reaching your highest-ranked choice? If yes, what are they? If no, what could they be?

4.2 Setting Goals for Reducing the Gap between Your Ideal Future and Your Current Reality

Think of an aspect of your life where there is a gap between what you hoped it would be (the ideal) and what it is (the reality). On the lines that follow, identify goals you could pursue to reduce this gap.

Long-range goal: _____

Mid-range goal: _____

Short-range goal: _____

Use the form that follows to identify strategies for reaching each of these three goals. Consider the following areas for each goal:

* Actions to be taken:
* Available resources:
* Possible roadblocks:
* Potential solutions to roadblocks:

Long-range goal: _____

* Actions to be taken:
* Available resources:
* Possible roadblocks:
* Potential solutions to roadblocks:

Mid-range goal: _____

* Actions to be taken:
* Available resources:
* Possible roadblocks:
* Potential solutions to roadblocks:

Short-range goal: _____

- Actions to be taken:
- Available resources:
- Possible roadblocks:
- Potential solutions to roadblocks:

4.3 Converting Setbacks into Comebacks: Transforming Pessimism into Optimism through Positive Self-Talk

In *Hamlet*, Shakespeare wrote, "There is nothing good or bad, but thinking makes it so." His point was that experiences have the potential to be positive or negative, depending on how people interpret them and react to them.

Listed here is a series of statements representing negative, motivation-destroying interpretations and reactions to a situation or experience:

1. "I'm just not good at this."
2. "There's nothing I can do about it."
3. "Nothing is going to change."
4. "This always happens to me."
5. "Everybody is going to think I'm a loser."

For each of the preceding statements, replace the negative statement with a statement that represents a more positive, self-motivating interpretation or reaction.

No Goals, No Direction

Amy Aimless decided to go to college because it seemed like that was what she was expected to do. All of her closest friends were going and her parents had talked to her about going to college as long as she could remember.

Now that she's in her first term, Amy isn't sure she made the right decision. She has no educational or career goals, nor does she have any idea about what her major might be. None of the subjects she took in high school and none of the courses she's taking in her first term of college have really sparked her interest. Since she has no goals or sense of purpose, she's beginning to think that being in college is a waste of time and money, so she's considering withdrawing at the end of her first term.

Reflection and Discussion Questions

1. What advice would you give Amy about whether she should remain in college or withdraw?

2. What suggestion would you have for Amy that might help her find some sense of educational purpose or direction?

3. How could you counter Amy's claim that no subjects interest her as possible college majors?

4. Would you agree that Amy is currently wasting her time and her parents' money? Why?

5. Would you agree that Amy shouldn't have begun college in the first place? Why?

Time Management

Preventing Procrastination and Promoting Self-Discipline

ACTIVATE YOUR THINKING | *Reflection* **5.1** | **LEARNING GOAL**

Complete the following sentence with the first thought that comes to your mind:

For me, time is . . .

LEARNING GOAL

To help you appreciate the significance of managing time and supply you with a powerful set of time-management strategies that can be used to promote your success in college and beyond.

The Importance of Time Management

Reaching goals requires managing time because it takes time to successfully complete the series of steps that lead to those goals. For first-year college students, time management is especially essential for achieving their goals because the beginning of college brings with it the challenge of independent living and managing their new-found freedom. Even for first-year students who have lived on their own for some time, managing time remains a crucial skill because they will be juggling multiple responsibilities, including school, family, and work.

In addition, the academic calendar and class scheduling patterns in college differ radically from high school. There's less "seat time" in class each week and more "free time" outside of class, which leaves you with a lot more personal time to manage. Your time is not as closely monitored by school authorities or family members, and you are expected to do more academic work on your own outside of class. Personal time-management skills grow in importance when one's time is less structured and controlled by others, leaving the individual with more decision-making power about how to spend personal time. Thus, it's not surprising that research shows the ability to manage time effectively plays a crucial role in college success (Erickson, Peters, & Strommer, 2006). Simply stated, college students who have difficulty managing their time have difficulty managing college.

Studies also indicate that managing time plays a pivotal role in the lives of working adults. Setting priorities and balancing multiple responsibilities (e.g., work and family) that compete for limited time and energy can be a stressful juggling act for people of all ages (Harriott & Ferrari, 1996). Thus, good time management serves as good stress management. Time management should be viewed not only as a college-success strategy, but also as a life-management and life-success skill. In short, when you gain greater control of your time, you become more satisfied with your life.

Student
Perspective

"The major difference [between high school and college] is time. You have so much free time on your hands that you don't know what to do for most of the time."

—First-year college student (Erickson & Strommer, 1991)

Student
Perspective

"I cannot stress enough that you need to intelligently budget your time."

—Advice to new college students from a first-year student

Strategies for Managing Time

Effective time management involves three key mental processes:

1. **Analysis.** Breaking down time into specific segments and work into smaller tasks;
2. **Itemizing.** Identifying all key tasks that need to be done and by what dates;
3. **Prioritizing.** Organizing and attacking tasks in order of their importance.

The following steps can help you apply these skills to find more time in your schedule and use this time more productively.

1. **Break time down into smaller units to become more aware about how your time is being spent.** Have you ever asked yourself, "Where did all the time go?" or told yourself, "I just can't seem to find the time"? One way to find out where your time went is by taking a time inventory. Conduct a time analysis by tracking your time and recording what you do and when you do it. By mapping out how you spend time, you become more aware of how much total time you actually have and where it goes, including patches of wasted time during which you get little or nothing accomplished. You just need to do this time analysis for more than a week or two to see where your time is going and to get started on strategies for using your time more productively.

Reflection 5.2

Do you have time gaps between your classes this term? If you do, what have you been doing during those "free" periods between classes?

What would you say is your greatest time waster?

Do you see a need to stop or eliminate it?

If you don't, why not? If yes, what could you do to convert your wasted time into productive time?

2. **Identify the key tasks you need to accomplish and when you need to accomplish them.** People make lists to be sure they don't forget items they need from the grocery store or people they want to be sure are invited to a party. You can use the same list-making strategy for work tasks so that you don't forget to do them or forget to do them on time. Studies of effective people show that they are list makers; they write out lists not only for grocery items and wedding invitations, but also for things they want to accomplish each day (Covey, 2004).

    You can itemize the tasks on your lists by using the following time-management tools:

    • **Personal digital assistant (PDA) or cell phone.** You can use these to do a lot more than check social networking sites and send and receive text messages. Use the calendar tools in these devices to record due dates and set up the alert functions to remind you of these deadlines. Many PDAs and smartphones will also allow you to set up task or "to-do" lists and to set priorities for each item you enter.
    • **Small, portable planner.** List all your major assignments and exams for the term, along with their due dates. Putting all work tasks from different

courses in one place makes it easier to keep track of what you have to do and when you have to do it.

- **Large, stable calendar.** In the calendar's date boxes, record your major assignments for the academic term and when they are due. Place the calendar in a position or location where it's in full view and you can't help but see it every day (e.g., on your bedroom or refrigerator door). If you regularly and literally "look" at the things you have to do, you're less likely to "overlook" them, forget about them, or subconsciously push them out of your mind because you don't really want to do them.

3. **Rank your tasks in order of their importance.** Once you've itemized your work by listing all tasks you need to do, prioritize them—determine the order in which you will do them. Prioritizing basically involves ranking your tasks in terms of their importance, with the highest-ranked tasks appearing at the top of your list to ensure that they are tackled first. How do you determine which tasks are most important and should be ranked highest? Two criteria or standards of judgment can be used to help determine which tasks should be your highest priorities:

- **Urgency.** Tasks that are closest to their deadline or due date should receive high priority. For example, finishing an assignment that's due tomorrow should receive higher priority than starting an assignment that's due next month.

- **Gravity.** Tasks that carry the heaviest weight (count the most) should receive highest priority. For example, if an assignment worth 100 points and another worth 10 points are due at the same time, the 100-point task should receive higher priority. Just like investing money, you want to invest your time in tasks that yield the greatest dividends or payoff.

> "Things that matter most must never be at the mercy of things that matter least."
>
> —Johann Wolfgang von Goethe, German poet, dramatist, and author of the epic *Faust*

Reflection 5.3

Do you have a calendar that you carry with you, or do you use the calendar tool on your PDA or cell phone?

If yes, why?

If no, why do you think you don't?

One strategy for prioritizing your tasks is to divide them into A, B, and C lists (Lakein, 1973; Morgenstern, 2004). Your "A" list is for *essential* tasks—what you *must* do now; your "B" list is for *important* tasks—what you *should* do soon; and your "C" list is for *optional* tasks—what you *could* or *might* do if there is time remaining after you've completed the tasks on the A and B lists. Organizing your tasks in this fashion can help you decide how to divide your labor in a way that ensures you put first things first. Don't waste time doing unimportant things to deceive yourself into thinking that you're keeping busy and getting things done; in reality, all you're doing is taking time (and your mind) away from the more important things you should be doing.

Remember

"First things first." Plan your work by placing the most important and most urgent tasks at the top of your list, and work your plan by attacking tasks in the order in which you have listed them.

At first glance, itemizing and prioritizing may appear to be rather boring chores. However, if you look at these mental tasks carefully, they require higher-level thinking skills, such as:

1. **Analysis.** Dividing time into component elements or segments and breaking down work into specific tasks;
2. **Evaluation.** Critically evaluating the relative importance or value of tasks; and
3. **Synthesis.** Organizing individual tasks into classes or categories based on their level of priority.

> **Remember**
>
> *Developing self-awareness about how your time is spent is more than a brainless, clerical activity. When it's done with thoughtful reflection, it becomes an exercise in higher-level thinking. It's also a good values-clarification exercise because it makes us aware of whether we're actually spending our time on those things that we say we really value.*

Develop a Time-Management Plan

Humans are creatures of habit. Routines help you organize and gain control of your life. Doing things by design, rather than leaving them to chance or accident, is the first step toward making things happen for you rather than allowing them to happen. By developing an intentional plan for how you're going to spend your time, you're developing a plan to gain greater control of your life.

Don't buy into the myth that you don't have time to plan because it takes too much time that could be spent getting started and getting things done. Time-management experts estimate that the amount of time you spend planning your work reduces your total work time by a factor of three (Goldsmith, 2010; Lakein, 1973). In other words, for every one unit of time you spend planning, you save three units of work time. Thus, five minutes of planning time will typically save you 15 minutes of total work time, and 10 minutes of planning time will save you 30 minutes of work time. You save work time by engaging in planning time because you end up with a clearer understanding of what needs to be done and the order of steps you need to take to get it done. This clearer sense of direction reduces the likelihood of losing time to "false starts"—having to restart your work because you started off in the wrong direction. If you have no plan of attack, you're more likely to go off track; when you discover this at some point after you've started, you're then forced to retreat and start all over again.

As the proverb goes, "A stitch in time saves nine." Planning your time represents the "stitch" (unit of time) that saves you nine additional stitches (units of time). Similar to successful chess players, successful time managers plan ahead and anticipate their next moves.

Elements of a Comprehensive Time-Management Plan

Once you've accepted the notion that taking the time to plan your time saves you time in the long run, you're ready to design a time-management plan. The following are elements of a comprehensive, well-designed plan for managing time.

1. **A good time-management plan includes short, mid- and long-range time frames.** For instance, a good academic time-management plan for the term should include:

- A *long-range* plan for the entire term that identifies deadline dates for reports and papers that are due toward the end of the term;
- A *mid-range* plan for the upcoming month and week; and
- A *short-range* plan for the following day.

Here's how you can put this three-stage plan into action this term:

- Review the *course syllabus (course outline)* for each class you are enrolled in this term, and highlight all major exams, tests, quizzes, assignments, and papers and the dates on which they are due
- Obtain a *large calendar* for the academic term (available at your campus bookstore or learning center) and record all your exams, assignments, and so on, for all your courses in the calendar boxes that represent their due dates. To fit this information within the calendar boxes, use creative abbreviations to represent different tasks, such as E for exam and TP for term paper (not toilet paper). When you're done, you'll have a centralized chart or map of deadline dates and a potential master plan for the entire term. Get in the habit of not only doing short-range academic planning and calendaring for the upcoming day or week, but long-range planning for the academic semester or term.
- Activate the calendar and task lists functions on your PDA or cell phone. Enter your schedule, important dates, and deadlines, and set alert reminders. Since you carry your PDA or cell phone with you regularly, you will always have this information at your fingertips.

Work backward from this long-range plan to:

- **Plan your week.**
  a. Make a map of your *weekly schedule* that includes times during the week when you are in class, when you typically eat and sleep, and if you are employed, when you work.
  b. If you are a full-time college student, find *at least 25 total hours per week* when you can do academic work outside the classroom. (These 25 hours can be pieced together in any way you like, including time between daytime classes and work commitments, evening time, and weekend time.) When adding these 25 hours to the time you spend in class each week, you will end up with a 40-hour workweek, similar to any full-time job. If you are a part-time student, you should plan on spending at least two hours on academic work outside of class for every hour that you're in class.
  c. Make good use of your *free time between classes* by working on assignments and studying in advance for upcoming exams. See Do It Now! 5.1 for a summary of how you can use your out-of-class time to improve your academic performance and course grades.
- Plan your day.
  a. Make a *daily to-do list.*
  b. Attack daily tasks in *priority order.*
- Carry a *small calendar, planner, or appointment book* at all times. This will enable you to record appointments that you may make on the run during the day and will allow you to jot down creative ideas or memories of things you need to do—which can sometimes pop into your mind at the most unexpected times.
- Take *portable work* with you during the day that you can carry with you and do in any place at any time. This will enable you to take advantage of "dead time" during the day. For example, carry material with you that you can read while sit-

Remember

College professors are more likely than high school teachers to expect you to rely on your course syllabus to keep track of what you have to do and when you have to do it.

Student
Perspective

"The amount of free time you have in college is much more than in high school. Always have a weekly study schedule to go by. Otherwise, time slips away and you will not be able to account for it."

—Advice to new college students from a first-year student (Rhoads, 2005)

Student
Perspective

"In high school we were given a homework assignment every day. Now we have a large task assigned to be done at a certain time. No one tells [us] when to start or what to do each day."

—First-year college student (Rhoads, 2005)

Remember

If you write it out, you're less likely to block it out and forget about it.

Student
Perspective

"I was constantly missing important meetings during my first few weeks because I did not keep track of the dates and times. I thought I'd be told again when the time was closer, just as had been done in high school. Something I should have done to address that would have been to keep a well-organized planner for reference."

—College sophomore (Walsh, 2005)

ting and waiting for appointments or transportation, allowing you to resurrect this dead time and convert it to "live" work time. (Not only is this a good time-management strategy, it's a good stress-management strategy because it puts you in control of "wait time," enabling you to use it to save time later and reducing the likelihood that you'll feel frustrated, anxious, or bored.)

- Wear a *watch* or carry a cell phone that can accurately and instantly tell you what time it is and what date it is. You can't even begin to manage time if you don't know what time it is, and you can't plan a schedule if you don't know what date it is. (Try setting the time on your watch or cell phone slightly ahead of the actual time to help ensure that you arrive to class, work, or meetings on time.)

Reflection 5.4

Do you make a to-do list of things you need to get done each day? (Circle one.)

never   seldom   often   almost always

If you circled "never" or "seldom," why don't you?

2. **A good time-management plan includes planning reserve time to take care of the unexpected.** Always hope for the best, but always be prepared for the worst. Your time-management plan should include a buffer zone or safety net of extra time in case you encounter unforeseen developments or unexpected emergencies. Just as you should plan to have extra funds in your account to pay for unexpected costs (e.g., an auto repair), you should plan to have extra time in your schedule for unexpected events (e.g., a random emergency).

3. **A good time-management plan should balance work and recreation.** Don't only plan work time: plan time to relax, refuel, and recharge. Your overall time-management plan shouldn't turn you into an obsessive-compulsive workaholic. Instead, it should represent a balanced blend of work and play, including activities that promote your mental and physical wellness, such as relaxation, recreation, and reflection. If your schedule makes room for the things you like to do, you're more likely do to the things you have to do. You could also arrange your schedule of work and play as a self-motivation strategy by using your play time to reward completion of your work time.

Remember

A good time-management plan should help you stress less, learn more, and earn higher grades while leaving you time for other important aspects of your life. A good plan not only enables you to get your work done on time, but also enables you to attain and maintain balance in your life.

Reflection 5.5

What activities do you engage in for fun or recreation?

What do you do to relax or relieve stress?

Do you build these activities into your daily or weekly schedule?

5.1

Making Productive Use of Free Time Outside the Classroom

Unlike in high school, homework in college often does not involve turning things in to your instructor daily or weekly. The academic work you do outside the classroom may not even be collected and graded. Instead, it is done for your own benefit to help prepare yourself for upcoming exams and major assignments (e.g., term papers or research reports). Rather than formally assigning work to you as homework, your professors expect that you will do this work on your own and without supervision. Listed below are strategies for working independently and in advance of college exams and assignments. These strategies will increase the quality of your time management in college and the quality of your academic performance.

Working Independently in Advance of Exams

Use the following strategies to use out-of-class time wisely to prepare for exams:

- **Complete reading assignments** relating to lecture topics before the topic is discussed in class. This will make lectures easier to understand and will prepare you to participate intelligently in class (e.g., ask meaningful questions of your instructor and make informed comments during class discussions).
- **Review your class notes** between class periods so that you can construct a mental bridge from one class to the next and make each upcoming lecture easier to follow. When reviewing your notes before the next class, rewrite any class notes that may be sloppily written the first time. If you find notes related to the same point all over the place, reorganize them by combining them into one set of notes. Lastly, if you find any information gaps or confusing points in your notes, seek out the course instructor or a trusted classmate to clear them up before the next class takes place.
- **Review information** you highlighted in your reading assignments to improve your retention of the information. If certain points are confusing to you, discuss them with your course instructor during office hours or with a fellow classmate outside of class.
- **Integrate key ideas** in your class notes with information that you have highlighted in your assigned reading, which relates to the same major point or general category. In other words, put related information from your lecture notes and your reading in the same place (e.g., on the same index card).
- **Use a part-to-whole study method** whereby you study material from your class notes and assigned reading in small pieces during short, separate study sessions that take place well in advance of the exam; then make your last study session before the exam a longer review session during which you restudy all the small parts together as a whole. It's a myth that studying in advance is a waste of time because you'll forget it all anyway by test time. As you'll see in Chapter 5, information studied in advance of an exam remains in your brain and is still there when you later review it. Even if you cannot recall the previously studied information when you first start reviewing it, you will relearn it faster than you did the first time, thus proving that some memory of it was retained from your earlier study sessions.

Work Independently Well in Advance of Due Dates for Term Papers and Research Reports

Work on large, long-range assignments by breaking them into the following smaller, short-term tasks:

1. Search for and select a topic.
2. Locate sources of information on the topic.
3. Organize the information obtained from these sources into categories.
4. Develop an outline of the report's major points and the order or sequence in which you plan to discuss them.
5. Construct a first draft of the paper (and, if necessary, a second draft).
6. Write a final draft of the paper.
7. Proofread the final draft of your paper for minor mechanical mistakes, such as spelling and grammatical errors, before submitting it to your instructor.

Remember

When you create a personal time-management plan, remember that it's your plan—you own it and you run it. It shouldn't run you.

4. **A good time-management plan has some flexibility.** Some students are immediately turned off by the idea of developing a schedule and planning their time because they feel it over-structures their lives and limits their freedom. It's only natural for you to prize your personal freedom and resist anything that appears to restrict your freedom in any way. However, a good time-management plan doesn't limit freedom: it preserves freedom by helping you get done what you must do and reserves free time to do what you want and like to do.

5. **A good time-management plan shouldn't enslave you to a rigid work schedule.** The plan should be flexible enough to allow you to occasionally bend it without breaking it. Just as work commitments and family responsibilities can crop up unexpectedly, so, too, can opportunities for fun and enjoyable activities. Your plan should allow you the freedom to modify your schedule so that you can take advantage of these enjoyable opportunities and experiences. However, you should plan to make up the work time you lost. In other words, you can borrow or trade work time for play time, but don't "steal" it; plan to pay back the work time you borrowed by substituting it for play time that was planned for another time. If you can't do something you planned to do, the next best thing is to re-plan when you'll do it.

Converting a Time-Management Plan into an Action Plan

Once you've planned the work, the next step is to work the plan. A good action plan is one that enables you to (1) preview what you intend to accomplish and (2) review what you actually accomplished. You can begin to implement an action plan by constructing a daily to-do list, bringing that list with you as the day begins, and checking off items on the list as you get them done throughout the day. At the end of the day, review your list and identify what was completed and what still needs to be done. The uncompleted tasks should become high priorities for the next day.

5.6

Reflection

By the end of a typical day, how often do you find that you accomplished most of the important tasks you hoped to accomplish? (Circle one.)

never   seldom   often   almost always

Why?

At the end of the day, if you find many unchecked items remain on your daily to-do list, this may mean that you're spreading yourself too thin by trying to do too many things in a day. You may need to be more realistic about the number of items you can accomplish per day by shortening your daily to-do list.

Being unable to complete many of your intended daily tasks may also mean that you need to modify your time-management plan by adding more work time or subtracting activities that are drawing time and attention away from your work (e.g., responding to phone calls and text messages during your planned work times).

Dealing with Procrastination

Procrastination Defined

The word *procrastination* derives from two roots: *pro* (meaning "forward") plus *crastinus* (meaning "tomorrow"). As these roots suggest, procrastinators don't abide by the proverb "Why put off to tomorrow what can be done today?" Their philosophy is just the opposite: "Why do today what can be put off until tomorrow?" Adopting this philosophy promotes a perpetual pattern of postponing what needs to be done until the last possible moment, forcing a frantic rush to finish the job in time, which results in a product of poorer quality (or not finishing the product at all).

Research shows that the vast majority of college students procrastinate and almost half of them procrastinate consistently (Onwuegbuzie, 2000). Procrastination is such a serious issue for college students that some colleges and universities have opened "procrastination centers" to provide help exclusively for students who are experiencing problems with procrastination (Burka & Yuen, 2008).

Myths That Promote Procrastination

Before there can be any hope of putting a stop to procrastination, procrastinators need to let go of two popular myths (misconceptions) about time and performance.

Myth 1. "I work better under pressure" (e.g., on the day or night before something is due). Procrastinators often confuse desperation with motivation. Their belief that they work better under pressure is often just a rationalization to justify or deny the reality that they *only* work when they're under pressure—that is, when they've run out of time and have no choice but to do it under the gun of the final deadline.

It's true that some people will only start to work and will work really fast when they're under pressure, but that does not mean they're working more *effectively* and

"Many people take no care of their money 'til they come nearly to the end of it, and others do just the same with their time."

—Johann Wolfgang von Goethe, German poet, dramatist, and author of the epic *Faust*

Student *Perspective*

"I believe the most important aspect of college life is time management. DO NOT procrastinate because, although this is the easy thing to do at first, it will catch up with you and make your life miserable."

—Advice to new college students from a first-year student

Next time I'll start sooner!

A procrastinator's idea of planning ahead and working in advance often boils down to this scenario.

"Haste makes waste."

—Benjamin Franklin

producing work of better *quality*. Because they're playing "beat the clock," the procrastinator's focus is no longer is on doing the job *well* but is on doing the job *fast* so that it gets done before they run out of time. This typically results in a work product that turns out to be incomplete or inferior to what could have been produced if the work process began earlier.

Myth 2. **"Studying in advance is a waste of time because you will forget it all by test time."** The misconception that information learned early will be forgotten is commonly used to justify procrastinating with respect to preparing for upcoming exams. As will be discussed in Chapter 5, studying that is distributed (spread out) over time is more effective than massed (crammed) studying. Furthermore, last-minute studying that takes place the night before exams often results in lost sleep time resulting from pulling "late-nighters" or "all-nighters." This fly-by-night strategy interferes with retention of information that has been studied and elevates test anxiety because of lost dream sleep (a.k.a. rapid eye movement, or REM) that the brain needs to store memories and manage stress (Hobson, 1988; Voelker, 2004). Research indicates that procrastinators experience higher rates of stress-related physical disorders, such as insomnia, stomach problems, colds, and flu (McCance & Pychyl, 2003).

Working under time pressure adds to performance pressure because procrastinators are left with no margin of error to correct mistakes, no time to seek help on their work, and no chance to handle random catastrophes that may arise at the last minute (e.g., an attack of the flu or a family emergency).

Reflection 5.7

Do you tend to put off work for so long that getting it done turns into an emergency or panic situation?

If your answer is yes, why do you think you find yourself in this position? If your answer is no, what is it that prevents this from happening to you?

Psychological Causes of Procrastination

"Procrastinators would rather be seen as lacking in effort than lacking in ability."

—Joseph Ferrari, professor of psychology and procrastination researcher

Sometimes, procrastination has deeper psychological roots. People may procrastinate for reasons that do not relate directly to poor time-management habits but to emotional issues. For instance, studies show that procrastination is sometimes used as a psychological strategy to protect self-esteem. Referred to as *self-handicapping* (Rhodewalt & Vohs, 2005), this strategy is used consciously or unconsciously by some procrastinators to give themselves a "handicap" or disadvantage. Thus, if their performance turns out to be less than spectacular, they can conclude (rationalize) that it was because they were performing under a handicap—lack of time rather than lack of ability (Chu & Cho, 2005).

For example, if they receive a low grade on a test or paper, they can "save face" (self-esteem) by concluding that it was because they waited until the last minute and didn't put much time or effort into it. In other words, they had enough ability or intelligence to earn a high grade; they just didn't have enough time. Better yet, if they happened to luck out and get a good grade—despite doing it at the last minute—they can think it proves just how smart they are because they were able to get that good grade without putting in much time at all! Thus, self-handicapping creates a fail-safe or win-win scenario that's guaranteed to protect the procrastinator's self-image. If the work performance or product is less than excellent, it can be blamed on external factors (e.g., lack of time); if it happens to earn them a high grade, they can attribute the result to themselves—their extraordinary ability enabled them to do so well despite working at the last minute.

In addition to self-handicapping, other psychological factors have been found to contribute to procrastination, including the following:

- **Fear of failure.** The procrastinator feels better about not completing the work on time than doing it and experiencing failure (Burka & Yuen, 2008; Solomon & Rothblum, 1984).
- **Perfectionism.** Having unrealistically high personal standards or expectations, which leads to the procrastinator's belief that it's better to postpone work or not do it than to risk doing it less than perfectly (Kachgal, Hansen, & Nutter, 2001).
- **Fear of success.** Fearing that doing well will show others that the procrastinator has the ability to achieve success and will lead others to expect the procrastinator to maintain those high standards in the future (Beck, Koons, & Milgram, 2000; Ellis & Knaus, 2002).
- **Indecisiveness.** The procrastinator has difficulty making decisions, including decisions about what to do first, when to do it, or whether to do it (Anderson, 2003; Steel, 2007).
- **Thrill seeking.** The procrastinator enjoys the adrenaline rush triggered by hurrying to get things done just before a deadline (Szalavitz, 2003).

> "We didn't lose the game; we just ran out of time."
>
> —Vince Lombardi, football coach

> "Striving for excellence motivates you; striving for perfection is demoralizing."
>
> —Harriet Braiker, psychologist and bestselling author

Reflection 5.8

How often do you procrastinate? (Circle one.)

rarely   occasionally   frequently   consistently

When you do procrastinate, what's the usual cause?

If these underlying psychological issues are at the root of procrastination, they must be dealt with before procrastination can be overcome. Because they have deeper roots, it may take some time and professional assistance to uproot them. A good place to get such assistance is the Counseling Center on campus, where there are counseling psychologists who are professionally trained to deal with emotional issues, including those that may be contributing to procrastination.

Self-Help Strategies for Beating the Procrastination Habit

Once inaccurate beliefs or emotional issues underlying procrastination have been identified and dealt with, the next step is to take direct action on the procrastination habit itself. What follows are seven key strategies for minimizing or eliminating the procrastination habit.

1. **Continually practice effective time-management strategies.** If effective time-management practices, such as those previously cited in this chapter, are implemented consistently, they can turn into a habit. When people repeatedly practice

effective time-management strategies, these practices gradually become part of their routine and develop into habits. For instance, studies show that when procrastinators repeatedly practice effective time-management strategies with respect to tasks that they procrastinate on, their procrastination tendencies begin to fade and are gradually replaced by good habits of good time management (Ainslie, 1992; Baumeister, Heatherton, & Tice, 1994).

2. **Make the start of work as inviting or appealing as possible.** Getting started can be a stumbling block for many procrastinators. They experience what's called "start-up stress"—when they're about to begin a task, they start to experience negative feelings about the task being unpleasant, difficult, or boring (Burka & Yuen, 2008). If you have trouble starting your work, one way to give yourself a jump-start is to arrange your work tasks in an order that allows you to start with tasks that you're likely to find most interesting or to succeed in. Once you've overcome the initial inertia and get going, you can ride the momentum you've created to attack other tasks that you find less appealing or more daunting.

You're also likely to discover that the dreaded work wasn't as difficult, boring, or time-consuming as it appeared to be. When you sense that you're making some progress toward getting work done, your anxiety begins to decline. As with many experiences in life that are feared and avoided, the anticipation of the event turns out to be worse than the event itself. Research on students who hadn't started a project until it was about to be due indicates that they experienced anxiety and guilt about delaying their work, but once they begin working these negative emotions subsided and were replaced by more positive feelings of progress and accomplishment (McCance & Pychyl, 2003).

3. **Make the work manageable.** Work becomes less overwhelming and less stressful when it's handled in small chunks or pieces. You can conquer procrastination for large tasks by using a "divide and conquer" strategy: divide the large task into smaller, more manageable units, and then attack and complete them one at a time.

Don't underestimate the power of short work sessions. They can be more effective than longer sessions because it's easier to maintain momentum and concentration for shorter periods of time. If you're working on a large project or preparing for a major exam, dividing your work into short sessions will enable you to take quick jabs and poke small holes in it, reducing its overall size with each successive punch. This approach will also give you the sense of satisfaction that comes with knowing that you're making steady progress toward completing a big task—by continually jabbing at it in short strokes and gradually reducing the pressure associated with having to go for a big knockout punch right before the final bell (deadline).

4. **Organization matters.** Research indicates that disorganization is a factor that contributes to procrastination (Steel, 2007). How well you organize your workplace and manage your work materials can reduce your risk of procrastination. Ask yourself, "Can I just go in and do it?" Having the right materials in the right place at the right time can make it easier to get to your work and get going on your work. Once you've made a decision to start working, you don't want to delay acting on that decision by looking for the tools you need to get started. For procrastinators, this time delay may be just the amount of time they need to change their minds and decide not to start working!

One simple but effective way to organize your college work materials is to develop your own file system. You can begin to create an effective academic file system by filing (storing) materials from different courses in different-colored folders or notebooks. This will allow you to keep all materials related to the same course in the same place, giving you direct and immediate access to the materials you need as soon as you need them. Such a system helps you get organized, reduces stress associated with having things all over the place, and reduces the risk of procrastination by reducing the time it takes for you to start working.

5. **Location matters.** Where you choose to work can influence whether you work. Research on procrastinators demonstrates that distraction is a factor that can contribute to procrastination (Steel, 2007). Thus, you can reduce your risk of procrastinating by working in an environment whose location and arrangement prevent distraction and promote concentration.

Reflection 5.9

List your two most common sources of distraction while working. Next to each distraction, identify a strategy that you might use to reduce or eliminate it.

Source of Distraction   Strategy for Reducing This Distraction

1.

2.

Distractions tend to come in two major forms: social distractions, e.g., people nearby who are not working, and media distractions, e.g., cell phones, e-mails, text messages, CDs, and TV. Research on college students indicates that the number of hours per week they spend watching TV is *negatively* associated with success: more TV is associated with lower grade point averages, less likelihood of graduating with honors, and lower levels of personal development (Astin, 1993).

Remember

Select a workplace and arrange your workspace to minimize distraction from people and media. Try to remove everything from your work site that's not relevant or directly related to your work.

You can arrange your work environment in a way that not only disables distraction but also enables concentration. Your concentration is easier to maintain when you work in an environment that allows you easy access to (1) work support materials, e.g., class notes, textbooks, and a dictionary, and (2) social support networks, e.g., a group of motivated students who will help you stay focused, on task, and on track toward completing your work.

6. **Arrange the order or sequence of work tasks to intercept procrastination at times when you're most likely to experience it.** While procrastination often involves difficulty starting work, it can also involve difficulty continuing and completing work (Lay & Silverman, 1996). As previously mentioned, if you have trouble starting work, it might be best to first do the tasks that you find most interesting or easiest. However, if you have difficulty maintaining or sustaining your work until it's finished, you might try to schedule work tasks that you find easier and more interesting *in the middle or toward the end* of your planned work time. If you perform tasks of greater interest and ease at a time when you typically lose interest or energy, you may be able to restore or revive your interest and energy. Also, doing your most enjoyable and easiest tasks later can provide

an incentive or reward for completing your less enjoyable tasks first.

7. **If you're close to completing a task, don't stop until you complete it.** It's often harder to restart a task than it is to finish a task that you've already started because you've overcome the initial inertia needed to get started and can ride the momentum you've created until you finish. Furthermore, finishing a task can give you a sense of *closure*—the feeling of personal accomplishment and self-satisfaction that comes from knowing that you "closed the deal." Placing a checkmark next to a completed task can serve as a source of positive self-reinforcement that increases your motivation to complete other tasks on your to-do list.

Summary and Conclusion

To manage time effectively, you need to:

- **Analyze.** Break down time and become aware of how you spend it;
- **Itemize.** Identify the tasks you need to accomplish and their due dates; and
- **Prioritize.** Tackle your tasks in their order of importance.

Developing a comprehensive time-management plan for academic work involves long-, mid-, and short-range components that include:

- Planning the total term (long-range);
- Planning your week (mid-range); and
- Planning your day (short-range).

A good time-management plan also has the following features:

- It sets aside time to take care of unexpected developments;
- It takes advantage of your natural peak periods and down times;
- It balances work and recreation; and
- It gives you the flexibility to accommodate unforeseen opportunities.

The enemy of effective time management is procrastination, which is often rooted in the following myths:

- Better work occurs on the day or night before something is due.
- Studying in advance is a waste of time because everything you study will be forgotten by test time.

Effective strategies for beating the procrastination habit include the following:

- Start with the work that is the most inviting or appealing.
- Divide large tasks into smaller, more manageable units.
- Organize your work materials to make it easy and convenient for you to start working.
- Organize your work place or space so that you work in a location that minimizes distractions and temptations not to work.
- Intentionally arrange your work tasks so that you're working on more enjoyable or stimulating tasks at times when you're vulnerable to procrastination.
- If you're close to finishing a task, finish it, because it's often harder to restart a task than to complete one you've already started.

Mastering the skill of managing time is critical for success in college and beyond. Time is one of our most powerful personal resources; the better we manage it, the more likely we are to achieve our goals and gain control of our lives.

"Dost thou love life? Then do not squander time, for that is the stuff life is made of."

—Benjamin Franklin, 18th-century inventor, newspaper writer, and signer of the *Declaration of Independence*

Learning More through the World Wide Web

Internet-Based Resources for Further Information on Time Management

For additional information related to the ideas discussed in this chapter, we recommend the following Web sites:

Time-Management Strategies for All Students:

www.studygs.net/timman.htm

www.pennstatelearning.psu.edu/resources/study-tips/time-mgt

Time-Management Strategies for Adult Students:

www.essortment.com/lifestyle/timemanagement_sjmu.htm

Beating Procrastination:

www.mindtools.com

Chapter 5 Exercises

5.1 Term at a Glance

Term _____, Year _____

Review the syllabus (course outline) for all classes you're enrolled in this term, and complete the following information for each course.

Course	Professor	Exams	Projects & Papers	Other Assignments	Attendance Policy	Late & Makeup Assignment Policy

Self-Assessment Questions

1. Is the overall workload what you expected? Are your surprised by the amount of work required in any particular course or courses?

2. At this point in the term, what do you see as your most challenging or demanding course or courses? Why?

3. Do you think you can handle the total workload required by the full set of courses you're enrolled in this term?

4. What adjustments or changes could you make to your personal schedule that would make it easier to accommodate your academic workload this term?

5.2 Taking a Personal Time Inventory

On the blank Week-at-a-Glance Grid that follows, map out your typical or average week for this term. Start by recording what you usually do on these days, including when you have class, when you work, and when you relax or recreate. You can use abbreviations (e.g., J for job and R&R for rest and relaxation) or write tasks out in full if you have enough room in the box. List the abbreviations you created at the bottom of the page so that your instructor can follow them.

If you're a *full-time* student, find *25 hours* in your week that you could devote to homework (HW). These 25 hours could be found between classes, during the day, in the evenings, or on the weekends. If you can find 25 hours per week for homework (in addition to the time you spend in class), you'll have a 40-hour workweek for coursework, which research has shown to result in good grades and success in college.

If you're a *part-time* student, find two *hours* you could devote to homework *for every hour* that you're in class (e.g., if you're in class nine hours per week, find 18 hours of homework time).

Week-at-a-Glance Grid

	Sunday	Monday	Tuesday	Wednesday	Thursday	Friday	Saturday
7:00 a.m.							
8:00 a.m.							
9:00 a.m.							
10:00 a.m.							
11:00 a.m.							
12:00 p.m.							
1:00 p.m.							
2:00 p.m.							
3:00 p.m.							
4:00 p.m.							
5:00 p.m.							
6:00 p.m.							
7:00 p.m.							
8:00 p.m.							
9:00 p.m.							
10:00 p.m.							
11:00 p.m.							

1. Go to the following Web site: pennstatelearning.psu.edu/resources/study-tips/time-mgt
   Click on the link for the "time-management exercise."

2. Complete the time-management exercise at this site. The exercise asks you to estimate the hours per day or week that you spend doing various activities (e.g., sleeping, employment, and commuting). As you enter the amount of time you engage in these activities, the total number of remaining hours available in the week for academic work will be automatically computed.

3. After completing your entries, look at your Week-At-A-Glance grid and answer the following questions (or provide your best estimate).

   a. How many hours per week do you have available for academic work?

   b. Do you have two hours available for academic work outside of class for each hour you spend in class?

   c. What time wasters do you detect that might be easily eliminated or reduced to create more time for academic work outside of class?

Procrastination: The Vicious Cycle

Delilah has a major paper due at the end of the term. It's now past midterm and she still hasn't started to work on her paper. She tells herself, "I should have started sooner."

However, Delilah continues to postpone starting her work on the paper and begins to feel anxious and guilty about it. To relieve her growing anxiety and guilt, she starts doing other tasks instead, such as cleaning her room and returning e-mails. This makes Delilah feel a little better because these tasks keep her busy, take her mind off the term paper, and give her the feeling that at least she's getting something accomplished. Time continues to pass; the deadline for the paper is growing dangerously close. Delilah now finds herself in the position of having lots of work to do and little time in which to do it.

Source: Burka & Yuen, *Procrastination: Why You Do It, and What to Do about It.*

Reflection and Discussion Questions

1. What do you predict Delilah will do at this point?

2. Why did you make the above prediction?

3. What grade do you think Delilah will receive on her paper?

4. What do you think Delilah will do on the next term paper she's assigned?

5. Other than starting sooner, what recommendations would you have for Delilah (and other procrastinators like her) to break this cycle of procrastination and prevent it from happening repeatedly?

Learning Style and Intelligence

Knowing about your learning style can help you to choose effective strategies for learning in school and on the job. Knowing about your preferred learning environment can help you increase productivity. Discovering your multiple intelligences will help you to gain an appreciation of your gifts and talents that can be used to develop your self-confidence, study effectively, and choose the career that is right for you.

What Is Learning Style?

Just as each individual has a unique personality, each individual has a unique learning style. It is important to remember that there are no good or bad learning styles. Learning style is simply your preferred way of learning. It is how you like to learn and how you learn best. By understanding your learning style, you can maximize your potential by choosing the learning techniques that work best for you. This chapter explores the many factors that determine how you learn best. Each individual also has a preferred learning environment. Knowing about your preferred learning environment and learning style helps you be more productive, increase achievement, be more creative, improve problem solving, make good decisions, and learn effectively. Personality type also influences how we learn. Knowing about how you learn best helps to reduce frustration and increase your confidence in learning.

I LEARN BY:

DOING ⊙

READING ○

© 2014, iQoncept. Used under license with Shutterstock, Inc.

Gary Price[1] developed the Productivity Environmental Preference Survey (PEPS) which is included in the textbook. He identified sixteen different elements of learning style and environmental factors that influence productivity and satisfaction in school and on the job. As you read the description of each of these elements, think about your preferences and place a checkmark next to them.

1. **Visual.** Some students learn through reading, observing, or seeing things.
   - Those who prefer visual learning benefit from pictures and reading.
   - Those who are not visual learners may dislike reading. If auditory learning is preferred, attend the lecture first to hear the lecturer talk about the subject and then do the reading. It is important to do the reading because not all the material is covered in the lecture.

2. **Design.** Some students study best in a more formal environment or less formal environment.
   - If you prefer a formal environment, sit in a straight chair and use a desk.
   - If you prefer an informal environment, sit on the sofa or a soft chair or on some pillows on the floor.

3. **Persistence.** Some students may finish what they start, whereas others have many things going on at once and may not finish what they started. Persistence may indicate whether or not you procrastinate in finishing tasks.
   - If you are persistent, you generally finish what you start.
   - If you lack persistence, you may get bored or easily distracted. You may find it easier to break tasks into small steps and work steadily toward completing assignments on time. Think about your college and career goals to increase motivation and persistence.

4. **Motivation.** Some students are self-motivated to learn, and others lack motivation.
   - If you are self-motivated, you usually like school and enjoy learning on your own.
   - If you lack motivation, think about your reasons for attending college and review the material in the motivation chapter in this book.

5. **Time of day.** Some students are most awake and learn easier early in the day while others are most awake and learn better in the afternoon or evening.
   - If you are most alert in the morning, schedule your classes and learning for earlier in the day and your routine tasks for later in the day when you are tired.
   - If you are most alert in the late afternoon or evening, schedule your classes and learning during that time.

6. **Light.** Some students prefer bright light for studying and others find bright light uncomfortable or irritating. Having the right light can help you to be more productive.
   - If you prefer bright light, study near a window with light shining over your shoulder or invest in a good study lamp.
   - If you prefer dim lights, sit away from direct sunlight or use a shaded light.

7. **Intake.** Some students like to eat or drink something while studying while others find eating or drinking to be distracting.
   - If you prefer intake while learning, drink water and have nutritious snacks such a fruits and vegetables.
   - Some students do not need intake to study.

8. **Tactile.** Some students prefer to touch the material or use a "hands-on" approach to learning while others do not need to touch what they are learning.
   - Students who prefer tactile learning like manipulative and three-dimensional materials. They learn from working with models and writing. Taking notes is one of the best tactile learning strategies.
   - Students who are not tactile learners can focus on visual or auditory strategies for learning.

9. **Kinesthetic.** Kinesthetic learning is related to tactile learning. Some students learn best by movement and experiencing what they are learning while other students do not use movement to learn.
   - Students who prefer kinesthetic learning enjoy field trips, drama, and becoming physically involved with learning. For example, they can learn fractions by slicing an apple into parts. It is important to be actively involved in learning.
   - Students who are not kinesthetic learners will use another preferred method of learning such as auditory or visual learning.

10. **Structure.** Some students prefer more or less structure. This preference may also be related to your personality type (judging or perceptive).
    - Students who prefer more structure want the teacher to give details and directions about how to complete the assignment.
    - Students who prefer less structure want the teacher to give assignments in which the students can choose the topic and organize the material on their own.
11. **Authority.** Some students are more or less independent learners.
    - Some students prefer to have the professor or a tutor to guide learning. In the college environment, students may prefer traditional face-to-face classes.
    - Others prefer to work on their own. In the college environment, students may prefer online classes or independent study.
12. **Mobility.** Some students like to move around frequently while studying while others can sit still for longer periods of time.
    - If you prefer mobility, you may find it difficult to sit still for a long time. Take a break every 15–20 minutes to move around. When choosing an occupation, consider one that requires you to move around.
    - If you don't need to move around while studying, a desk and chair are sufficient to help you concentrate on learning.
13. **Sound.** Some students need a quiet environment for study while others find it distracting if it is too quiet.
    - If you prefer quiet, use the library or find another quiet place. If you cannot find a quiet place, sound-blocking earphones or earplugs may be helpful.
    - If you study better with sound, play soft music or study in open areas. Use headphones for your music if you are studying with those who prefer quiet.
14. **Temperature.** Some students perform better in cool temperatures and others prefer warmer temperatures.
    - If you prefer a warm environment, remember to bring your sweater or jacket. Sit near a window or other source of heat.
    - If you prefer a cooler environment, study in a well-ventilated environment or even outside in the shade.
15. **Auditory.** Some students learn through listening and talking while others find it distracting.
    - Those who prefer auditory learning find it easier to learn through lectures, audio materials, discussion, and oral directions.
    - Those who do not prefer auditory learning may find their mind wandering during lectures and become confused by oral directions. It is helpful to read the material before the lecture and take notes during the lecture. Review the notes periodically to remember the material.
16. **Alone or with peers.** Some students prefer to study alone and others prefer to study in groups. This may be related to your personality type (introvert, extravert).
    - You may find other people distracting and prefer to study alone. Find a private area to study.
    - You may enjoy working in a group because talking with others helps you to learn.

Review the 16 elements of learning style and environment in this chapter and in the PEPS learning style assessment included with this textbook. Write a paragraph about your ideal learning environment.

What are your strongest learning preferences?

What environment makes you most productive?

"What I hear, I forget. What I see, I remember. What I do, I know."

Chinese Proverb

© 2014, VLADGRIN. Used under license with Shutterstock, Inc.

Learning Techniques

It is important to connect specific learning strategies to your preferred learning style. Even if you have definite preferences, you can experiment with other styles to improve your learning. If you become frustrated with a learning task, first try a familiar technique that you have used successfully in the past. If that does not work, experiment with different ways of learning. If one technique does not work, try another. It is powerful to combine techniques. For example, it is a good idea to make pictures of what you want to remember (visual), recite the ideas you want to remember (auditory), and take notes (tactile).

The following are specific techniques for each type of learner. Underline or highlight techniques that are useful to you.

Auditory Learning Techniques

You like to learn by listening. You are good at listening to lectures, audio materials, and learning through discussions. You generally understand, comprehend, and remember oral instructions. Here are some auditory learning strategies that you might find useful.

- Before reading, skim through the textbook and look at the major headings. As you are reading, ask questions or say out loud what you think will be important to remember.
- Since you learn by listening, you may not think you need to take notes on college lectures. However, note taking is needed for review and long-term recall. Focus on writing down the key ideas in your notes and leave spaces to fill in the details. Immediately after the lecture, review your lecture notes to add details you heard in the lecture. To review your notes, read them aloud.
- To prepare for exams, rehearse or say information verbally. For example, while studying math, say the equations out loud.
- Use auditory tools for learning such as lectures, videos, discussions, and recordings.
- Work in a quiet area to avoid distractions.
- Make it a priority to attend lectures and participate in discussion sessions. Sit near the front of the classroom so that you can hear clearly. Ask questions in class.
- Discuss what you are learning with other students. Discuss what you are learning with a friend or form a study group where you can discuss what you are learning.

- Participate actively in class discussions.
- Use memory devices, rhymes, poems, rhythms, or music to remember what you are studying. For example, turn facts into a rap song or a musical jingle to aid in recall.
- Memorize key concepts by repeating them aloud.
- Read the textbook and any directions for assignments or tests out loud if possible. Hear the words or directions in your mind if you cannot read them aloud.
- When learning new or difficult material, begin with auditory learning techniques and then reinforce the learning with visual, kinesthetic, and tactile learning strategies according to your preferences.

Visual Learning Techniques

You learn best by reading, observing, and seeing things. You remember what you read and see.

- Use color to highlight the important points in the text while reading. Review the important points by looking at the highlighted passages again.
- Take notes and use underlining and highlighting in different colors to highlight the important points. Include flow charts, graphs, and pictures in your notes. Make summary sheets or mind maps to summarize or review your notes.
- Use pictures, diagrams, flow charts, maps, graphs, time lines, video, and multimedia to aid in learning and prepare for exams. Use flash cards to remember important details and facts.
- Sit in front of the class so you can carefully observe the professor. Copy what is written on the board.
- Organize your work area to avoid visual distractions.
- Create visual reminders to keep on track. Make lists on note pads or use sticky notes as reminders.
- Make a visual image of what you are learning. For example, while reading history, picture in your mind's eye what it would be like to live in that historical period.
- Before answering an essay question, picture the answer in your mind, create a mind map, or write a quick outline.
- Use outlines or mind maps to review for exams.
- When learning new or difficult material, begin with visual learning strategies and then reinforce your learning with audio, kinesthetic, and tactile learning strategies.
- Practice remembering what you hear for those situations where you cannot get the material or instructions in writing. Using mnemonic memory devices may be helpful in remembering what you hear.

Tactile Learning Techniques

You need to be involved in your learning by doing things with your hands and your sense of touch. You prefer to touch the material as you learn and you need "hands-on" kinds of activities, which will help you learn by doing.

- Try to select educational courses that allow you to "do" things. For example, take courses that involve science experiments, writing, practicing math problems, etc.
- As you are reading, mark or highlight the key ideas and review them to enhance recall. Writing a journal or making a summary sheet of key ideas will help you to remember what you have read.
- Attend lectures and take notes. The physical act of writing will help you to remember the important points in the lecture.

- To prepare for exams, use a mind map, outline or drawing to help you to remember.
- Use real objects to help you to learn. For example, in a physics class, if you are studying levers, create a simple lever and observe how it functions. If you are studying geography, use a globe or map to aid in studying.
- Keep your desk clear of distracting objects.
- Use flash cards to review for exams.
- When learning new or difficult material, begin with tactile learning strategies and then reinforce your learning with visual, auditory, and kinesthetic learning strategies according to your preferences.

Kinesthetic Learning Techniques

You learn better when you are able to move around while learning. You prefer to be active and it is important for you to be actively involved to remember. Here are some learning strategies for kinesthetic learners:

- Quickly skim through material before reading it in detail. As you are reading, think about how the material applies to your personal life. Underline the key ideas and review them to enhance recall.
- Writing a journal or make a summary sheet of key ideas to help you to remember what you have read.
- Take notes on lectures. You are more likely to remember what you have written down.
- To prepare for exams, use flashcards to learn detailed information and review them while walking around.
- Move while studying. For example, read while using your exercise bike or stair stepper.
- Use kinesthetic learning experiences such as drama, building, designing, visiting, interviewing, and going on field trips.
- Actively participate in discussions to increase motivation and recall.
- Use all of your senses (sight, touch, taste, smell, and hearing) to help you to remember. For example, when studying Spanish, picture yourself speaking the language, use flash cards you can touch to remember the vocabulary, imagine the smell of Mexican food, say the words out loud, and listen to recordings of the language.
- Actively participate in classroom exercises to involve yourself in learning and motivate yourself to learn.
- Avoid long classes if possible. For example, choose a class that meets one hour on Mondays, Wednesdays, and Fridays instead of three hours on Monday.
- If you have a choice on how to do your assignments, do a skit or create a video.
- Look for courses or majors with hands-on activities, labs, or field trips.
- Take frequent breaks and study in different locations.
- Use a study group to teach the material to someone else.
- Use bright colors to highlight reading material.
- If you find it helpful, listen to music while you are studying.
- Chew gum to stay alert while studying.
- To prepare for exams, write practice answers and essays. Break the material to be reviewed into small parts and review frequently.
- When learning new and difficult material, begin with kinesthetic learning strategies and then reinforce your learning with visual, tactile, and auditory techniques according to your preferences.

My Learning Strategies

If you are having difficulties learning some new material in college, list some strategies that you might try:

1. _____
2. _____
3. _____
4. _____
5. _____
  _____
  _____
  _____
  _____
  _____
  _____

Developing Your E-Learning Style

There are many opportunities for learning online, including online courses, professional development, or learning for your personal life. Students who are independent learners or introverts who enjoy individual learning in a quiet place may prefer online learning. Students who prefer having a professor to guide learning with immediate feedback and extraverts who are energized by social interaction may prefer traditional classroom education. Because of work, family, and time constraints, online learning might be a convenient way to access education. No matter what your learning style, you are likely to be in situations where you may want to take advantage of online learning.

If you have never taken an online course, be aware of some of the myths of online learning. One of the most popular myths is than online courses are easier than traditional courses. Online courses cover the same content and are just as rigorous as traditional face-to-face courses. It is likely that your online course will require more writing; instead of responding verbally in discussions, you will have to write your answer. Online courses generally require the same amount of time as traditional courses. However, you will save time in commuting to class and have the added convenience of working on your class at any time or place where you can access the Internet.

© 2014, Naypong. Used under license with Shutterstock, Inc.

"The illiterate of the 21st century will not be those who cannot read and write, but those who cannot learn, unlearn, and relearn."
Alvin Toffler

Here are some suggestions for a successful e-learning experience.

- The most important factor in online learning is to **log in regularly** and complete the work in a systematic way. Set goals for what you need to accomplish each week and do the work a step at a time. Get in the habit of regularly doing your online study, just as you would attend a traditional course each week.
- It is important to **carefully read the instructions** for the assignments and **ask for help** if you need it. Your online professor will not know when you need help.

- Begin your online work by getting familiar with the requirements and components of the course. Generally online courses have reading material, quizzes, discussion boards, chat rooms, assignments, and multimedia presentations. Make sure that you **understand all the resources, components, and requirements** of the course.
- **Have a backup plan** if your computer crashes or your Internet connection is interrupted. Colleges generally have computer labs where you can do your work if you have technical problems at home.
- Remember to **participate** in the online discussions or chats. It is usually part of your grade and a good way to learn from other students and apply what you have learned. The advantage of online communication is that you have time to think about your responses.
- **Check your grades** online to make sure you are completing all the requirements. Celebrate your success as you complete your online studies. Online learning becomes easier with experience.

Personality and Learning Preferences

Learning preferences are also connected to personality type. As a review, personality has four dimensions:

1. Extraversion or Introversion
2. Sensing or Intuition
3. Thinking or Feeling
4. Judging or Perceiving

What is your personality type? To review, read the following brief descriptions and think about your preferences:

Extraverts focus their energy on the world outside themselves. They enjoy interaction with others and get to know a lot of different people. They enjoy and are usually good at communication. They are energized by social interaction and prefer being active. These types are often described as talkative and social.

Introverts focus their energy on the world inside of themselves. They enjoy spending time alone and think about the world in order to understand it. Introverts like more limited social contacts, preferring smaller groups or one-on-one relationships. These types are often described as quiet or reserved.

Sensing persons prefer to use the senses to take in information (what they see, hear, taste, touch, smell). They focus on "what is" and trust information that is concrete and observable. They learn through experience.

INtuitive persons rely on instincts and focus on "what could be." While we all use our five senses to perceive the world, the intuitive person is interested in relationships, possibilities, meanings, and implications. They value inspiration and trust their "sixth sense" or hunches. We all use our senses and intuition in our daily lives, but we usually have a preference for one mode or another.

Thinking individuals make decisions based on logic. They are objective and analytical. They look at all the evidence and reach an impersonal conclusion. They are concerned with what they think is right.

Feeling individuals make decisions based on what is important to them and matches their personal values. They are concerned about what they feel is right.

6.1 | ACTIVITY

Circle your personality type.

Extravert	or	Introvert	Sensing	or	Intuitive
Thinking	or	Feeling	Judging	or	Perceptive

Each personality type has a natural preference for how to learn. When learning something new, it may be easiest and most efficient to use the style that matches your personality type. It is also a good idea to experiment with using new techniques commonly used by other types. There is no learning style that works best in all situations. You may need to adapt your learning style based on the learning activity. As you look at the chart below, think about your personality type and learning preferences:

Learning Preferences Associated with Personality Types[2]

Extraversion	Introversion
Learn best when in action	Learn best by pausing to think
Value physical activity	Value reading
Like to study with others	Prefer to study individually
Say they're above average in verbal and interpersonal skills	Say they're below average in verbal expression
Say they need training in reading and writing papers	Say they need training in public speaking
Background sounds help them study	Need quiet for concentration
Want faculty who encourage discussion	Want faculty who give clear lectures

Sensing	INtuition
Seek specific information	Seek quick insights
Memorize facts	Use imagination to go beyond facts
Value what is practical	Value what is original
Follow instructions	Create their own directions
Like hands-on experience	Like theories to give perspective
Trust material as presented	Read between the lines
Want faculty who give clear assignments	Want faculty who encourage independent thinking

Thinking	Feeling
Want objective material to study	Want to be able to relate to the material personally
Logic guides learning	Personal values are important
Like to critique new ideas	Like to please instructors
Can easily find flaws in an argument	Can easily find something to appreciate
Learn by challenge and debate	Learn by being supported and appreciated
Want faculty who make logical presentations	Want faculty who establish personal rapport with students

Judging	Perceiving
Like formal instructions for solving problems	Like to solve problems informally
Value dependability	Value change
Plan work well in advance	Work spontaneously
Work steadily toward goals	Work impulsively with bursts of energy
Like to be in charge of events	Like to adapt to events
Drive toward closure (finish)	Stay open to new information
Want faculty to be organized	Want faculty to be entertaining and inspiring

Judging types like to live in a structured, orderly, and planned way. They are happy when their lives are structured and matters are settled. They like to have control over their lives. Judging does not mean to judge others. Think of this type as orderly and organized.

Perceptive types like to live in a spontaneous and flexible way. They are happy when their lives are open to possibilities. They try to understand life rather than control it. Think of this type as spontaneous and flexible.

© 2014, Monkey Business Images. Used under license with Shutterstock, Inc.

Learning Strategies for Different Personality Types

Based on the above descriptions of learning preferences, the following learning strategies are suggested along with some cautions for each type. As you read these descriptions, think about those suggestions and cautions that apply to you.

Extravert

1. Since extraverts learn best when talking, discuss what you have learned with others. Form a study group.
2. Extraverts like variety and action. Take frequent breaks and do something active during your break such as walking around.
3. *Caution!* You may become so distracted by activity and socialization that your studying does not get done.

Introvert

1. Since introverts like quiet for concentration, find a quiet place to study by yourself.
2. Plan to study for longer periods of time and in a way that minimizes interruptions. Turn off the phone or study in the library.
3. *Caution!* You may miss out on sharing ideas and the fun social life of college.

Sensing

1. Sensing types are good at mastering facts and details.
2. Think about practical applications in order to motivate yourself to learn. Ask, "How can I use this information?"
3. *Caution!* You may miss the big picture or general outline by focusing too much on the facts and details. Make a general outline to see the relationship and meaning of the facts.

Intuitive

1. Intuitive types are good at learning concepts and theories.
2. As you are reading, ask yourself, "What is the main point?"
3. *Caution!* Because this type focuses on general concepts and theories, they are likely to miss details and facts. To learn details, organize them into broad categories that have meaning for you.

Thinking

1. Thinking types are good at logic.
2. As you are reading, ask yourself, "What do I think of these ideas?" Discuss or debate your ideas with others.
3. Allow time to think and reflect on your studies.
4. If possible, pick instructors whom you respect and who are intellectually challenging.
5. *Caution!* Others may be offended by your logic and love of debate. Learn to respect the ideas of others.

Feeling

1. Feeling types need a comfortable environment in order to concentrate.
2. For motivation, search for personal meaning in your studies. Ask how the material affects you or others. Look for a supportive environment or study group.
3. Help others to learn.
4. When possible, choose classes that relate to your personal interests.
5. If possible, select instructors who get to know the students and establish a positive learning environment.
6. *Caution!* You may neglect studying because of time spent helping others or may find it difficult to pay attention to material that is not personally meaningful.

Judging

1. Judging types are orderly and organized. Find ways to organize the material to learn it easier.
2. If possible, select instructors who present material in an organized way.
3. Set goals and use a schedule to motivate yourself. This type is naturally good at time management.
4. Use a daily planner, calendar, or to-do list.
5. *Caution!* Being too structured and controlled may limit your creativity and cause conflict with others who are different. Judging types are sometimes overachievers who get stressed easily.

Perceptive

1. Perceptive students are good at looking at all the possibilities and keeping options open.
2. Allow enough time to be thorough and complete your work.
3. Keep learning fun and interesting.
4. Study in groups that have some perceptive types and some judging types. In this way, you can explore possibilities, have fun, and be organized.
5. *Caution!* Work on managing your time to meet deadlines. Be careful not to overextend yourself by working on too many projects at once.

Journal Entry **6.2**

Write a paragraph about your personality type and how it affects your learning style. Begin your paragraph by listing the four letters of your personality type. Tell how these personal characteristics affect your learning style. Include at least four learning strategies that match your personality type. For example:

My personality type is ISFJ. Being an introvert, I like quiet for concentration and prefer to study quietly in the library. I am also a sensing type . . .

"The wisest mind has something yet to learn."

George Santayana

"Tell me and I forget. Teach me and I remember. Involve me and I learn."

Benjamin Franklin

Understanding Your Professor's Personality

Different personality types have different expectations of teachers.

- Extraverts want faculty who encourage class discussion.
- Introverts want faculty who give clear lectures.
- Sensing types want faculty who give clear assignments.
- Intuitive types want faculty who encourage independent thinking.
- Thinking types want faculty who make logical presentations.
- Feeling types want faculty who establish personal rapport with students.
- Judging types want faculty to be organized.
- Perceptive types want faculty to be entertaining and inspiring.

What can you do if your personality and the professor's personality are different? This is often the case. In a study reported by *Consulting Psychologist Press,* college faculty were twice as likely as students to be introverted intuitive types interested in abstractions and learning for its own sake.[3] College students are twice as likely as faculty to be extraverted sensing types who are interested in practical learning. There are three times more sensing and perceptive students than faculty. Faculty tend to be intuitive and judging types. Students expect faculty to be practical, fun, and flexible. Faculty tend to be theoretical and organized. In summary:

College faculty tend to be	College students tend to be
Introverted	Extraverted
Intuitive	Sensing
Judging	Perceptive

Of course, the above is not always true, but there is a good probability that you will have college professors who are very different from you. First, try to understand the professor's personality. This has been called "psyching out the professor." You can usually tell the professor's personality type on the first day of class by examining class materials and observing his or her manner of presentation. If you understand the professor's personality type, you will know what to expect. Next, try to appreciate what the professor has to offer. You may need to adapt your style to fit. If you are a perceptive type, be careful to meet the due dates of your assignments. Experiment with different study techniques so that you can learn the material presented.

© 2014, Alexander Raths. Used under license with Shutterstock, Inc.

Journal Entry 6.3

How can you use your knowledge of personality type to understand your professor's teaching style and expectations? What should you do if your personality does not match the professor's personality? For example, if your professor is a judging type and you are a perceptive type, how can you adapt to be successful in this course?

6.1 QUIZ: LEARNING STYLE

Test what you have learned by selecting the correct answers to the following questions.

1. The best environment for learning

   a. matches your learning style.
   b. is a straight chair and a desk.
   c. includes music in the background.

2. Kinesthetic types learn best by

   a. listening to lectures.
   b. reading the textbook.
   c. taking notes and reviewing them.

3. If you become frustrated in learning, it is best to

   a. keep trying.
   b. take a long break.
   c. take a short break and then apply your preferred learning style.

4. Introverts would probably prefer

   a. studying quietly in the library.
   b. participating in a study group.
   c. learning through classroom discussions.

5. When working on a term paper, perceptive types would probably prefer

   a. organizing the project and completing it quickly.
   b. making a plan and finishing early.
   c. looking at all the possibilities and keeping their options open.

How did you do on the quiz? Check your answers: 1. a, 2. c, 3. c, 4. a, 5. c

Multiple Intelligences

© 2014, VLADGRIN. Used under license with Shutterstock, Inc.

In 1904, the French psychologist Alfred Binet developed the IQ test, which provided a single score to measure intelligence. This once widely used and accepted test came into question because it measured the intelligence of individuals in schools in a particular culture. In different cultures and different situations, the test was less valid. As an alternative to traditional IQ tests, Harvard professor Howard Gardner developed the theory of multiple intelligences. He looked at intelligence in a broader and more inclusive way than people had done in the past.

Howard Gardner observed famous musicians, artists, athletes, scientists, inventors, naturalists, and others who were recognized contributors to society to formulate a more meaningful definition of intelligence. He defined intelligence as **the human ability to solve problems or design or compose something valued in at least one culture.** His definition broadens the scope of human potential. He identified nine different intelligences: musical, interpersonal, logical-mathematical, spatial, bodily-kinesthetic, linguistic, intrapersonal, naturalist and existential. He selected these intelligences because they are all represented by an area in the brain and are valued in different cultures. His theory can help us to understand and use many different kinds of talents.

Within the theory of multiple intelligences, learning style is defined as intelligences put to work. These intelligences are measured by looking at performance in activities associated with each intelligence. A key idea in this theory is that most people can develop all of their intelligences and become relatively competent in each area. Another key idea is that these intelligences work together in complex ways to make us unique. For example, an athlete uses bodily-kinesthetic intelligence to run, kick, or jump. They use spatial intelligence to keep their eye on the ball and hit it. They also need linguistic and interpersonal skills to be good members of a team.

Developing intelligences is a product of three factors:

1. Biological endowment based on heredity and genetics
2. Personal life history
3. Cultural and historical background[4]

For example, Wolfgang Amadeus Mozart was born with musical talent (biological endowment). Members of his family were musicians who encouraged Mozart in music (personal life history). Mozart lived in Europe during a time when music flourished and wealthy patrons were willing to pay composers (cultural and historical background).

Each individual's life history contains **crystallizers** that promote the development of the intelligences and **paralyzers** that inhibit the development of the intelligences. These crystallizers and paralyzers often take place in early childhood. For example, Einstein was given a magnetic compass when he was four years old. He became so interested in the compass that he started on his journey of exploring the universe. An example of a paralyzer is being embarrassed or feeling humiliated about your math skills in elementary school so that you begin to lose confidence in your ability to do math. Paralyzers involve shame, guilt, fear, and anger and prevent intelligence from being developed.

"I have no special talent. I am only passionately curious."

Albert Einstein

6.2 ACTIVITY: DESCRIBING YOUR MULTIPLE INTELLIGENCES

Below are some definitions and examples of the different intelligences. As you read each section, think positively about your intelligence in this area. Place a checkmark in front of each item that is true for you.

Musical

Musical intelligence involves hearing and remembering musical patterns and manipulating patterns in music. Some occupations connected with this intelligence include musician, performer, composer, and music critic. Place a checkmark next to each skill that you possess in this area.

_____ I enjoy singing, humming, or whistling.

_____ One of my interests is playing recorded music.

_____ I have collections of recorded music.

_____ I play or used to play a musical instrument.

_____ I can play the drums or tap out rhythms.

_____ I appreciate music.

_____ Music affects how I feel.

_____ I enjoy having music on while working or studying.

_____ I can clap my hands and keep time to music.

_____ I can tell when a musical note is off key.

_____ I remember melodies and the words to songs.

_____ I have participated in a band, chorus, or other musical group.

Look at the items you have checked above and summarize your musical intelligence.

_____

_____

_____

Interpersonal

Interpersonal intelligence is defined as understanding people. Occupations connected with this intelligence involve working with people and helping them, as in education or health care. Place a checkmark next to each skill that you possess in this area.

_____ I enjoy being around people.

_____ I am sensitive to other people's feelings.

_____ I am a good listener.

_____ I understand how others feel.

_____ I have many friends.

_____ I enjoy parties and social gatherings.

_____ I enjoy participating in groups.

_____ I can get people to cooperate and work together.

6.2   **ACTIVITY CONTINUED...**

_____ I am involved in clubs or community activities.

_____ People come to me for advice.

_____ I am a peacemaker.

_____ I enjoy helping others.

Look at the items you have checked above and summarize your interpersonal intelligence.

_____

_____

_____

Logical-Mathematical

Logical-mathematical intelligence involves understanding abstract principles and manipulating numbers, quantities, and operations. Some examples of occupations associated with logical-mathematical intelligence are mathematician, tax accountant, scientist, and computer programmer. Place a checkmark next to each skill that you possess. Keep an open mind. People usually either love or hate this area.

_____ I can do arithmetic problems quickly.

_____ I enjoy math.

_____ I enjoy doing puzzles.

_____ I enjoy working with computers.

_____ I am interested in computer programming.

_____ I enjoy science classes.

_____ I enjoy doing the experiments in lab science courses.

_____ I can look at information and outline it easily.

_____ I understand charts and diagrams.

_____ I enjoy playing chess or checkers.

_____ I use logic to solve problems.

_____ I can organize things and keep them in order.

Look at the items you have checked above and summarize your logical-mathematical intelligence.

_____

_____

_____

Spatial

Spatial intelligence involves the ability to manipulate objects in space. For example, a baseball player uses spatial intelligence to hit a ball. Occupations associated with spatial intelligence include pilot, painter, sculptor, architect, inventor, and surgeon. This intelligence is often used in athletics, the arts, or the sciences. Place a checkmark next to each skill that you possess in this area.

_____ I can appreciate a good photograph or piece of art.

_____ I think in pictures and images.

_____ I can use visualization to remember.

_____ I can easily read maps, charts, and diagrams.

_____ I participate in artistic activities (art, drawing, painting, photography).

_____ I know which way is north, south, east, and west.

_____ I can put things together.

_____ I enjoy jigsaw puzzles or mazes.

_____ I enjoy seeing movies, slides, or photographs.

_____ I can appreciate good design.

_____ I enjoy using telescopes, microscopes, or binoculars.

_____ I understand color, line, shape, and form.

Look at the items you have checked above and summarize your spatial intelligence.

_____

_____

_____

Bodily-Kinesthetic

Bodily-kinesthetic intelligence is defined as being able to use your body to solve problems. People with bodily-kinesthetic intelligence make or invent objects or perform. They learn by doing, touching, and handling. Occupations connected to this type of intelligence include athlete, performer (dancer, actor), craftsperson, sculptor, mechanic, and surgeon. Place a checkmark next to each skill that you possess in this area.

_____ I am good at using my hands.

_____ I have good coordination and balance.

_____ I learn best by moving around and touching things.

_____ I participate in physical activities or sports.

_____ I learn new sports easily.

_____ I enjoy watching sports events.

_____ I am skilled in a craft such as woodworking, sewing, art, or fixing machines.

_____ I have good manual dexterity.

_____ I find it difficult to sit still for a long time.

_____ I prefer to be up and moving.

_____ I am good at dancing and remember dance steps easily.

_____ It was easy for me to learn to ride a bike or skateboard.

Look at the items you checked above and describe your bodily-kinesthetic intelligence.

_____

_____

_____

Linguistic

People with linguistic intelligence are good with language and words. They have good reading, writing, and speaking skills. Linguistic intelligence is an asset in any occupation. Specific related careers include writing, education, and politics. Place a checkmark next to each skill that you possess in this area.

_____ I am a good writer.

_____ I am a good reader.

_____ I enjoy word games and crossword puzzles.

_____ I can tell jokes and stories.

_____ I am good at explaining.

_____ I can remember names, places, facts, and trivia.

_____ I'm generally good at spelling.

_____ I have a good vocabulary.

_____ I read for fun and relaxation.

_____ I am good at memorizing.

_____ I enjoy group discussions.

_____ I have a journal or diary.

Look at the items you have checked above and summarize your linguistic intelligence.

_____

_____

_____

Intrapersonal

Intrapersonal intelligence is the ability to understand yourself and how to best use your natural talents and abilities. Examples of careers associated with this intelligence include novelist, psychologist, or being self-employed. Place a checkmark next to each skill that you possess in this area.

_____ I understand and accept my strengths and weaknesses.

_____ I am very independent.

_____ I am self-motivated.

_____ I have definite opinions on controversial issues.

_____ I enjoy quiet time alone to pursue a hobby or work on a project.

_____ I am self-confident.

_____ I can work independently.

_____ I can help others with self-understanding.

_____ I appreciate quiet time for concentration.

_____ I am aware of my own feelings and sensitive to others.

_____ I am self-directed.

_____ I enjoy reflecting on ideas and concepts.

Look at the items you have checked above and summarize your intrapersonal intelligence.

_____

_____

_____

Naturalist

The naturalist is able to recognize, classify, and analyze plants, animals, and cultural artifacts. Occupations associated with this intelligence include botanist, horticulturist, biologist, archeologist, and environmental occupations. Place a checkmark next to each skill you possess in this area.

_____ I know the names of minerals, plants, trees, and animals.

_____ I think it is important to preserve our natural environment.

_____ I enjoy taking classes in the natural sciences such as biology.

_____ I enjoy the outdoors.

_____ I take care of flowers, plants, trees, or animals.

_____ I am interested in archeology or geology.

_____ I would enjoy a career involved in protecting the environment.

_____ I have or used to have a collection of rocks, shells, or insects.

_____ I belong to organizations interested in protecting the environment.

_____ I think it is important to protect endangered species.

_____ I enjoy camping or hiking.

_____ I appreciate natural beauty.

Look at the items you have checked above and describe your naturalist intelligence.

_____

_____

_____

ACTIVITY CONTINUED...

Existential

Existential intelligence is the capacity to ask profound questions about the meaning of life and death. This intelligence is the cornerstone of art, religion, and philosophy. Related occupations include minister, philosopher, psychologist, and artist. Place a checkmark next to each skill that you possess in this area.

_____ I often think about the meaning and purpose of life.

_____ I have strong personal beliefs and convictions.

_____ I enjoy thinking about abstract theories.

_____ I have considered being a philosopher, scientist, theologian, or artist.

_____ I often read books that are philosophical or imaginative.

_____ I enjoy reading science fiction.

_____ I like to work independently.

_____ I like to search for meaning in my studies.

_____ I wonder if there are other intelligent life forms in the universe.

Look at the items you have checked above and describe your existential intelligence.

_____

_____

Journal Entry **6.4**

Look at the above charts and see where you have the most checkmarks. What do you think are your highest intelligences?

Build on Your Strengths

Consider your personal strengths when deciding on a career. People in each of the multiple intelligence areas have different strengths:

* Musical strengths include listening to music, singing, playing a musical instrument, keeping a beat, and recognizing musical patterns. People with this intelligence are "musical smart."
* Interpersonal strengths include communication skills, social skills, helping others, understanding other's feelings, and the ability to resolve conflicts. People with this intelligence are "people smart."
* Logical—mathematical strengths include math aptitude, interest in science, problem-solving skills, and logical thinking. People with this intelligence are "number/reasoning smart."
* Spatial strengths include visualization, understanding puzzles, navigation, visual arts, reading, and writing. People with this intelligence are "picture smart."

- Bodily-kinesthetic strengths include hand and eye coordination, athletics, dance, drama, cooking, sculpting, and learning by doing. People with this intelligence are "body smart."
- Linguistic strengths include good reading, writing, vocabulary, and spelling skills; good communication skills; being a good listener; having a good memory; and learning new languages easily. People with this intelligence are "word smart."
- Intrapersonal strengths include good self-awareness. They are aware of their feelings and emotions and are often independent and self-motivated to achieve. People with this intelligence are "self-smart."
- Naturalist strengths include exploring and preserving the environment and are very aware of natural surroundings. People with this intelligence are "nature smart."
- Existential strengths include reflecting on important questions about the universe, the purpose of life, and religious beliefs. People with this intelligence are "curiosity smart."

6.3 ACTIVITY: DESCRIBING YOUR MULTIPLE INTELLIGENCES

In what areas are you "smart"?_____

_____

© 2014, DeiMosz. Used under license with Shutterstock, Inc.

Some Careers and Multiple Intelligences

Circle any careers that seem interesting to you		
Musical	**Interpersonal**	**Logical–Mathematical**
disc jockey	cruise director	engineer
music teacher	mediator	accountant
music retailer	human resources	computer analyst
music therapist	dental hygienist	physician
recording engineer	nurse	detective
singer	psychologist	researcher
song writer	social worker	scientist
speech pathologist	administrator	computer programmer
music librarian	marketer	database designer
choir director	religious leader	physicist
music critic	teacher	auditor
music lawyer	counselor	economist

Spatial	Bodily-Kinesthetic	Linguistic
architect	athlete	journalist
artist	carpenter	writer
film animator	craftsperson	editor
mechanic	mechanic	attorney
pilot	jeweler	curator
webmaster	computer game designer	newscaster
interior decorator	firefighter	politician
graphic artist	forest ranger	speech pathologist
sculptor	physical therapist	translator
surveyor	personal trainer	comedian
urban planner	surgeon	historian
photographer	recreation specialist	librarian
		marketing consultant

Intrapersonal	Naturalist	Existential
career counselor	park ranger	counselor
wellness counselor	dog trainer	psychologist
therapist	landscaper	psychiatrist
criminologist	meteorologist	social worker
intelligence officer	veterinarian	ministry
entrepreneur	animal health technician	philosopher
psychologist	ecologist	artist
researcher	nature photographer	scientist
actor	wilderness guide	researcher
artist	anthropologist	motivational speaker
philosopher	environmental lawyer	human resources
writer	water conservationist	writer

Using Emotional Intelligence in Your Personal Life and Career

Emotional intelligence is related to interpersonal and intrapersonal intelligences. It is the ability to recognize, control, and evaluate your own emotions while realizing how they affect people around you. Emotional intelligence affects career and personal success because it is related to the ability to build good relationships, communicate, work as part of a team, concentrate, remember, make decisions, deal with stress, overcome challenges, deal with conflict, and empathize with others. Research has shown emotional intelligence can predict career success and that workers with high emotional intelligence are more likely to end up in leadership positions in which workers are happy with their jobs.

The premise of emotional intelligence is that you can be more successful if you are aware of your own emotions as well as the emotions of others. There are two aspects of emotional intelligence:

- Understanding yourself, your goals, intentions, responses, and behavior.
- Understanding others and their feelings.

Daniel Goleman has identified the five most important characteristics of emotional intelligence:[5]

1. **Self-Awareness**
   People with high emotional intelligence are aware of their emotions including strengths and weaknesses.
2. **Self-Regulation**
   This involves the ability to control emotions and impulses. Being impulsive can lead to careless decisions like attending a party the night before a final exam. Characteristics of self-regulation include comfort with change, integrity, and the ability to say no.
3. **Motivation**
   People with high emotional intelligence can defer immediate results for long-term success. For example, investing your time in education can lead to future career opportunities and income.
4. **Empathy**
   Empathy is the ability to understand the needs and viewpoints of others around you and avoiding stereotypes. It involves good listening skills that enhance personal relationships.
5. **Social Skills**
   People with good social skills are good team players and willing to help others to be successful.

You can enhance your personal and career success by developing your emotional intelligence. Here are some tips for developing good relationships in your personal life and on the job.

- Be empathetic when working with others by trying to put yourself in their place to understand different perspectives and points of view. Don't be quick to jump to conclusions or stereotype others.
- Think about how your actions affect others. Always treat others as you would like to be treated.
- Be open-minded and intellectually curious. Consider the opinions of others in a positive manner. Be willing to examine and change your mind-set.
- Give others credit for their accomplishments in your personal life and in the workplace. When speaking about your own accomplishments, confidently state what you accomplished without trying to seek too much attention.
- Evaluate your own strengths and weaknesses. Focus on your strengths, but be aware of the weaknesses and work to improve them. The personality assessment in the previous chapter helps you to understand your personal strengths and weaknesses.
- Work on stress management by finding some stress reduction techniques that work for you. In stressful situations, it is helpful to remain calm and in control. Seek workable solutions without blaming others. Your college health services office often provides workshops on stress management.
- Take a college course to improve verbal as well as nonverbal communication. When talking with others, focus on what they are saying rather than what you are going to say next. Learn how to make "I statements" that effectively communicate your thoughts without blaming others. Become aware of nonverbal communication which adds a significant dimension to communication.
- Use humor to help you deal with challenges. Humor helps you to keep things in perspective, deal with differences, relax, and come up with creative solutions.

- Deal with conflicts in a way that builds trust. Focus on win-win solutions that allow both parties to have their needs met.
- Take responsibility for your actions. Admit when you make mistakes and work to improve the situation in the future.
- Use critical thinking to analyze the pros and cons of the situation.
- Be goal oriented and focus on the task and the steps needed to achieve your goals.
- Be optimistic. Optimism leads to greater opportunities and results in better personal relationships.

© 2014, arka38. Used under license with Shutterstock, Inc.

> "The best years of your life are the ones in which you decide your problems are your own. You do not blame them on your mother, the ecology, or the president. You realize that you control your own destiny."
>
> Albert Ellis

Journal Entry 6.5

Comment on your emotional intelligence and how you can use it to be successful in your personal life and your career.

6.2   QUIZ: MULTIPLE INTELLIGENCES

Test what you have learned by selecting the correct answers to the following questions.

1. Multiple intelligences are defined as
   a. the many parts of intelligence as measured by an IQ test.
   b. the ability to design something valued in at least one culture.
   c. the ability to read, write, and do mathematical computations.

2. The concept of multiple intelligences is significant because
   a. it measures the intelligence of students in schools.
   b. it does not use culture in measuring intelligence.
   c. it broadens the scope of human potential and includes all cultures.

3. Intelligences are measured by
   a. IQ tests.
   b. performance in activities related to the intelligence.
   c. performance in the classroom.

4. Each individual's life history contains crystallizers that
   a. promote the development of the intelligences.
   b. inhibit the development of the intelligences.
   c. cause the individual to be set in their ways.

5. Multiple intelligences include
   a. getting good grades in college.
   b. bodily kinesthetic skills.
   c. good test-taking skills.

How did you do on the quiz? Check your answers: 1. b, 2. c, 3. b, 4. a, 5. b

KEYS TO SUCCESS

Create Your Success

We are responsible for what happens in our lives. We make decisions and choices that create the future. Our behavior leads to success or failure. Too often we believe that we are victims of circumstance. When looking at our lives, we often look for others to blame for how our lives are going:

- My grandparents did it to me. I inherited these genes.
- My parents did it to me. My childhood experiences shaped who I am.
- My teacher did it to me. He gave me a poor grade.
- My boss did it to me. She gave me a poor evaluation.
- The government did it to me. All my money goes to taxes.
- Society did it to me. I have no opportunity.

These factors are powerful influences in our lives, but we are still left with choices. Concentration camp survivor Viktor Frankl wrote a book, Man's Search for Meaning, in which he describes his experiences and how he survived his ordeal. His parents, brother, and wife died in the camps. He suffered starvation and torture. Through all of his sufferings and imprisonment, he still maintained that he was a free man because he could make choices.

> We who lived in concentration camps can remember the men who walked through the huts comforting others, giving away their last piece of bread. They may have been few in number, but they offer sufficient proof that everything can be taken from a man but one thing: the last of the human freedoms— to choose one's attitude in any given set of circumstances, to choose one's own way. . . . Fundamentally, therefore, any man can, even under such circumstances, decide what shall become of him—mentally and spiritually. He may retain his human dignity even in a concentration camp.[6]

Viktor Frankl could not choose his circumstances at that time, but he did choose his attitude. He decided how he would respond to the situation. He realized that he still had the freedom to make choices. He used his memory and imagination to exercise his freedom. When times were the most difficult, he would imagine that he was in the classroom lecturing to his students about psychology. He eventually did get out of the concentration camp and became a famous psychiatrist.

Hopefully none of you will ever have to experience the circumstances faced by Viktor Frankl, but we all face challenging situations. It is empowering to think that our behavior is more a function of our decisions than of our circumstances. It is not productive to look around and find someone to blame for your problems. Psychologist Abraham Maslow says that instead of blaming, we should see how we can make the best of the situation.

> One can spend a lifetime assigning blame, finding a cause, "out there" for all the troubles that exist. Contrast this with the responsible attitude of confronting the situation, bad or good, and instead of asking, "What caused the trouble? Who was to blame?" asking, "How can I handle the present situation to make the best of it?"[7]

Author Stephen Covey suggests that we look at the word responsibility as "response-ability."[8] It is the ability to choose responses and make decisions about the future. When you are dealing with a problem, it is useful to ask yourself what decisions you made that led to the problem. How did you create the situation? If you created the problem, you can create a solution.

At times, you may ask, "How did I create this?" and find that the answer is that you did not create the situation. We certainly do not create earthquakes or hurricanes, for example. But we do create or at least contribute to many of the things that happen to us. Even if you did not create your circumstances, you can create your reaction to the situation. In the case of an earthquake, you can decide to panic or find the best course of action at the moment.

Stephen Covey believes that we can use our resourcefulness and initiative in dealing with most problems. When his children were growing up and they asked him how to solve a certain problem, he would say, "Use your R and I!" He meant resourcefulness and initiative. He notes that adults can use this R and I to get good jobs.

> But the people who end up with the good jobs are the proactive ones who are solutions to problems, not problems themselves, who seize the initiative to do whatever is necessary, consistent with correct principles, to get the job done.[9]

Use your resourcefulness and initiative to create the future that you want.

JOURNAL ENTRIES

Learning Style and Intelligence

Go to http://www.collegesuccess1.com/ JournalEntries.htm for Word files of the Journal Entries

Success over the Internet

Visit the *College Success Website* at http://www.collegesuccess1.com/

The *College Success Website* is continually updated with new topics and links to the material presented in this chapter. Topics include:

- Learning style assessments
- Learning style and memory
- Learning style and personality type

Contact your instructor if you have any problems in accessing the *College Success Website*.

Notes

1. Gary E. Price, "Productivity Environmental Preference Survey," Price Systems, Inc., Box 1818, Lawrence, KS 66044-8818.
2. Modified and reproduced by special permission of the Publisher, Consulting Psychologist Press, Inc., Palo Alto, CA 94303, from *Introduction to Type in College* by John K. Ditiberio and Allen L. Hammer. Copyright 1993 by Consulting Psychologist Press, Inc. All rights reserved. Further reproduction is prohibited without the Publisher's written consent.
3. John K. Ditiberio and Allen L. Hammer, *Introduction to Type in College* (Palo Alto, CA: Consulting Psychologist Press, 1993), 7.
4. Howard Gardner, *Intelligence Reframed: Multiple Intelligences for the Twenty-First Century* (Boulder, CO: Basic Books, 1999).
5. Thomas Armstrong, *Multiple Intelligences in the Classroom* (Alexandria, VA: Association for Curriculum Development, 1994).
6. Viktor Frankl, *Man's Search for Meaning* (New York: Pocket Books, 1963), 104–5.
7. Quoted in Rob Gilbert, ed., *Bits and Pieces*, November 4, 1999.
8. Stephen Covey, *The Seven Habits of Highly Effective People* (New York: Simon and Schuster, 1989), 71.
9. Ibid., 75.

Learning Style Quiz

Name _____ Date _____

Read the following questions and circle the letter of the best answer for each in your opinion. There are no right or wrong answers in this quiz. Just circle what you usually prefer.

1. When learning how to use my computer, I prefer to
   a. read the manual first.
   b. have someone explain how to do it first.
   c. just start using the computer and get help if I need it.

2. When getting directions to a new location, it is easier to
   a. look at a map.
   b. have someone tell me how to get there.
   c. follow someone or have him or her take me there.

3. To remember a phone number, I
   a. look at the number and dial it several times.
   b. repeat it silently or out loud to myself several times.
   c. remember the number by the pattern pressed on the keypad, the tones of each number, or writing it down.

4. For relaxation, I prefer to
   a. read a book or magazine.
   b. listen to or play music.
   c. go for a walk or do something physical.

5. I am better at
   a. reading.
   b. talking.
   c. physical activities.

6. In school, I learn best by
   a. reading.
   b. listening.
   c. hands-on activities.

7. I tend to be a
   a. thinker.
   b. talker.
   c. doer.

8. When I study for a test, it works best when I
   a. read and picture the information in my head.
   b. read and say the ideas out loud or silently.
   c. highlight, write notes, and outline.

9. It is easier for me to remember
    a. faces.
    b. names.
    c. events.

10. On a Saturday, I would prefer to
    a. see a movie.
    b. go to a concert.
    c. participate in athletics or be outside.

11. In a college class, it is most important to have
    a. a good textbook with pictures, graphs, and diagrams.
    b. a good teacher who gives interesting lectures.
    c. hands-on activities.

12. It is easier for me to study by
    a. reading and reviewing the material.
    b. discussing the subject with others.
    c. writing notes or outlines.

13. When I get lost, I prefer to
    a. look at the map.
    b. call or ask for directions.
    c. drive around the area until I recognize familiar landmarks.

14. When cooking, I often
    a. look for new recipes.
    b. talk to others to get new ideas.
    c. just put things together and it generally comes out okay.

15. When assembling a new toy or piece of furniture, I usually
    a. read the instructions first.
    b. talk myself through each step.
    c. start putting it together and read the directions if I get stuck.

16. When solving a problem, it is more useful to
    a. read a bestselling book on the topic.
    b. talk over the options with a trusted friend.
    c. do something about it.

17. Which statement do you like the best?
    a. A picture is worth a thousand words.
    b. Talk to me and I can understand.
    c. Just do it.

18. When I was a child, my mother said I
    a. spent a lot of time reading, taking photos, or drawing.
    b. had lots of friends and was always talking to someone on the phone.
    c. was always taking things apart to see how they worked.

Score your quiz:

Number of A answers	_____	Visual Learner
Number of B answers	_____	Auditory Learner
Number of C answers	_____	Kinesthetic/Tactile Learner

What did you discover as a result of taking this quiz?

Learning Style Applications

Name _____   Date _____

How would you use the knowledge of your learning style to deal with the following college situations? Your instructor may use this exercise for a group activity and class discussion.

1. You have just been assigned a 10-page term paper.

2. You have to study for a challenging math test.

3. You have to write up a lab report for a biology class. It includes drawings of a frog you have dissected.

4. You are taking a required course for your major and it is taught by only one professor. You dislike this professor.

5. You are taking a business class and have been assigned a group project to design a small business. It is worth 50 percent of your grade.

6. You have signed up for an economics course and find it difficult to stay awake during the lecture.

7. You signed up for a philosophy course to meet a humanities requirement. The vocabulary in this course is unfamiliar.

8. As part of the final exam, you have to prepare a five-minute presentation for your art history class.

Taking Notes, Writing, and Speaking

7

LEARNING GOALS

Read to answer these key questions:
- Why is it important to take notes?
- What are some good listening techniques?
- What are some tips for taking good lecture notes?
- What are some note-taking systems?
- What is the best way to review my notes for the test?
- What is power writing?
- How can I make a good speech?

Knowing how to listen and take good notes can make your college life easier and may help you in your future career as well. Professionals in many occupations take notes as a way of recording key ideas for later use. Whether you become a journalist, attorney, architect, engineer, or other professional, listening and taking good notes can help you to get ahead in your career.

Good writing and speaking skills are important to your success in college and in your career. In college, you will be asked to write term papers and complete other writing assignments. The writing skills you learn in college will be used later in jobs involving high responsibility and good pay; on the job, you will write reports, memos, and proposals. In college, you will probably take a speech class and give oral reports in other classes; on the job, you will present your ideas orally to your colleagues and business associates.

Why Take Notes?

The most important reason for taking notes is to remember important material for tests or for future use in your career. If you just attend class without taking notes, you will forget most of the material by the next day.

How does taking notes enhance memory?

- In college, the lecture is a way of supplementing the written material in the textbook. Without good notes, an important part of the course is missing. Note taking provides material to rehearse or recite, so that it can be stored in long-term memory.

- When you take notes and impose your own organization on them, the notes become more personally meaningful. If they are meaningful, they are easier to remember.

- Taking notes helps you to make new connections. New material is remembered by connecting it to what you already know.

- For kinesthetic and tactile learners, the physical act of writing the material is helpful in learning and re-membering it.

© 2014, Monkey Business Images. Used under license with Shutterstock, Inc.

- For visual learners, notes provide a visual map of the material to be learned.

- For auditory learners, taking notes is a way to listen carefully and record information to be stored in the memory.

- Note taking helps students to concentrate, maintain focus, and stay awake.
- Attending the lectures and taking notes helps you to understand what the professor thinks is important and to know what to study for the exam.

The College Lecture

You will experience many different types of lectures while in college. At larger universities, many of the beginning-level courses are taught in large lecture halls with 300 people or more. More advanced courses tend to have fewer students. In large lecture situations, it is not always possible or appropriate to ask questions. Under these circumstances, the large lecture is often supplemented by smaller discussion sessions where you can ask questions and review the lecture material. Although attendance may not be checked, it is important to attend both the lectures and the discussion sessions.

A formal college lecture is divided into four parts. Understanding these parts will help you to be a good listener and take good notes.

1. **Introduction.** The professor uses the introduction to set the stage and to introduce the topic of the lecture. Often an overview or outline of the lecture is presented. Use the introduction as a way to begin thinking about the organization of your notes and the key ideas you will need to write down.
2. **Thesis.** The thesis is the key idea in the lecture. In a one-hour lecture, there is usually one thesis statement. Listen carefully for the thesis statement and write it down in your notes. Review the thesis statement and related ideas for the exam.
3. **Body.** The body of the lecture usually consists of five or six main ideas with discussion and clarification of each idea. As a note taker, your job is to identify the main ideas, write them in your notes, and put in enough of the explanation or examples to understand the key ideas.
4. **Conclusion.** In the conclusion, the professor summarizes the key points of the lecture and sometimes asks for questions. Use the conclusion as an opportunity to check your understanding of the lecture and to ask questions to clarify the key points.

"Education is not a problem. It is an opportunity."

Lyndon B. Johnson

How to Be a Good Listener

Effective note taking begins with good listening. What is good listening? Sometimes students confuse listening with hearing. Hearing is done with the ears. Listening is a more active process done with the ears and the brain engaged. Good listening requires attention and concentration. Practice these ideas for good listening:

- **Be physically ready.** It is difficult to listen to a lecture if you are tired, hungry, or ill. Get enough sleep so that you can stay awake. Eat a balanced diet without too much caffeine or sugar. Take care of your health and participate in an exercise program so that you feel your best.
- **Prepare a mental framework.** Look at the course syllabus to become familiar with the topic of the lecture. Use your textbook to read, or at least survey, the material to be covered in the lecture. If you are familiar with the key concepts from the textbook, you will be able to understand the lecture and know what to write down in your notes. If the material is in your book, there is no need to write it down in your notes.

The more complex the topic, the more important it is for you to read the text first. If you go to the lecture and have no idea what is being discussed, you may be overwhelmed and find it difficult to take notes on material that is totally new to you. Remember that it is easier to remember material if you can connect it to material you already know.

- **Find a good place to sit.** Arrive early to get a good seat. The best seats in the classroom are in the front and center of the room. If you were buying concert tickets, these would be the best and most expensive seats. Find a seat that will help you to hear and focus on the speaker. You may need to find a seat away from your friends to avoid distractions.

- **Have a positive mental attitude.** Convince yourself that the speaker has something important to say and be open to new ideas. This may require you to focus on your goals and to look past some distractions. Maybe the lecturer doesn't have the best speaking voice or you don't like his or her appearance. Focus on what you can learn from the professor rather than outward appearances.

- **Listen actively to identify the main points.** As you are listening to the lecture, ask yourself, "What is the main idea?" In your own words, write the main points down in your notes. Do not try to write down everything the professor says. This will be impossible and unnecessary. Imagine that your mind is a filter and you are actively sorting through the material to find the key ideas and write them down in your notes. Try to identify the key points that will be on the test and write them in your notes.

- **Stay awake and engaged in learning.** The best way to stay awake and focused is to listen actively and take notes. Have a mental debate with the professor. Listen for the main points and the logical connection between ideas. The physical act of writing the notes will help to keep you awake.

Tips for Good Note Taking

Here are some suggestions for taking good notes:

1. Attend all of the lectures. Because many professors do not take attendance, students are often tempted to miss class. If you do not attend the lectures, however, you will not know what the professor thinks is important and what to study for the test. There will be important points covered in the lectures that are not in the book.

2. Have the proper materials. A three-ring notebook and notebook paper are recommended. Organize notes chronologically and include any handouts given in class. You can have a small notebook for each class or a single large notebook with dividers for each class. Just take the notebook paper to class and later file it in your notebook at home. Use your laptop as an alternative to a paper notebook.

3. Begin your notes by writing the date of the lecture, so you can keep your notes in order.

4. Write notes on the front side only of each piece of paper. This will allow you to spread the pages out and see the big picture or pattern in the lectures when you are reviewing.

5. Write notes neatly and legibly so you can read and review them easily.

6. Do not waste time recopying or typing your notes. Your time would be better spent reviewing your notes.

7. As a general rule, do not rely on a tape recorder for taking notes. With a tape recorder, you will have to listen to the lecture again on tape. For a semester course, this would be about 45 hours of tape! It is much faster to review carefully written notes.

8. Copy down everything written on the board and the main points from Power-Point or other visual presentations. If it is important enough for the professor to write on the board, it is important enough to be on the test.

9. Use key words and phrases in your notes. Leave out unimportant words and don't worry about grammar.

10. Use abbreviations as long as you can read them. Entire sentences or paragraphs are not necessary and you may not have time to write them.

11. Don't loan your whole notebook to someone else because you may not get it back. If you want to share your notes, make copies.

12. If the professor talks too fast, listen carefully for the key ideas and write them down. Leave spaces in your notes to fill in later. You may be able to find the information in the text or get the information from another student.

13. Explore new uses of technology for note taking. Students are taking notes and sharing them on Facebook and GradeGuru, for example.

Journal Entry 7.1

Write one paragraph giving advice to a new student about taking notes in college. Use any of these questions to guide your thinking:

• Why is note taking necessary in college?

• How can you be a good listener?

• What are some tips for taking good notes?

• What are some ideas that don't work?

Note-Taking Systems
• Cornell format
• Outline method
• Mind map

Note-Taking Systems

There are several systems for taking notes. How you take notes will depend on your learning style and the lecturer's speaking style. Experiment with these systems and use what works best for you.

The Cornell Format

The Cornell format is an efficient method of taking notes and reviewing them. It appeals to students who are logical, orderly, and organized and have lectures that fit into this pattern. The Cornell format is especially helpful for thinking about key points as you review your notes.

Step 1: Prepare. To use the Cornell format, you will need a three-ring notebook with looseleaf paper. Draw or fold a vertical line 2½ inches from the left side of the paper. This is the recall column that can be used to write key ideas when reviewing. Use the remaining section of the paper for your notes. Write the date and title of the lecture at the top of the page.

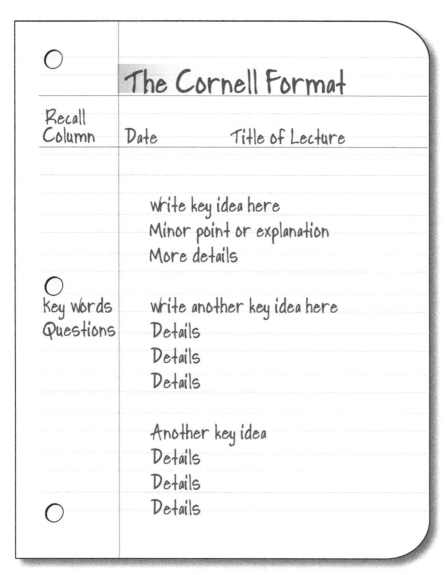

Figure 7.1 The Cornell format is an efficient way of organizing notes and reviewing them.

Step 2: Take notes. Use the large area to the right of the recall column to take notes. Listen for key ideas and write them just to the right of the recall column line, as in the diagram above. Indent your notes for minor points and illustrative details. Then skip a space and write the next key idea. Don't worry about using numbers or letters as in an outline format. Just use the indentations and spacing to highlight and separate key ideas. Use short phrases, key words, and abbreviations. Complete sentences are not necessary, but write legibly so you can read your notes later.

Step 3: Use the recall column for review. Read over your notes and write down key words or ideas from the lecture in the recall column. Ask yourself, "What is this about?" Cover up the notes on the right-hand side and recite the key ideas of the lecture. Another variation is to write questions in the margin. Find the key ideas and then write possible exam questions in the recall column. Cover your notes and see if you can answer the questions.

The Outline Method

If the lecture is well organized, some students just take notes in outline format. Sometimes lecturers will show their outline as they speak.

- Use Roman numerals to label main topics. Then use capital letters for main ideas and Arabic numerals for related details or examples.
- You can make a free-form outline using just indentation to separate main ideas and supporting details.
- Leave spaces to fill in material later.
- Use a highlighter to review your notes as soon as possible after the lecture.

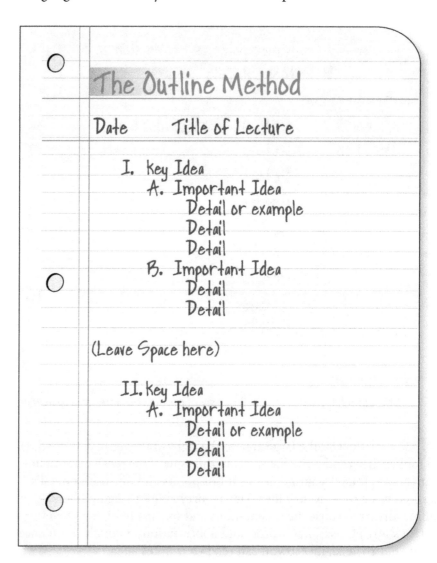

Figure 7.2 If a lecture is well organized, the outline format of taking notes works well.

The Mind Map

A mind map shows the relationship between ideas in a visual way. It is much easier to remember items that are organized and linked together in a personally meaningful way. As a result, recall and review is quicker and more effective. Mind maps have appeal to visual learners and those who do not want to be limited by a set structure, as in the outline formats. They can also be used for lectures that are not highly structured. Here are some suggestions for using the mind-mapping technique:

- Turn your paper sideways to give you more space. Use standard-size notebook paper or consider larger sheets if possible.
- Write the main idea in the center of the page and circle it.
- Arrange ideas so that more important ideas are closer to the center and less important ideas are farther out.

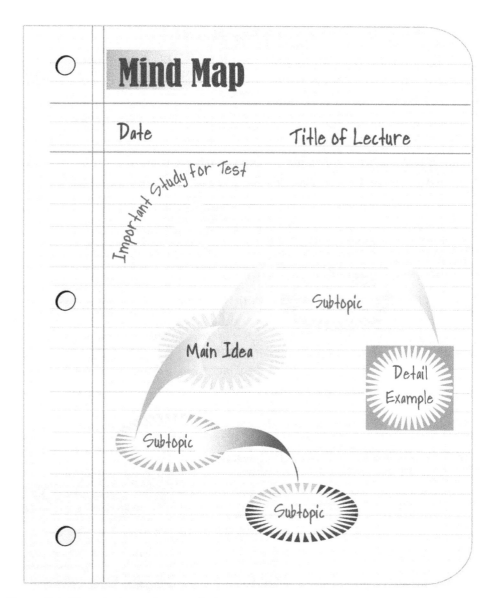

Figure 7.3 The mind map format of taking notes shows the relationship between ideas in a visual way.

- Show the relationship of the minor points to the main ideas using lines, circles, boxes, charts, and other visual devices. Here is where you can use your creativity and imagination to make a visual picture of the key ideas in the lecture.
- Use symbols and drawings.
- Use different colors to separate main ideas.
- When the lecturer moves to another main idea, start a new mind map.
- When you are done with the lecture, quickly review your mind maps. Add any written material that will be helpful in understanding the map later.
- A mind map can also be used as:
  - a review tool for remembering and relating the key ideas in the textbook;
  - a preparation tool for essay exams in which remembering main ideas and relationships is important; and
  - the first step in organizing ideas for a term paper.

Improving Note-Taking Efficiency

Improve note-taking efficiency by listening for key words that signal the main ideas and supporting details. Learn to write faster by using telegraphic sentences, abbreviations, and symbols.

Telegraphic Sentences

Telegraphic sentences are short, abbreviated sentences used in note taking. They are very similar to the text messages sent on a cell phone. There are four rules for telegraphic sentences:

1. Write key words only.
2. Omit unnecessary words (*a, an, the*).
3. Ignore rules of grammar.
4. Use abbreviations and symbols.

Here is an example of a small part of a lecture followed by a student's telegraphic notes:

Heavy drinking of alcoholic beverages causes students to miss class and to fall behind in schoolwork. College students who are considered binge drinkers are at risk for many alcohol-related problems. Binge drinking is simply drinking too much alcohol at one time. Binge drinking is defined by researchers as drinking five or more drinks in a row for men or four or more drinks in a row for women. Researchers estimate that two out of five college students (40 percent) are binge drinkers.

Binge drinking—too much alcohol at one time
    Men = 5 in row
    Women = 4
    2 out of 5 (40%) college students binge

Signal Words

Signal words are clues to understanding the structure and content of a lecture. Recognizing signal words can help you identify key ideas and organize them in your notes. The table on the following page lists some common signal words and their meaning.

© 2014, Lightspring. Used under license with Shutterstock, Inc.

Signal Words

Type	Examples	Meaning
Main idea words	And most important A major development The basic concept is Remember that The main idea is We will focus on The key is	Introduce the key points that need to be written in your notes.
Example words	To illustrate For example For instance	Clarify and illustrate the main ideas in the lecture. Write these examples in your notes after the main idea. If multiple examples are given, write down the ones you have time for or the ones that you understand the best.
Addition words	In addition Also Furthermore	Add more important information. Write these points down in your notes.
Enumeration words	The five steps First, second, third Next	Signal a list. Write down the list in your notes and number the items.
Time words	Before, after Formerly Subsequently Prior Meanwhile	Signal the order of events. Write down the events in the correct order in your notes.
Cause and effect words	Therefore As a result If . . ., then	Signal important concepts that might be on the exam. When you hear these words, label them "cause" and "effect" in your notes and review these ideas for the exam.
Definition words	In other words It simply means That is In essence	Provide the meanings of words or simplify complex ideas. Write these definitions or clarifications in your notes.
Swivel words	However Nevertheless Yes, but Still	Provide exceptions, qualifications, or further clarification. Write down qualifying comments in your notes.
Compare and contrast words	Similarly Likewise In contrast	Present similarities or differences. Write these similarities and differences in your notes and label them.
Summary words	In conclusion To sum up In a nutshell	Restate the important ideas of the lecture. Write the summaries in your notes.
Test words	This is important. Remember this. You'll see this again. You might want to study this for the test.	Provide a clue that the material will be on the test. Write these down in your notes and mark them in a way that stands out. Put a star or asterisk next to these items or highlight them. Each professor has his or her own test clue words.

Abbreviations

If you have time, write out words in their entirety for ease of reading. If you are short on time, use any abbreviation as long as you can read it. Here are some ideas:

1. Use the first syllable of the word.

democracy	dem
education	ed
politics	pol
different	diff
moderate	mod
characteristic	char
develop	dev

2. Use just enough of the word so that you can recognize it.

republican	repub
prescription	prescrip
introduction	intro
intelligence	intell
association	assoc

3. Abbreviate or write out the word the first time, then use an acronym. For example, for the United States Department of Agriculture, abbreviate it as "US Dept of Ag" and then write it as USDA in subsequent references. Other examples:

short-term memory	STM
as soon as possible	ASAP

4. Omit vowels.

background	bkgrnd
problem	prblm
government	gvt

5. Use g in place of ing.

checking	ckg
decreasing	decrg

6. Write your notes in text message format.

Symbols

Use common symbols or invent your own to speed up the note-taking process.

Common Symbols Used in Note Taking

Symbol	Meaning	Symbol	Meaning
&	and	B4	before
w	with	BC	because
wo	without	esp	especially
wi	within	diff	difference
<	less than	min	minimum
>	more than	gov	government
@	at	ex	example

Symbol	Meaning	Symbol	Meaning
/	per	↑	increasing
2	to, two, too	↓	decreasing
∴	therefore	=	equal
vs	versus, against	≠	not equal

How to Review Your Notes

Immediate review. Review your notes as soon as possible after the lecture. The most effective review is done immediately or at least within 20 minutes. If you wait until the next day to review, you may already have forgotten much of the information. During the immediate review, fill in any missing or incomplete information. Say the important points to yourself. This begins the process of rehearsal for storing the information in long-term memory.

© 2014, Terence. Used under license with Shutterstock, Inc.

There are various methods for review depending on your note-taking system:

- For the Cornell format, use the recall column to write in key words or questions. Cover your notes and see if you can recall the main ideas. Place checkmarks by the items you have mastered. Don't worry about mastering all the key points from the beginning. With each review, it will be easier to remember the information.
- For the outline format, use a highlighter to mark the key ideas as you repeat them silently to yourself.
- For mind maps, look over the information and think about the key ideas and their relationships. Fill in additional information or clarification. Highlight important points or relationships with color.

Intermediate review. Set up some time each week for short reviews of your notes and the key points in your textbook from previous weeks. Quickly look over the notes and recite the key points in your mind. These intermediate reviews will help you to master the material and avoid test anxiety.

Test review. Complete a major review as part of your test preparation strategy. As you look through your notes, turn the key ideas into possible test questions and answer them.

Final review. The final review occurs after you have received the results of your test. Ask yourself these questions:

- What percentage of the test questions came from the lecture notes?
- Were you prepared for the exam? If so, congratulate yourself on a job well done. If not, how can you improve next time?
- Were your notes adequate? If not, what needs to be added or changed?

"You have to get your education. Then nobody can control your destiny."
Charles Barkley

7.1   QUIZ: LISTENING AND NOTE TAKING

Test what you have learned by selecting the correct answer to the following questions.

1. When taking notes on a college lecture, it is most important to

   a. write down everything you hear.
   b. write down the main ideas and enough explanation to understand them.
   c. write down names, dates, places, and numbers.

2. To be a good listener,

   a. read or skim over the material before you attend the lecture.
   b. attend the lecture first and then read the text.
   c. remember that listening is more important than note taking.

3. To stay awake during the lecture,

   a. drink lots of coffee.
   b. sit near your friends so you can make some comments on the lecture.
   c. listen actively by taking notes.

4. Since attendance is not always checked in college classes,

   a. it is not necessary to attend class if you read the textbook.
   b. it is acceptable to miss lectures as long as you show up for the exams.
   c. it is up to you to attend every class.

5. The best time to review your notes is

   a. as soon as possible after the lecture.
   b. within 24 hours.
   c. within one week.

How did you do on the quiz? Check your answers: 1. b, 2. a, 3. c, 4. c, 5. a

---

"The highest reward for a person's toil is not what they get for it, but what they become by it."

John Ruskin

Journal Entry   7.2

Write five intention statements about improving your note-taking skills. Consider your note-taking system, how to take notes more efficiently, and the best way to review your notes. I intend to . . .

Power Writing

- Prepare
- Organize
- Write
- Edit
- Revise

Power Writing

Effective writing will help you in school, on the job, and in your personal life. Good writing will help you to create quality term papers. The writing skills that you learn in college will be used later in jobs involving high responsibility and good pay. You can become an excellent writer by learning about the steps in POWER writing: prepare, organize, write, edit, and revise.

Prepare

"The most valuable of all education is the ability to make yourself do the thing you have to do, when it has to be done, whether you like it or not."

Aldous Huxley

Plan your time. The first step in writing is to plan your time so that the project can be completed by the due date. Picture this scene: It is the day that the term paper is due. A few students proudly hand in their term papers and are ready to celebrate their accomplishments. Many of the students in the class are absent, and some will never return to the class. Some of the students look as though they haven't slept the night before. They look stressed and weary. At the front of the class is a line of students wanting to talk with the instructor. The instructor has heard it all before:

- I had my paper all completed and my printer jammed.
- My hard drive crashed and I lost my paper.
- I was driving to school and my paper flew off my motorcycle.
- I had the flu.
- My children were sick.
- I had to take my dog to the vet.
- My dog ate my paper.
- My car broke down and I could not get to the library.
- My grandmother died and I had to go to the funeral.
- My roommate accidentally took my backpack to school.
- I spilled salad dressing on my paper, so I put it in the microwave to dry it out and the writing disappeared!

To avoid being in this uncomfortable and stressful situation, plan ahead. Plan to complete your project at least one week ahead of time so that you can deal with life's emergencies. Life does not always go as planned. You or your children may get sick, or your dog may do strange things to your homework. Your computer may malfunction, leading you to believe it senses stress and malfunctions just to frustrate you even more.

To avoid stress and do your best work, start with the date that the project is due and then think about the steps needed to finish. Write these dates on your calendar or on your list of things to do. Consider all these components:

© 2014, Benjamin Howell. Used under license with Shutterstock, Inc.

Project due date:

To do	By when?
1. Brainstorm ideas.	_____
2. Choose a topic.	_____
3. Gather information.	_____
4. Write a thesis statement.	_____
5. Write an outline.	_____
6. Write the introduction.	_____
7. Write the first draft.	_____
8. Prepare the bibliography.	_____
9. Edit.	_____
10. Revise.	_____
11. Print and assemble.	_____

Find a space and time. Find a space where you can work. Gather the materials that you will need to write. Generally, writing is best done in longer blocks of time. Determine when you will work on your paper and write the time on your schedule. Start right away to avoid panic later.

Choose a general topic. This task will be easy if your topic is already clearly defined by your instructor or your boss at work. Make sure that you have a clear idea of what is required, such as length, format, purpose, and method of citing references and topic. Many times the choice of a topic is left to you. Begin by doing some brainstorming. Think about topics that interest you. Write them down. You may want to focus your attention on brainstorming ideas for five or 10 minutes, and then put the project aside and come back to it later. Once you have started the process of thinking about the ideas, your mind will continue to work and you may have some creative inspiration. If inspiration does not come, repeat the brainstorming process.

Gather information. Go to your college library and use the Internet to gather your information. As you begin, you can see what is available, what is interesting to you, and what the current thinking is on your topic. Note the major topics of interest that might be useful to you. Once you have found some interesting material, you will feel motivated to continue your project. As you find information relevant to your topic, make sure to write down the sources of your information to use in your bibliography. The bibliography contains information about where you found your material. Write down the author, the title of the publication, the publisher, and the place and date of publication. For Internet resources, list the address of the website and the date accessed.

Write the thesis statement. The thesis statement is the key idea in your paper. It provides a direction for you to follow. It is the first step in organizing your work. To write a thesis statement, review the material you have gathered and then ask these questions:
- What is the most important idea?
- What question would I like to ask about it?
- What is my answer?

For example, if I decide to write a paper for my health class on the harmful effects of smoking, I would look at current references on the topic. I might become interested in how the tobacco companies misled the public on the dangers of smoking. I would think about my thesis statement and answer the questions stated above.

© 2014, Elena Elisseeva. Used under license with Shutterstock, Inc.

- **What is the most important idea?** Smoking is harmful to your health.
- **What question would I like to ask about it?** Did the tobacco companies mislead the public about the health hazards of smoking?
- **What is my answer?** The tobacco companies misled the public about the hazards of smoking in order to protect their business interests.
- **My thesis statement:** Tobacco companies knew that smoking was hazardous to health, but to protect their business interests, they deliberately misled the public.

The thesis statement helps to narrow the topic and provide direction for the paper. I can now focus on reference material related to my topic: research on health effects of smoking, congressional testimony relating to regulation of the tobacco industry, and how advertising influences people to smoke.

Organize

At this point you have many ideas about what to include in your paper, and you have a central focus, your thesis statement. Start to organize your paper by listing the topics that are related to your thesis statement. Here is a list of topics related to my thesis statement about smoking:

- Tobacco companies' awareness that nicotine is addictive
- Minimizing health hazards in tobacco advertisements
- How advertisements encourage people to smoke
- Money earned by the tobacco industry
- Health problems caused by smoking
- Statistics on numbers of people who have health problems or die from smoking
- Regulation of the tobacco industry
- Advertisements aimed at children

> **Organize**
> - List related topics
> - Arrange in logical order
> - Have an organizational structure

Think about the topics and arrange them in logical order. Use an outline, a mind map, a flowchart, or a drawing to think about how you will organize the important topics. Keep in mind that you will need an introduction, a body, and a conclusion. Having an organizational structure will make it easier for you to write because you will not need to wonder what comes next.

Write

Write the First Sentence

Begin with the main idea.

Write the Introduction

This is the road map for the rest of the paper. The introduction includes your thesis statement and establishes the foundation of the paper. It introduces topics that will be discussed in the body of the paper. The introduction should include some interesting points that provide a "hook" to motivate the audience to read your paper. For example, for a paper on the hazards of smoking, you might begin with statistics on how many people suffer from smoking-related illnesses and premature death. Note the large profits earned by the tobacco industry. Then introduce other topics: deception, advertisements, and regulation. The introduction provides a guide or outline of what will follow in the paper.

> **Write**
> - First sentence
> - Introduction
> - Body
> - Conclusion
> - References

Write the Body of the Paper

The body of the paper is divided into paragraphs that discuss the topics that you have introduced. As you write each paragraph, include the main idea and then explain it and give examples. Here are some good tips for writing:

1. Good writing reflects clear thinking. Think about what you want to say and write about it so the reader can understand your point of view.
2. Use clear and concise language. Avoid using too many words or scholarly-sounding words that might get in the way of understanding.
3. Don't assume that the audience knows what you are writing about. Provide complete information.
4. Provide examples, stories, and quotes to support your main points. Include your own ideas and experiences.
5. Beware of plagiarism. Plagiarism is copying the work of others without giving them credit. It is illegal and can cause you to receive a failing grade on your project or even get you into legal trouble. Faculty regularly uses software programs that identify plagiarized material in student papers. You can avoid plagiarism by using quotation marks around an author's words and providing a reference indicating where you found the material. Another way to avoid plagiarism is by carefully reading your source material while using critical thinking to evaluate it. Then look away from the source and write about the ideas in your own words, including your critical thinking about the subject. Don't forget to include a reference for the source material in your bibliography.

Write the Conclusion

The conclusion summarizes the topics in the paper and presents your point of view. It makes reference to the introduction and answers the question posed in your thesis statement. It often makes the reader think about the significance of your point and the implications for the future. Make your conclusion interesting and powerful.

Include References

No college paper is complete without references. References may be given in footnotes, endnotes, a list of works cited, or a bibliography. You can use your computer to insert these references. There are various styles for citing references depending on your subject area. There are computer programs that put your information into the correct style. Ask your instructor which style to use for your particular class or project. Three frequently used styles for citing references are APA, Chicago, and MLA.

1. The American Psychological Association (APA) style is used in psychology and other behavioral sciences. Consult the *Publication Manual of the American Psychological Association*, 6th ed. (Washington, DC: American Psychological Association, 2010). You can find this source online at www.apastyle.org.
2. Chicago style is used by many professional writers in a variety of fields. Consult the *Chicago Manual of Style*, 16th ed. (Chicago: University of Chicago Press, 2010). You can find this source online at www.chicagomanualofstyle.org/home.html.
3. The Modern Language Association (MLA) style is used in English, classical languages, and the humanities. Consult the *MLA Handbook for Writers of Research Papers*, 7th ed. (New York: Modern Language Association, 2009). This source is available online at www.mla.org/style.

Each of these styles uses a different format for listing sources, but all include the same information. Make sure you write down this information as you collect your reference material. If you forget this step, it is very time-consuming and difficult to find later.

- Author's name
- Title of the book or article
- Journal name
- Publisher
- City where book was published
- Publication date
- Page number (and volume and issue numbers, if available)

Here are some examples of citations in the APA style:

- **Book.** Include author, date of publication, title, city of publication, and publisher.

Fralick, M. (2014). *College and career success* (6th ed.). Dubuque, IA: Kendall Hunt.

- **Journal article.** Include author, date, title, name of journal, volume and issue numbers, pages.

Fralick, M. (1993). College success: A study of positive and negative attrition. *Community College Review, 20*(5), 29–36.

- **Website.** Include author, date listed or updated, document title or name of website, URL or website address, and date accessed. Include as many of the above items as possible. Methods of citing information from the Internet are still evolving.

Fralick, M. (2014, October). *Note taking*. Retrieved October 2013 from College Success 1 at www.collegesuccess1.com/

Save Your Work

As soon as you have written the first paragraph, save it on your computer. If your computer is not backed up by a remote server such as iCloud or Carbonite, save another copy on a flash drive. When you are finished, print your work and save a paper copy. Then, if your hard drive crashes, you will still have your work at another location. If your file becomes corrupted, you will still have the paper copy. Following these procedures can save you a lot of headaches. Any writer can tell you stories of lost work because of computer problems, lightning storms, power outages, and other unpredictable events.

Put It Away for a While

The last step in writing the first draft is easy. Put it away for a while and come back to it later. In this way, you can relax and gain some perspective on your work. You will be able to take a more objective look at your work to begin the process of editing and revising.

"All things are difficult before they are easy."
John Norley

Writer's Block

Many people who are anxious about writing experience "writer's block." You have writer's block if you find yourself staring at that blank piece of paper or computer screen not knowing how to begin or what to write. Here are some tips for avoiding writer's block.

- **Write freely.** Just write anything about your topic that comes to mind. Don't worry about organization or perfection at this point. Don't censure your ideas. You can always go back to organize and edit later. Free-writing helps you to overcome one of the main causes of writer's block: you think it has to be perfect from the beginning. This expectation of perfection causes anxiety. You freeze up and become unable to write. Perhaps you have past memories of writing where the teacher made many corrections on your paper. Maybe you lack confidence in your writing skills. The only way you will become a better writer is to keep writing and perfecting your writing skills, so to start the writing process, just write what comes to mind. Don't worry how great it is. You can fix it later. Just begin.

- **Use brainstorming if you get stuck.** For five minutes, focus your attention on the topic and write whatever comes to mind. You don't even need to write full sentences; just jot down ideas. If you are really stuck, try working on a different topic or take a break and come back to it later.

- **Realize that it is only the first draft.** It is not the finished product and it does not have to be perfect. Just write some ideas on paper; you can revise them later.

- **Read through your reference materials.** The ideas you find can get your mind working. Also, reading can make you a better writer.

- **Break the assignment up into small parts.** If you find writing difficult, write for five minutes at a time. Do this consistently and you can get used to writing and can complete your paper.

- **Find a good place for writing.** If you are an introvert, look for a quiet place for concentration. If you are an extrovert, go to a restaurant or coffee shop and start your writing.

- **Beware of procrastination.** The more you put off writing, the more anxious you will become and the more difficult the task will be. Make a schedule and stick to it.

© 2014, Creativa. Used under license with Shutterstock, Inc.

Edit and Revise

The editing and revising stage allows you to take a critical look at what you have written. It takes some courage to do this step. Once people see their ideas in writing, they become attached to them. With careful editing and revising, you can turn in your best work and be proud of your accomplishments. Here are some tips for editing and revising:

1. **Read your paper as if you were the audience.** Pretend that you are the instructor or another person reading your paper. Does every sentence make sense? Did you say what you meant to say? Read what you have written, and the result will be a more effective paper.

2. **Read paragraph by paragraph.** Does each paragraph have a main idea and supporting details? Do the paragraphs fit logically together? Use the cut-and-paste feature on your computer to move sentences and paragraphs around if needed.

3. **Check your grammar and spelling.** Use the spell check and grammar check on your computer. These tools are helpful, but they are not thorough enough. The spell check will pick up only misspelled words. It will skip words that are spelled correctly but not the intended word—for example, if you use "of" instead of "on" or "their" instead of "there." To find such errors, you need to read your paper after doing a spell check.

4. **Check for language that is biased in terms of gender, disability, or ethnic group.** Use words that are gender neutral. If a book or paper uses only the pronoun "he" or "she," half of the population is left out. You can often avoid sexist language by using the plural forms of nouns:

   (singular)   The successful student knows *his* values and sets goals for the future.

   (plural)   Successful students know *their* values and set goals for the future.

> **Tips for Editing and Revising**
>
> 1. Read your paper objectively
> 2. Read paragraph by paragraph
> 3. Check grammar and spelling
> 4. Check for biased language
> 5. Have someone else read your paper
> 6. Review the introduction and conclusion
> 7. Prepare final copy
> 8. Prepare title page

After all, we are trying to make the world a better place, with opportunity for all. Here are some examples of biased language and better alternatives.

Biased Language	*Better Alternatives*
policeman	police officer
chairman	chair
fireman	firefighter
postman	mail carrier
mankind	humanity
manmade	handcrafted
housewife	homemaker
crippled	persons with disabilities

5. **Have someone else read your paper.** Ask your reader to check for clarity and meaning. After you have read your paper many times, you do not really see it anymore. If you need assistance in writing, colleges offer tutoring or writing labs where you can get help with editing and revising.

6. **Review your introduction and conclusion.** They should be clear, interesting, and concise. The introduction and conclusion are the most powerful parts of your paper.

7. **Prepare the final copy.** Check your instructor's instructions on the format required. If there are no instructions, use the following format:
   • Use double-spacing.

- Use 10- or 12-point font.
- Use one-inch margins on all sides.
- Use a three-inch top margin on the first page.
- Single-space footnotes and endnotes.
- Number your pages.

8. **Prepare the title page.** Center the title of your paper and place it one third of the page from the top. On the bottom third of the page, center your name, the professor's name, the name of the class, and the date.

Final Steps

Make sure you follow instructions about using a folder or cover for your paper. Generally professors dislike bulky folders or notebooks because they are difficult to carry. Imagine your professor trying to carry 50 notebooks to his or her office! Unless asked to do so, do not use plastic page protectors. Professors like to write comments on papers, and it is extremely difficult to write on papers with page protectors.

Turning your paper in on time is very important. Some professors do not accept late papers. Others subtract points if your paper is late. Put your paper in the car or someplace where you will have to see it before you go to class. **Then reward yourself for a job well done!**

Journal Entry **7.3**

Write five intention statements about improving your writing. While thinking about your statements, consider the steps of POWER writing: prepare, organize, write, edit, and revise. Do you need to work on problems such as writer's block or getting your writing done on time? I intend to . . .

> "Let us think of education as the means of developing our greatest abilities, because in each of us there is a private hope and dream which, fulfilled, can be translated into greater benefit for everyone and greater strength for our nation."
>
> John F. Kennedy

Effective Public Speaking

You may need to take a speech class in order to graduate from college, and many of your classes will require oral presentations. Being a good speaker can contribute to your success on the job as well. A study done at Stanford University showed that one of the top predictors of success in professional positions was the ability to be a good public speaker.[1] You will need to present information to your boss, your colleagues, and your customers or clients.

© 2014, Sanjay Deva. Used under license with Shutterstock, Inc.

Learn to Relax

Whenever I tell students that they will need to take a speech class or make an oral presentation, I see a look of panic on their faces. Good preparation can help you to feel confident about your oral presentation. Professional speaker Lilly Walters believes that you can deal with 75 percent of your anxiety by being well prepared.[2] You can deal with the remaining 25 percent by using some relaxation techniques.

- If you are anxious, admit to yourself that you are anxious. If it is appropriate, as in a beginning speech class, you can even admit to the audience that you are anxious. Once you have admitted that you are anxious, visualize yourself confidently making the speech.
- You do not have to be perfect; it is okay to make mistakes. Making mistakes just shows you are human like the rest of us.
- If you are anxious before your speech, take three to five deep breaths. Breathe in slowly and hold your breath for five seconds, and then breathe out slowly. Focus your mind on your breathing rather than your speech.
- Use positive self-talk to help you to relax. Instead of saying to yourself, "I will look like a fool up there giving the speech," tell yourself, "I can do this" or "It will be okay."
- Once you start speaking, anxiety will generally decline.
- With experience, you will gain confidence in your speaking ability and will be able to relax more easily.

Preparing and Delivering Your Speech

Write the Beginning of the Speech

The beginning includes a statement of your objective and what your speech will be about. It should prepare the audience for what comes next. You can begin your speech with a personal experience, a quote, a news article, or a joke. Jokes can be effective, but they are risky. Try out your joke with your friends to make sure that it is funny. Do not tell jokes that put down other people or groups.

Write the Main Body of the Speech

The main body of the speech consists of four or five main points. Just as in your term paper, state your main points and then provide details, examples, or stories that illustrate them. As you present the main points of your speech, consider your audience. Your speech will be different depending on whether it is made to a group of high school students, your college classmates, or a group of professionals. You can add interest to your speech by using props, pictures, charts, PowerPoint, music, or video clips. College students today are increasingly using PowerPoint software to make classroom presentations. If you are planning to enter a professional career, learning how to make PowerPoint presentations will be an asset.

Write the Conclusion

In your conclusion, summarize and review the key points of your speech. The conclusion is like the icing on a cake. It should be strong, persuasive, and interesting. Invest some time in your ending statement. It can be a call to action, a recommendation for the future, a quote, or a story.

Practice Your Speech

Practice your speech until you feel comfortable with it. Prepare a memory system or notes to help you deliver your speech. You will want to make eye contact with your audience, which is difficult if you are trying to read your speech. A memory system useful for delivering speeches is the loci system. Visualize a house, for example: the entryway is the introduction, and each room represents a main point in the speech. Visualize walking into each room and what you will say in each room. Each room can have items that remind you of what you are going to say. At the conclusion, you say good-bye at the door. Another technique is to prepare brief notes or outlines on index cards or sheets of paper. When you are practicing your speech, time it to see how long it is. Keep your speech within the time allowed. Most people tend to speak longer than necessary.

Review the Setup

If you are using props, make sure that you have them ready. If you are using equipment, make sure it is available and in working condition. Make arrangements in advance for the equipment you need and, if possible, check to see that it is running properly right before your presentation.

Deliver the Speech

Wear clothes that make you feel comfortable, but not out of place. Remember to smile and make eye contact with members of the audience. Take a few deep breaths if you are nervous. You will probably be less nervous once you begin. If you make a mistake, keep your sense of humor. I recall the famous chef Julia Child doing a live television production on how to cook a turkey. As she took the turkey out of the oven, it slipped and landed on the floor right in front of the television cameras. She calmly picked it up and said, "And remember that you are the only one that really knows what goes on in the kitchen." It was one of the shows that made her famous.

7.2   QUIZ: WRITING AND SPEAKING

Test what you have learned by selecting the correct answers to the following questions.

1. To make sure to get your paper done on time,
   a. have someone remind you of the deadline.
   b. write the due date on your calendar and the date for completion of each step.
   c. write your paper just before the due date to increase motivation.

2. The thesis statement is the
   a. most important sentence in each paragraph.
   b. key idea in the paper.
   c. summary of the paper.

3. If you have writer's block, it is helpful to
   a. delay writing your paper until you feel relaxed.
   b. make sure that your writing is perfect from the beginning.
   c. begin with brainstorming or free writing.

4. No college paper is complete without
   a. the references.
   b. a professional-looking cover.
   c. printing on quality paper.

5. You can deal with most of your anxiety about public speaking by
   a. striving for perfection.
   b. visualizing your anxiety.
   c. being well prepared.

How did you do on the quiz? Check your answers: 1. b, 2. b, 3. c, 4. a, 5. c

Journal Entry 7.4

Write one paragraph giving advice to a new college student on how to make a speech. Use any of these questions to guide your thinking:

- What are some ways to deal with anxiety about public speaking?
- How can you make your speech interesting?
- What are some steps in preparing a speech?
- What are some ideas that don't work?

KEYS TO SUCCESS

Be Selective

Psychologist and philosopher William James said, "The essence of genius is knowing what to overlook."[3] This saying has a variety of meanings. In reading, note taking, marking a college textbook, and writing, it is important to be able to pick out the main points first and then identify the supporting details. Imagine you are trying to put together a jigsaw puzzle. You bought the puzzle at a garage sale and all the pieces are there, but the lid to the box with the picture of the puzzle is missing. It will be very difficult, if not impossible, to put this puzzle together. Reading, note taking, marking, and writing are very much like putting a puzzle together. First you will need an understanding of the main ideas (the big picture) and then you can focus on the details.

How can you get the overall picture? When reading, you can get the overall picture by skimming the text. As you skim the text, you get a general outline of what the chapter contains and what you will learn. In note taking, actively listen for the main ideas and write them down in your notes. In marking your text, try to pick out about 20 percent of the most important material and underline or highlight it. In writing, think about what is most important, write your thesis statement, and then provide the supporting details. To select what is most important, be courageous, think, and analyze.

Does this mean that you should forget about the details? No, you will need to know some details too. The supporting details help you to understand and assess the value of the main idea. They help you to understand the relationship between ideas. Being selective means getting the general idea first, and then the details will make sense to you and you will be able to remember them. The main ideas are like scaffolding or a net that holds the details in some kind of framework so you can remember them. If you focus on the details first, you will have no framework or point of reference for remembering them.

Experiment with the idea of being selective in your personal life. If your schedule is impossibly busy, be selective and choose to do the most important or most valuable activities. This takes some thinking and courage too. If your desk drawer is stuffed with odds and ends and you can never find what you are looking for, take everything out and only put back what you need. Recycle, give away, or throw away surplus items around the house. You can take steps toward being a genius by being selective and taking steps to simplify and organize your life and your work.

Journal Entry   **7.5**

How can being selective help you achieve success in college and in life? Use any of these questions to guide your thinking:
- How can being selective help you to be a better note taker, writer, or speaker?
- How can being selective help you to manage your time and your life?
- What is the meaning of this quote by William James: "The essence of genius is knowing what to overlook?"

JOURNAL ENTRIES

Taking Notes, Writing, and Speaking

Go to http://www.collegesuccess1.com/JournalEntries.htm for Word files of the Journal Entries

Success over the Internet

Visit the *College Success Website* at http://www.collegesuccess1.com/

The *College Success Website* is continually updated with new topics and links to the material presented in this chapter. Topics include:

- Note taking
- Mind maps
- Memory and note taking
- Telegraphic sentences
- Signal words
- Listening to lectures
- Grammar and style
- Quotes to use in speeches and papers
- The virtual public speaking assistant
- Researching, organizing, and delivering a speech
- Best speeches in history

Contact your instructor if you have any problems accessing the *College Success Website*.

Notes

1. T. Allesandra and P. Hunsaker, *Communicating at Work* (New York: Fireside, 1993), 169.
2. Lilly Walters, *Secrets of Successful Speakers: How You Can Motivate, Captivate, and Persuade* (New York: McGraw-Hill, 1993), 203.
3. Quoted in Rob Gilbert, ed., *Bits and Pieces*, August 12, 1999, 15.

Note-Taking Checklist

Name _____ Date _____

Place a checkmark next to the note-taking skills you have now.

_____ I attend every (or almost every) lecture in all my classes.

_____ I check the syllabus to find out what is being covered before I go to class.

_____ I read or at least skim through the reading assignment before attending the lecture.

_____ I attend lectures with a positive attitude about learning as much as possible.

_____ I am well rested so that I can focus on the lecture.

_____ I eat a light, nutritious meal before going to class.

_____ I sit in a location where I can see and hear easily.

_____ I have a laptop or a three-ring binder, looseleaf paper, and a pen for taking notes.

_____ I avoid external distractions (friends, sitting by the door).

_____ I am alert and able to concentrate on the lecture.

_____ I have a system for taking notes that works for me.

_____ I am able to determine the key ideas of the lecture and write them down in my notes.

_____ I can identify signal words that help to understand key points and organize my notes.

_____ I can write quickly using telegraphic sentences, abbreviations, and symbols.

_____ If I don't understand something in the lecture, I ask a question and get help.

_____ I write down everything written on the board or on visual materials used in the class.

_____ I review my notes immediately after class.

_____ I have intermediate review sessions to review previous notes.

_____ I use my notes to predict questions for the exam.

_____ I have clear and complete notes that help me to prepare adequately for exams.

Evaluate Your Note-Taking Skills

Name _____   Date _____

Use the note-taking checklist on the previous page to answer these questions.

1. Look at the items that you checked. What are your strengths in note taking?

2. What are some areas that you need to improve?

3. Write at least three intention statements about improving your listening and note-taking skills.

Assess Your College Writing Skills

Name _____   Date _____

Read the following statements and rate how true they are for you at the present time. Use the following scale:

5 Definitely true
4 Mostly true
3 Somewhat true
2 Seldom true
1 Never true

_____ I am generally confident in my writing skills.

_____ I have a system for reminding myself of due dates for writing projects.

_____ I start writing projects early so that I am not stressed by finishing them at the last minute.

_____ I have the proper materials and a space to write comfortably.

_____ I know how to use the library and the Internet to gather information for a term paper.

_____ I can write a thesis statement for a term paper.

_____ I know how to organize a term paper.

_____ I know how to write the introduction, body, and conclusion of a paper.

_____ I can cite references in the appropriate style for my subject.

_____ I know where to find information about citing material in APA, MLA, or Chicago style.

_____ I know what plagiarism is and know how to avoid it.

_____ I can deal with "writer's block" and get started on my writing project.

_____ I know how to edit and revise a paper.

_____ I know where I can get help with my writing.

_____ **Total**

60–70   You have excellent writing skills, but can always learn new ideas.

50–59   You have good writing skills, but there is room for improvement.

Below 50   You need to improve writing skills. The skills presented in this chapter will help. Consider taking a writing class early in your college studies.

Fiscal Literacy

Managing Money and Minimizing Debt

8

ACTIVATE YOUR THINKING *Reflection* **8.1**

LEARNING GOAL

To become more self-aware, knowledgeable, and strategic with respect to managing money and financing a college education.

Complete the following sentence with the first thought that comes to your mind:

For me, money is . . .

The beginning of college often marks the beginning of greater personal independence and greater demands for effective financial self-management and fiscal decision-making. The importance of money management for college students is growing for two major reasons. The first reason is the rising cost of a college education, which has resulted in more students working more hours while they're in college (Levine & Cureton, 1998; Perna & DuBois, 2010). The rising cost of a college education is also requiring students to make more difficult decisions about what options (or combination of options) to use to meet their college expenses. Unfortunately, research indicates that many students today are not making the most effective decisions about how to finance their college education in a way that best contributes to their academic success in college and their financial success beyond college (King, 2005).

A second reason money management is growing in importance for college students is the availability and convenience of credit cards. It has never been easier for college students to get access to, use, and abuse credit cards. A college graduate today can do everything right in college, such as earn good grades, get involved on campus, and get work experience before graduating, but a poor credit history resulting from irresponsible credit-card use while in college can reduce that student's chances of obtaining credit after college as well as their job prospects after graduation (Mae, 2005). Credit reporting agencies and bureaus collect information about how faithfully college students make credit-card payments and report their "credit scores" to credit-card companies and banks. Employers check these credit scores and use them as indicators or predictors of how responsible students will be as employees, because there's a statistical relationship between using credit cards responsibly and being a responsible employee (Ring, 1997; Susswein, 1995). Thus, being irresponsible with credit while you're in college can affect your ability to land a job after (or during) college. Your credit score report will also affect your likelihood of qualifying for car loans and home loans, as well as your ability to rent an apartment (Pratt, 2008).

Furthermore, research indicates that accumulating high levels of debt while in college is associated with higher levels of stress (Nelson, Lust, Story, & Ehlinger, 2008), lower academic performance (Susswein, 1995), and greater risk of withdrawing from college (Ring, 1997). On the positive side of the ledger, studies show that

"If we command our wealth, we shall be rich and free; if our wealth commands us, we are poor indeed."

—Edmund Burke, 18th-century author, political philosopher, and supporter of the American Revolution

when students learn to use effective money-management strategies, they reduce unnecessary spending, minimize accumulation of debt, and lower their level of stress (Health & Soll, 1996; Kidwell & Turrisi, 2004; Walker, 1996).

Strategies for Managing Money Effectively

Developing Financial Self-Awareness

Developing any good habit begins with the critical first step of self-awareness. The habit of effective money management begins with awareness of your *cash flow*—the amount of money you have flowing in and flowing out. As illustrated in Figure 8.1, you can track your cash flow by monitoring:

- The amount of money you have coming in (income) versus the amount going out (expenses or expenditures), and
- The amount of money you've earned and not spent (savings) versus the amount you've borrowed and not yet paid back (debt).

Student *Perspective*

"My money-management skills are poor. If I have money, I will spend it unless somebody takes it away from me. I am the kind of person who lives from paycheck to paycheck."

—First-year student

FIGURE 8.1

Income ⟷ Expenses

Savings ⟷ Debt

Two Key Avenues of Cash Flow

Income for college students typically comes from one or more of the following sources:

- Scholarships or grants, which don't have to be paid back
- Loans, which must be repaid
- Salary earned from part-time or full-time work
- Personal savings
- Gifts or other forms of monetary support from parents and other family members

Your sources of expenses or expenditures may be classified into three categories:

1. Basic needs or essential necessities—expenses that tend to be fixed because you cannot do without them (e.g., expenses for food, housing, tuition, textbooks, phone, transportation to and from school, and health-related costs)
2. Incidentals or extras—expenses that tend to be flexible because spending money on them is optional or discretionary, i.e., you choose to spend at your own discretion or judgment; these expenses typically include:
   a. money spent on entertainment, enjoyment, or pleasure (e.g., music, movies, and spring-break vacations), and
   b. money spent primarily for reasons of promoting personal status or self-image (e.g., buying expensive brand-name products, fashionable clothes, jewelry, and other personal accessories)
3. Emergency expenses—unpredicted, unforeseen, or unexpected costs (e.g., money paid for doctor visits and medicine needed to treat illnesses or injuries)

Reflection 8.2

What are your two or three most expensive incidentals (optional purchases)?

Do you think you should reduce these expenses or eliminate them?

Developing a Money-Management Plan

Once you're aware of the amount of money you have coming in (and from what sources) plus the amount of money you're spending (and for what reasons), the next step is to develop a plan for managing your cash flow. The bottom line is to ensure that the money coming in (income) is equal to or greater than the money going out (expenses). If the amount of money going out exceeds the amount coming in, you're "in the red" or have "negative cash flow."

Strategic Selection and Use of Financial Tools for Tracking Cash Flow

To track your cash flow and manage your money, there are a variety of tools available to you. These cash-flow tools include:

- Checking accounts
- Credit cards
- Charge cards
- Debit cards

What follows is a description of these different tools, along with specific strategies for using them effectively.

Checking Account

Long before credit cards were created, a checking account was the method most people used to keep track of their money. Many people still use checking accounts in addition to (or instead of) credit cards. A checking account may be obtained from a bank or credit union; its typical costs include a deposit ($20–$25) to open the account, a monthly service fee (e.g., $10), and small fees for checks. Some banks charge customers a service fee based on the number of checks written, which is a good option if you don't plan to write many checks each month. If you maintain a high enough balance of money deposited in your account, the bank may not charge any extra fees, and if you're able to maintain an even higher balance, the bank may also pay you interest—known as an interest-bearing checking account.

In conjunction with your checking account, banks usually provide you with an [ ] r machine (ATM) card that you can use to get cash. Look for a check-[ ]at doesn't charge a separate fee for ATM transactions, but offers it as a [ ]ng with your checking account. Also, look for a checking account that [ ]you if your balance drops below a certain minimum figure.

[ ]r Using Checking Accounts Effectively

[ ]wing strategies to make the best use of your checking account:

[ ]you write a check or make an ATM withdrawal, immediately subtract its amount from your *balance* (the amount of money remaining in your account) to determine your new balance.

- Keep a running balance in your checkbook; it will ensure that you know exactly how much money you have in your account at all times. This will reduce your risk of writing a check that *bounces*—a check that you don't have enough money in the bank to cover. If you do bounce a check, you'll probably have to pay a charge to the bank and possibly to the business that attempted to cash your bounced check.

- Double-check your checkbook balance with each monthly statement you receive from the bank. Be sure to include the service charges your bank makes to your account that appear on your monthly statement. This practice will make it easier to track errors—on either your part or the bank's part. (Banks can and do occasionally make mistakes.)

Advantages of a Checking Account

A checking account has several advantages:

- You can carry checks instead of cash.
- You have access to cash at almost any time through an ATM.
- It allows you to keep a visible track record of income and expenses in your checkbook.
- A properly managed checking account can serve as a good credit reference for future loans and purchases.

Credit Card (e.g., MasterCard®, Visa®, or Discover®)

A credit card is basically money loaned to you by the credit-card company that issues you the card, which you pay back to the company monthly. You can pay the whole bill or a portion of the bill each month, as long as some minimum payment is made. However, for any remaining (unpaid) portion of your bill, you are charged a high interest rate, which is usually about 18 percent.

Strategies for Selecting a Credit Card

If you decide to use a credit card, pay attention to *its annual percentage rate (APR)*—the interest rate you pay for previously unpaid monthly balances. This rate can vary from one credit-card company to the next. Credit-card companies also vary in terms of their annual service fee. You will likely find companies that charge higher interest rates tend to charge lower annual fees, and vice versa. As a rule, if you expect to pay the full balance every month, you're probably better off choosing a credit card that does not charge you an annual service fee. On the other hand, if you think you'll need more time to make the full monthly payments, you may be better off with a credit-card company that offers a low interest rate.

Another feature that differentiates one credit-card company from another is whether or not you're allowed a *grace period*—a certain period after you receive your monthly statement during which you can pay back the company without paying added interest fees. Some companies may allow you a grace period of a full month, while others may provide none and begin charging interest immediately after you fail to pay on the bill's due date.

Credit cards may also differ in terms of their *credit limit* (also called a *credit line* or *line of credit*), which refers to the maximum amount of money the credit-card company will make available to you. If you're a new customer, most companies will set a credit limit beyond which no additional credit is granted.

Advantages of a Credit Card

If a credit card is used responsibly, it has some key advantages as a money-management tool, such as those listed below.

- It helps you track your spending habits because the credit card company sends you a monthly statement that provides an itemized list of all your card-related purchases. This list supplies you with a "paper trail" of what you purchased that month and when you purchased it.

- It provides the convenience of making purchases online, which can save time and money that would otherwise be spent traveling to and from stores.
- It allows access to cash whenever and wherever you need it, because any bank or ATM that displays your credit card's symbol will give you cash up to a certain limit (usually for a small transaction fee). Keep in mind that some credit card companies charge a higher interest rate for cash advances than credit card purchases.
- It enables you to establish a personal credit history. If you use a credit card responsibly, you can establish a good credit history that you can use later in life for big-ticket purchases such as a car or home. In effect, responsible use of a credit card shows others from whom you wish to seek credit (or borrow money) that you're financially responsible.

Remember

Don't buy into the belief that the only way you can establish a good credit history is by using a credit card. It's not your only option; you can establish a good credit history through responsible use of a checking account and by paying your bills on time.

Strategies for Using Credit Cards Responsibly

While there may be advantages to using a credit card, you only reap those advantages if you use your card strategically. If not, the advantages of a credit card can be quickly and greatly outweighed by its disadvantages. Listed here are some strategies for using a credit card in a way that maximizes its advantages and minimizes its disadvantages.

1. **Use a credit card only as a convenience for making purchases and tracking the purchases you make; don't use it as a tool for obtaining a long-term loan.** A credit card's main money-management advantage is that it enables you to make purchases with plastic instead of cash. A credit card saves you the inconvenience of having to carry around cash and it provides you with a monthly statement of your purchases from the credit-card company, which makes it easier for you to track and analyze your spending habits.

   The credit provided by a credit card should be seen simply as a short-term loan that must be paid back at the end of every month. Do not use credit cards for long-term credit or long-term loans because their interest rates are outrageously high. Paying such a high rate of interest for a loan represents an ineffective (and irresponsible) money-management strategy.

2. **Limit yourself to one credit card.** The average college student has 2.8 credit cards (United College Marketing Service, cited in Pratt, 2008). More than one credit card just means more accounts to keep track of and more opportunities to accumulate debt. You don't need additional credit cards from department stores, gas stations, or any other profit-making business because they duplicate what your personal credit card already does (plus they charge extremely high interest rates for late payments).

3. **Pay off your balance each month in full and on time.** If you pay the full amount of your bill each month, this means that you're using your credit card effectively to obtain an interest-free, short-term (one-month) loan. You're just paying principal—the total amount of money borrowed and nothing more. However, if your payment is late and you need to pay interest, you end up paying more for the items you purchased than their actual ticket price. For instance, if you have an unpaid balance of $500 on your monthly credit bill for merchandise purchased

"You'll never get your credit card debt paid off if you keep charging on your card and make only the minimum monthly payment. Paying only the minimum is like using a Dixie cup to bail water from a sinking boat."

—Eric Tyson, financial counselor and national bestselling author of *Personal Finance for Dummies*

the previous month and you are charged the typical 18 percent credit-card interest rate for late payment, you end up paying $590: $500 (merchandise) + $90 (18 percent interest to the credit-card company).

Credit card companies make their profit from the interest they collect from cardholders who don't pay back their credit on time. Just as procrastinating about completing schoolwork is a poor time-management habit that can hurt your grades, procrastinating about paying your credit-card bills is a poor money-management habit that can hurt your pocketbook by forcing you to pay high interest rates.

Don't allow credit card companies to make profit at your expense. Pay your total balance on time and avoid paying exorbitantly high interest rates. If you can't pay the total amount owed at the end of the month, rather than making the minimum monthly payment, pay off as much of it as you possibly can. If you keep making only the minimum payment each month, you'll begin to pile up huge amounts of debt.

Remember

If you keep charging on your credit card while you have an unpaid balance or debt, you no longer have a grace period to pay back your charges; instead, interest is charged immediately on all your purchases.

Charge Card

A charge card works similar to a credit card in that you're given a short-term loan for one month; the only difference is that you must pay your bill in full at the end of each month and you cannot carry over any debt from one month to the next. Its major disadvantage relative to a credit card is that it has less flexibility—no matter what your expenses may be for a particular month, you must still pay up or lose your ability to acquire credit for the next month. For people who habitually fail to pay their monthly credit card bills on time, this makes a charge card a smarter money-management tool than a credit card because the cardholder cannot continue to accumulate debt.

Reflection 8.3

1. Do you have a credit card? Do you have more than one?

2. If you have at least one credit card, do you pay off your entire balance each month?

3. If you don't pay off your entire balance each month, what's your average unpaid balance per month?

4. What changes would you have to make in your money-management habits to be able to pay off your entire balance each month?

Debit Card

A debit card looks almost identical to a credit card (e.g., it has a MasterCard or Visa logo), but it works differently. When you use a debit card, money is immediately taken out or subtracted from your checking account. Thus, you're only using money that's already in your account (rather than borrowing money), and you don't receive a bill at the end of the month. If you attempt to purchase something with a debit card that costs more than the amount of money you have in your account, your card will not allow you to do so. Just like a bounced check, a debit card will not permit you to pay out any money that is not in your account. Like a check or ATM withdrawal, any purchase you make with a debit card should immediately be subtracted from your balance.

Like a credit card, a major advantage of the debit card is that it provides you with the convenience of plastic; however, unlike a credit card, it prevents you from spending beyond your means and accumulating debt. For this reason, financial advisors often recommend using a debit card rather than a credit card (Knox, 2004; Tyson, 2003).

> "Never spend your money before you have it."
>
> —Thomas Jefferson, third president of the United States and founder of the University of Virginia

Sources of Income for Financing Your College Education

Free Application for Federal Student Aid (FAFSA)

The Free Application for Federal Student Aid (FAFSA) is the application used by the U.S. Department of Education to determine financial aid eligibility for students. A formula is used to determine each student's *estimated family contribution (EFC)*—the amount of money the government has determined a family can contribute to the educational costs of the family member who is attending college. No fee is charged to complete the application, so you should complete one every year to determine your eligibility to receive financial aid, whether you believe you're eligible or not. See the Financial Aid Office on your campus for the FAFSA form and for help in completing it.

Snapshot Summary

8.1

Financial Literacy: Understanding the Language of Money Management

As you can tell from the number of financial terms used in this chapter, there is a fiscal vocabulary or language that we need to master in order to fully understand our financial options and transactions. In other words, we need to become *financially literate*. As you read the financial terms listed below, place a checkmark next to any term whose meaning you didn't already know.

Account. A formal business arrangement in which a bank provides financial services to a customer (e.g., checking account or savings account).

Annual percentage rate (APR). The interest rate that must be paid when monthly credit card balances are not paid in full.

Balance. The amount of money in a person's account or the amount of unpaid debt.

Bounced check. A check written for a greater amount of money than the amount contained in a personal checking account, which typically requires the person to pay a charge to the bank and possibly to the business that attempted to cash the bounced check.

Budget. A plan for coordinating income and expenses to ensure that sufficient money is available to cover personal expenses or expenditures.

Cash flow. Amount of money flowing in (income) and flowing out (expenses). "Negative cash flow" occurs when the amount of money going out exceeds the amount coming in.

Credit. Money obtained with the understanding that it will be paid back, either with or without interest.

Credit line (a.k.a. credit limit). The maximum amount of money (credit) made available to a borrower.

Debt. Amount of money owed.

Default. Failure to meet a financial obligation (e.g., a student who fails to repay a college loan "defaults" on that loan).

Emergency student loan. Immediate, interest-free loans provided by a college or university to help financially strapped students cover short-term expenses (e.g., cost of textbooks) or deal with financial emergencies (e.g., accidents and illnesses). Emergency student loans are typically granted within 24–48 hours, sometimes even the same day, and usually need to be repaid within two months.

Deferred student payment plan. A plan that allows student borrowers to temporarily defer or postpone loan payments for some acceptable reason (e.g., to pursue an internship or to do volunteer work after college).

Estimated family contribution (EFC). The amount of money the government has determined a family can contribute to the educational costs of the family member who is attending college.

Fixed interest rate. A loan with an interest rate that will remain the same for the entire term of the loan.

Grace period. The amount of time after a monthly credit card statement has been issued during which the credit card holder can pay back the company without paying added interest fees.

Grant. Money received that doesn't have to be repaid.

Gross income. Income generated before taxes and other expenses are deducted.

Insurance premium. The amount paid in regular installments to an insurance company to remain insured.

Interest. The amount of money paid to a customer for deposited money (as in a bank account) or money paid by a customer for borrowed money (e.g., interest on a loan). Interest is usually calculated as a percentage of the total amount of money deposited or borrowed.

Interest-bearing account. A bank account that earns interest if the customer keeps a sufficiently large sum of money in the bank.

Loan consolidation. Consolidating (combining) separate student loans into one larger loan to make the process of tracking, budgeting, and repayment easier. Loan consolidation typically requires the borrower to pay slightly more interest.

Loan premium. The amount of money loaned without interest.

Merit-based scholarship. Money awarded to a student on the basis of performance or achievement that doesn't have to be repaid.

Need-based scholarship. Money awarded to a student on the basis of financial need that doesn't have to be repaid.

Net income. Money earned or remaining after all expenses and taxes have been paid.

Principal. The total amount of money borrowed or deposited, not counting interest.

Variable interest rate. An interest rate on a loan that can vary or be changed by the lender.

Yield. Revenue or profit produced by an investment beyond the original amount invested. For example, the higher lifetime income and other monetary benefits acquired from a college education that exceed the amount of money invested in or spent on a college education.

Reflection **8.4**

Which of the terms in Snapshot Summary 8.1 were unfamiliar to you?

Which of the terms apply to your current financial situation or money-management plans?

Scholarships

Scholarships are available from many sources besides the institution you've chosen to attend. Typically, scholarships are awarded at the time of admission to college, but some scholarships may be awarded to students at a later point in their college experience. To find out about scholarships that you may still be eligible to receive, visit your Financial Aid Office. You can also conduct an Internet search to find many sites that offer scholarship information. (However, don't enter your credit card or bank account information on any site.)

Also, keep in mind that scholarships are very competitive and deadlines are strictly enforced.

Grants

Grants are considered to be gift aid, which typically does not have to be repaid. About two-thirds of all college students receive grant aid, which, on average, reduces their tuition bills by more than half (College Board, 2009). The Federal Pell Grant is the largest grant program; it provides need-based aid to low-income undergraduate students. The amount of the grant depends on criteria such as (1) the anticipated contribution of the family to the student's education (EFC), (2) the cost of the post-secondary institution that the student is attending, and (3) the enrollment status of the student (part-time or full-time).

Loans

Student loans need to be repaid once a student graduates from college. Listed below are some of the more common student loan programs. Snapshot Summary 8.2 lists the difference between federal loans and private loans.

- **The Federal Perkins Loan** is a 5 percent simple-interest loan awarded to exceptionally needy students. The repayment for this loan begins nine months after a student is no longer enrolled at least half-time.
- **The Federal Subsidized Stafford Loan** is available to students enrolled at least half time and has a fixed interest rate that's established each year on July 1. The federal government pays the interest on the loan while the student is enrolled. The repayment for this loan begins six months after a student is no longer enrolled half-time.
- **The Federal Unsubsidized Stafford Loan** is a loan that's not based on need and has the same interest rate as the Federal Subsidized Stafford Loan. Students are responsible for paying the interest on this loan while they're enrolled in college. The loan amount limits for Stafford loans are based on the classification of the student (e.g., freshman or sophomore).

Snapshot Summary

8.2   Federal Loan versus Private Loan: A Critical Difference

Private loans and federal loans are different, unrelated types of loans. Here are the key differences:

Federal loans have fixed interest rates that are comparatively low (currently less than 7 percent).

Private loans have variable interest rates that are very high (currently more than 15 percent) and can go higher at any time.

Note: Despite the high cost of private loans, they are the fastest-growing type of loans taken out by college students, largely because of aggressive, misleading, and sometimes irresponsible or unethical advertising on loan-shopping Web sites. Students sometimes think they're getting a federal loan only to find out later they have taken on a more expensive private loan.

"Apply for as much grant aid as possible before borrowing, and then seek lower-interest federal student loans before tapping private ones. There is a lot of student aid that can help make the expense [of college] more manageable."

—Sandy Baum, senior policy analyst, College Board (Gordon, 2009)

"Borrow money from a pessimist. He won't expect it back."

—Steven Wright, American comedian and first inductee to the Boston Comedy Hall of Fame

Source: Hamilton (2012); Kristof (2008).

Remember

Not all loans are created equally. Federally guaranteed student loans are relatively low-cost compared to private loans, and they may be paid off slowly after graduation. On the other hand, private lenders of student loans are like credit-card companies: they charge extremely high interest rates (that can go even higher at any time), and must be paid off as quickly as possible. They should not to be used as a primary loan to help pay for college, and they should only be used as a last resort when no other options are available for covering your college expenses.

Keep in mind that federal and state regulations require that if you're receiving financial aid, you must maintain "satisfactory academic progress." In most cases this means you must do the following:

1. **Maintain a satisfactory GPA.** Your entire academic record will be reviewed, even if you have paid for any of the classes with your own resources.
2. **Make satisfactory academic progress.** Your academic progress will be evaluated at least once per year, usually at the end of each spring semester.
3. **Complete a degree or certificate program within an established period of time.** Check with your institution's Financial Aid Office for details.

Salary Earnings

If you find yourself relying on your salary to pay for college tuition, check with your employer to see whether the company offers tuition reimbursement. Also, check with the Billing Office on your campus to determine whether payment plans are available for tuition costs. These plans may differ in terms of how much is due, deadlines for payments, and how any remaining debt owed to the institution is dealt with at the end of the term. You may find that the college you're attending will not allow you to register for the following term until the previous term is completely paid for.

Research shows that when students work on campus (versus off campus) they're more likely to succeed in college (Astin, 1993; Pascarella & Terenzini, 1991, 2005), probably because they become more connected to the college when they work on campus (Cermak & Filkins, 2004; Tinto, 1993) and also because on-campus employers are more flexible than off-campus employers in allowing students to meet their academic commitments (Leonard, 2008). For instance, campus employers are more willing to schedule students' work hours around their class schedule and allow students to modify their work schedules when their academic workload increases (e.g., at midterm and finals). Thus, if at all possible, rather than seeking work off campus, try to find work on campus and capitalize on its proven capacity to promote college success.

Money-Saving Strategies and Habits

The ultimate goal of money management is to save money and dodge debt. Here are some strategies for accomplishing this goal.

Prepare a personal budget. A budget is simply a plan for coordinating income and expenses to ensure that your cash flow leaves you with sufficient money to cover your expenses. A budget helps you maintain awareness of your financial state or condition, and enables you to be your own accountant who keeps an accurate account of your own money.

Just like managing and budgeting time, the first step in managing and budgeting money involves prioritizing. Money management requires identifying your most important expenses (indispensable necessities you can't live without) and distinguishing them from incidentals (dispensable luxuries you can live without). People can easily confuse essentials (what they need) and desirables (what they want). For instance, if a piece of merchandise happens to be on sale, it may be a desirable purchase at that time because of its reduced price, but it's not an essential purchase unless the person really needs that piece of merchandise at that particular time.

Postponing immediate or impulsive satisfaction of material desires is a key element of effective college financing and long-term financial success. We need to remain aware of whether we're spending money on impulse and out of habit or out of need and after thoughtful reflection. The truth is that humans spend money for a host of psychological reasons (conscious or subconscious), many of which are unrelated to actual need. For example, some people spend money to build their self-esteem or self-image, to combat personal boredom, or to seek an emotional "high" (Dittmar, 2004; Furnham & Argyle, 1998). Furthermore, people can become obsessed with spending money, shop compulsively, and develop an addiction to purchasing products. Just as Alcoholics Anonymous (AA) exists as a support group for alcoholics, Debtors Anonymous exists as a support group for shopaholics and includes a 12-step recovery program similar to AA.

Student *Perspective*

"I shouldn't buy random stuff (like hair dye) and other stuff when I don't need it."
—First-year student

Student *Perspective*

"I need to save money and not shop so much and impulse buy."
—First-year student

> **Remember**
> *Remaining consciously aware of the distinction between* essentials *that must be purchased and* incidentals *that may or may not be purchased is an important first step toward preparing an effective budget and avoiding debt.*

Make all your bills visible and pay them off as soon as possible. When your bills remain in your sight, they remain on your mind; you're less likely to forget to pay them or forget to pay them on time. Increase the visibility of your bill payments by keeping a financial calendar on which you record key fiscal deadlines for the academic year (e.g., due dates for tuition payments, residential bills, and financial aid applications). Also, try to get in the habit of paying a bill as soon as you open it and have it in your hands, rather than setting it aside and running the risk of forgetting to pay it (or losing it altogether).

Live within your means. To state it simply: Don't purchase what you can't afford. If you're spending more money than you're taking in, it means you're living *beyond* your means. To begin living *within* your means, you have two options:

1. Decrease your expenses (reduce your spending), or
2. Increase your income (earn more money).

Since most college students are already working while attending college (Orszag, Orszag, & Whitmore, 2001) and working so many hours that it's interfering with their academic performance or progress (King, 2005), the best option for most college students who find themselves in debt is to reduce their spending and begin living within their means.

Economize. By being intelligent consumers who use critical thinking skills when purchasing products, we can be frugal or thrifty without compromising the quality of our purchases. For example, we could pay less to see the same movie in the late afternoon than we could to see it at night. Why pay more for brand-name products that are the same as products with a different name? Why pay 33 percent more for Advil or Tylenol when the same amount of pain-relieving ingredient (ibuprofen or acetaminophen) is contained in generic brands? Often, what we're paying for when we buy brand-name products is all the advertising these companies pay to the media and to celebrities to publicly promote their products.

> "We choose to spend more money than we have today. Choose debt, or choose freedom, it's your choice."
>
> —Bill Pratt, *Extra Credit: The 7 Things Every College Student Needs to Know About Credit, Debt & Cash*

Reflection 8.5

Are you working for money while attending college?

If you're not working, are you sacrificing anything you want or need because you don't have the money to buy it?

If you are working:

1. How many hours per week do you currently work?
2. Do you think that working is interfering with your academic performance or progress?
3. Would it be possible for you to reduce the number of weekly hours you now work and still be able to make ends meet?

Remember

Advertising creates product familiarity, not product quality. The more money manufacturers pay for advertising and creating a well-known brand, the more money we pay for the product—not necessarily because we're acquiring a product of higher quality, but more likely because we're covering its high cost of advertising.

Downsize. Cut down or cut out spending for products that you don't need. Don't engage in conspicuous consumption just to keep up with the "Joneses" (your neighbors or friends), and don't allow peer pressure to determine your spending habits.

Let your spending habits reflect your ability to think critically rather than your tendency to conform socially.

Save money by living with others rather than living alone. Although you lose privacy when you share living quarters with others, you save money. Living with others also has the fringe social benefit of spending time with roommates or housemates whom you've chosen to live with and whose company you enjoy.

Give gifts of time rather than money. Spending money on gifts for family, friends, and romantic partners isn't the only way to show that you care. The point of gift giving isn't to show others you aren't cheap or show off by being a big-time spender; instead, show off your social sensitivity by doing something special or by making something meaningful for them. Gifts of time and kindness can often be more personal and more special than store-bought gifts.

Develop your own set of money-saving strategies and habits. You can save money by starting to develop little money-saving habits that eventually add up to big savings over time. Consider the following list of habit-forming tips for saving money that were suggested by students in a first-year seminar class:

- Don't carry a lot of extra money in your wallet. (It's just like food; if it's easy to get to, you'll be more likely to eat it up.)
- Shop with a list—get in, get what you need, and get out.
- Put all your extra change in a jar.
- Put extra cash in a piggy bank that requires you to smash the piggy to get at it.
- Seal your savings in an envelope.
- When you get extra money, get it immediately into the bank (and out of your hands).
- Bring (don't buy) your lunch.
- Take full advantage of your meal plan—you've already paid for it, so don't pay twice for your meals by buying food elsewhere.
- Use e-mail instead of the telephone.
- Hide your credit card or put it in the freezer so that you don't use it on impulse.
- Use cash (instead of credit cards) because you can give yourself a set amount of cash and clearly see how much of it you have at the start of a week (and how much is left at any point during the week).

Reflection 8.6

Do you use any of the strategies on the above list?

Have you developed any effective strategies that do not appear on the list?

When making purchases, always think in terms of their long-term total cost. It's convenient and tempting for consumers to think in the short term ("I see it; I like it; I want it; and I want it now.") However, long-term thinking is one of the essential keys to successful money management and financial planning. Those small (monthly) installment plans that businesses offer to get you to buy expensive products may make the cost of those products appear attractive and affordable in the short run. However, when you factor in the interest rates you pay on monthly installment plans, plus the length of time (number of months) you're making installment payments, you get a more accurate picture of the product's total cost over the long run. This longer-range perspective can quickly alert you to the reality that a prod-

> "It is preoccupation with possessions, more than anything else, that prevents us from living freely and nobly."
> —Bertrand Russell, British philosopher and mathematician

> "The richer your friends, the more they will cost you."
> —Elisabeth Marbury, legal agent for theatrical and literary stars in the late 19th and early 20th centuries

> "If you would be wealthy, think of saving as well as getting."
> —Benjamin Franklin, 18th-century inventor, newspaper writer, and signer of the Declaration of Independence

> "The safest way to double your money is to fold it over and put it in your pocket."
> —Kin Hubbard, American humorist, cartoonist, and journalist

uct's sticker price represents its partial and seemingly affordable short-term cost but its long-term total cost is much less affordable (and perhaps out of your league).

Furthermore, the long-term price for purchases sometimes involves additional "hidden costs" that don't relate directly to the product's initial price but must be paid to keep using the product. For example, the sticker price you pay for clothes doesn't include the hidden, long-term costs that may be involved if those clothes require dry cleaning. By just taking a moment to check the inside label, you can save yourself this hidden, long-term cost by purchasing clothes that are machine washable. To use an example of a big-ticket purchase, the extra money spent to buy a new car (instead of a used car) includes not only paying a higher sticker price but also paying the higher hidden costs of licensing and insuring the new car, as well as any interest fees if the new car was purchased on an installment plan. When you add in these hidden, long-term costs to a new car's total cost, buying a good used car is clearly a much more effective money-management strategy than buying a new one.

> ### Remember
> *Avoid buying costly items impulsively. Instead, take time to reflect on the purchase you intend to make, do a cost analysis of its hidden and long-term costs, and then integrate these invisible costs with the product's sticker price to generate an accurate synthesis and clearer picture of the product's total cost.*

Long-Range Fiscal Planning: Financing Your College Education

An effective money-management plan should be time-sensitive and include the following time frames:

- Short-range financial planning (e.g., weekly income and expenses)
- Mid-range financial planning (e.g., monthly income and expenses)
- Long-range financial planning (e.g., projected or anticipated income and expenses for the entire college experience)
- Extended long-range financial planning (e.g., expected income and debt after graduation, including a plan for repayment of college loans)

Thus far, our discussion has focused primarily on short-range and mid-range financial planning strategies that will keep you out of debt on a monthly or yearly basis. We turn now to issues involving long-term financial planning for your entire college experience. While no one "correct" strategy exists for financing a college education, there are some important research findings on the effectiveness of different financing strategies that you should be aware of when doing long-range financial planning for college and beyond.

Research shows that obtaining a student loan and working no more than 15 hours per week is an effective long-range strategy for students at all income levels to finance their college education and meet their personal expenses. Students who use this strategy are more likely to graduate from college, graduate in less time, and graduate with higher grades than students who work part-time for more than 15 hours per week while attending college full-time, or students who work full-time and attend college part-time (King, 2002; Perna & DuBois, 2010). Unfortunately, less than 6 percent of all first-year students use this strategy. Instead, almost 50 percent of first-year students choose a strategy that research shows to be least associated with college success: borrowing nothing and trying to work more than 15 hours per week. Students who use this strategy increase their risk of lowering their grades significantly and withdrawing from college altogether (King, 2005)—probably because they have difficulty finding enough time to handle the amount of academic work required by college on top of the more than the 15 hours they're working per week. Thus, a good strategy for balancing learning and earning is to try to limit work for pay to 15 hours per week (or as close to 15 hours as possible). Working longer hours increases the temptation to switch from full-time to part-time enrollment, which can increase the risk of delaying graduation or not graduating at all.

"People don't realize how much work it is to stay in college. It's its own job in itself, plus if you've got another job you go to, too. I mean, it's just a lot."

—College student (quoted in Engle & Bermeo, 2006)

"I work two jobs and go to school and it's hard, real hard. I go home at like 9 or 10, and I'm too tired to do my homework."

—College student (quoted in Engle & Bermeo, 2006)

Reflection 8.7

Do you need to work part-time to meet your college expenses?

If you answered "yes" to the above question, are you working more than 15 hours per week?

If you answered "yes" to the above question, can you reduce your work time to 15 or fewer hours per week and still make ends meet?

Some students decide to finance their college education by working full-time and going to college part-time. These students believe it will be less expensive in the long run to attend college part-time because it will allow them to avoid any debt from student loans. However, studies show that when students use this strategy, it lengthens their time to degree completion and increases the risk that they will never complete a degree (Orszag et al., 2001).

Students who manage to eventually graduate from college but take longer to do so because they have worked more than 15 hours per week will lose money in the long run. The longer they take to graduate, the longer they must wait to "cash in" on their college degrees and enter higher-paying, full-time positions that a college diploma would qualify them to enter. The hourly pay for most part-time jobs students hold while going to college is less than half what they will earn from working in full-time positions as college graduates (King, 2005).

Furthermore, studies show that two out of three college students have at least one credit card and nearly one of every two students with credit cards carries an average balance of more than $2,000 per month (Mae, 2005). A debt level this high is likely to push many students into working more than 15 hours a week to pay it off ("I owe, I owe, so off to work I go"). This often results in their taking longer to graduate and start earning a college graduate's salary because they end up taking fewer courses per term so they can work more hours to pay off their credit card debt.

Instead of paying almost 20 percent interest to credit card companies for their monthly debt, these students would be better off obtaining a student loan at a much lower interest rate, which they will not start paying back until 6 months after graduation—when they'll be making more money in full-time positions as college graduates. Despite this clear advantage of student loans compared to credit card loans, only about 25 percent of college students who use credit cards take out student loans (King, 2002).

"Unlike a car that depreciates in value each year that you drive it, an investment in education yields monetary, social, and intellectual profit. A car is more tangible in the short term, but an investment in education (even if it means borrowing money) gives you more bang for the buck in the long run."

—Eric Tyson, financial counselor and national bestselling author of *Personal Finance for Dummies*

"The cynic knows the price of everything and the value of nothing."

—Oscar Wilde, Irish playwright, poet, and author of numerous short stories

Remember

Student loans are provided by the American government with the intent of helping its citizens become better educated. In contrast, for-profit businesses such as credit-card companies lend students money with no intent of helping them become better educated, but with the clear intent of helping themselves make money—from the high rates of interest they collect from students who do not pay off their debt in full at the end of each month.

Keep in mind that not all debt is bad. Debt can be good if it represents an investment in something that will appreciate with time—i.e., something that will gain in value and eventually turn into profit for the investor. Purchasing a college education on credit is a good investment because, over time, it appreciates in the form of higher salaries for the remainder of the life of the investor (the college graduate). In contrast, purchasing a new car is a bad long-term investment because it immediately begins to depreciate or lose monetary value once it's purchased. The instant you drive that new car off the dealer's lot, you immediately become the proud owner of a used car that's worth much less than what you just paid for it.

Remember

What you're willing to sacrifice and save for, and what you're willing to go into debt for, say a lot about who you are and what you value.

"If a man empties his purse into his head, no one can take it away from him. An investment in knowledge always pays the best interest."

—Benjamin Franklin, 18th-century scientist, inventor, and a founding father of the United States

"I invested in myself—in study, in mastering my tools, in preparation. Many a man who is putting a few dollars a week into the bank would do much better to put it into himself."

—Henry Ford, founder of the Ford Motor Company and one of the richest people of the 20th century

You may have heard the expression that "time is money." One way to interpret this expression is that the more money you spend, the more time you must spend making money. If you're going to college, spending more time on earning money to cover your spending habits often means spending less time studying, learning, completing classes, and earning good grades. You can avoid this vicious cycle by viewing academic work as work that "pays" you back in terms of completed courses and higher grades. If you put in more academic time to complete more courses in less time and with higher grades, you're paid back by graduating and earning the full-time salary of a college graduate sooner—which will pay you about twice as much money per hour than you'll earn doing part-time work without a college degree (not to mention fringe benefits such as health insurance and paid vacation time). Furthermore, the time you put into earning higher grades in college should pay off immediately in your first full-time position after college, because research shows that students graduating in the same field who have higher grades receive higher starting salaries (Pascarella & Terenzini, 2005).

Reflection **8.8**

In addition to college, what might be other good long-term investments you could make now in the near future?

Summary and Conclusion

The following strategies for effectively managing money were recommended in this chapter:

- **Develop financial self-awareness.** Become aware of your cash flow—the amount of money flowing in and flowing out of your hands.
- **Develop a money-management plan.** Ensure that your income is equal to or greater than your expenses.
- **Manage your money effectively.** Use available financial tools and instruments to track and maximize your cash flow, such as checking accounts, credit cards, charge cards, or debit cards.
- **Finance your education wisely.** Explore all sources of income for financing your college education, including the FAFSA, scholarships, grants, loans, monetary gifts from family or friends, salary earnings, and personal savings.
- **Prepare a personal budget.** A budget helps you keep an accurate account of your money and ensures you have sufficient money to cover your expenses.
- **Pay your bills when they arrive.** Paying bills when you first lay your hands on them serves to reduce the risk that you'll forget to pay them or pay them late.
- **Live within your means.** Don't purchase what you can't afford.
- **Economize.** Be an intelligent consumer who uses critical thinking skills to evaluate and prioritize your purchases.
- **Downsize.** Don't buy products you don't need, and don't let peer pressure determine your spending habits.
- **Live with others, rather than live alone.** The reduction in privacy can be offset by the financial savings. Living with others can also bring the fringe social benefit of having roommates or housemates whom you've chosen to live with and whose company you enjoy.
- **Work for better grades now and better pay later.** Research shows that taking out a student loan and working part-time for 15 or fewer hours per week is the most effective financial and educational strategy for students at all income levels.
- **Take full advantage of your Financial Aid Office.** Check periodically to see if you qualify for additional sources of income, such as part-time employment on campus, low-interest loans, grants, or scholarships.

Money management is a personal skill that can either support or sabotage your success in college and life beyond college. As with time management, if you effectively manage your money and gain control of how you spend it, you gain greater control over the quality of your life. Research shows that accumulating high levels of debt while in college is associated with higher levels of stress, lower academic performance, and greater risk of withdrawing from college. The good news is that research demonstrates that students who learn to use effective money-management strategies are able to reduce unnecessary spending, decrease their risk of debt and stress, and increase the quality of their academic performance.

Learning More through the World Wide Web

Internet-Based Resources for Further Information on Money Management

For additional information related to the ideas discussed in this chapter, we recommend the following Web sites:

Fiscal Literacy and Money Management:

www.360financialliteracy.org

www.cashcourse.org

www.loveyourmoney.org

Financial Aid and Federal Funding Sources for a College Education:

studentaid.ed.gov

8.1 Self-Assessment of Financial Attitudes and Habits

Answer the following questions as accurately and honestly as possible.

	Agree	Disagree
1. I pay my rent or mortgage on time each month.	_____	_____
2. I avoid maxing out or going over the limit on my credit cards.	_____	_____
3. I balance my checkbook each month.	_____	_____
4. I set aside money each month for savings.	_____	_____
5. I pay my phone and utility bills on time each month.	_____	_____
6. I pay my credit card bills in full each month to avoid interest charges.	_____	_____
7. I believe it's important to buy the things I want when I want them.	_____	_____
8. Borrowing money to pay for college is a smart thing to do.	_____	_____
9. I have a monthly or weekly budget that I follow.	_____	_____
10. The thing I enjoy most about making money is spending money.	_____	_____
11. I limit myself to one credit card.	_____	_____
12. Getting a degree will get me a good job and a good income.	_____	_____

Sources: Cude et al. (2006); Niederjohn (2008).

Give yourself one point for each item that you marked "agree"—except for items 7, 9, and 10. For these items, give yourself a point if you marked "disagree."

A perfect score on this short survey would be 12.

Self-Assessment Questions

1. What was your total score?

2. Which items lowered your score?

3. Do you detect any pattern across the items that lowered your score?

4. Do you see any realistic way(s) for improving your score on this test?

8.2 Financial Self-Awareness: Monitoring Money and Tracking Cash Flow

1. Use the worksheet that follows to *estimate* your income and expenses per month, and enter them in column 2.

2. *Track* your actual income and expenses for a month and enter them in column 3. (To help you do this accurately, keep a file of your cash receipts, bills paid, and credit card or checking account records for the month.)

3. After one month of tracking your cash flow, answer the self-assessment questions.

    a. Were your estimates generally accurate?

    b. For what specific items were there the largest discrepancies between your estimated cost and the actual cost?

    c. Comparing your bottom-line totals for income and expenses, are you satisfied with how your monthly cash flow is going?

    d. What changes could you make to create more positive cash flow—i.e., to increase your income or savings and reduce your expenses or debt?

    e. How likely is it that you'll make the changes you mentioned in the previous question?

Financial Self-Awareness Worksheet

	Estimate	Actual
Income Sources		
Parents/Family		
Work/Job		
Grants/Scholarships		
Loans		
Savings		
Other:		
TOTAL INCOME		
Essentials (Fixed Expenses)		
Living Expenses:		
Food/Groceries		
Rent/Room & Board		
Utilities (gas/electric)		
Clothing		
Laundry/Dry Cleaning		
Phone		
Computer		
Household Items (dishes, etc.)		
Medical Insurance Expenses		
Debt Payments (loans/credit cards)		
Other:		
School Expenses:		
Tuition		
Books		
Supplies (print cartridges, etc.)		
Special Fees (lab fees, etc.)		
Other:		
Transportation:		
Public Transportation (bus fees, etc.)		
Car Insurance		
Car Maintenance		
Fuel (gas)		
Car Payments		
Other:		
Incidentals (*Variable* Expenses)		
Entertainment:		
Movies/Concerts		
DVDs/CDs		
Restaurants (eating out)		
Other:		
Personal Appearance/Accessories:		
Haircuts/Hairstyling		
Cosmetics/Manicures		
Fashionable Clothes		
Jewelry		
Other:		
Hobbies:		
Travel (trips home, vacations)		
Gifts		
Other:		
TOTAL EXPENSES		

Problems Paying for College

A college student posted the following message on the Internet:

"I went to college for one semester, failed some my classes, and ended with 900 dollars in student loans. Now I can't even get financial aid or a loan because of some stupid thing that says if you fail a certain amount of classes you can't get aid or a loan. And now since I couldn't go to college this semester they want me to pay for my loans already, and I don't even have a job. Any suggestions?"

Reflection and Discussion Questions

1. What suggestions would you offer this student? Which of your suggestions should the student do immediately? Which should the student do eventually?

2. What should the student have done to prevent this from happening in the first place?

3. Do you think that this student's situation is common or unusual? Why?

Diversity

Learning about and from Human Differences

9

ACTIVATE YOUR THINKING | *Reflection* 9.1

LEARNING GOAL

To further your appreciation of the value of human differences and develop skills for making the most of diversity in college and beyond.

Complete the following sentence:

When I hear the word *diversity*, the first thoughts that come to my mind are . . .

The Spectrum of Diversity

The word *diversity* derives from the Latin root *diversus*, meaning "various." Thus, human diversity refers to the variety of differences that exist among the people who comprise humanity (the human species). In this chapter, we use *diversity* to refer primarily to differences among the major groups of people who, collectively, comprise humankind or humanity. The relationship between diversity and humanity is represented visually in Figure 9.1.

The relationship between humanity and human diversity is similar to the relationship between sunlight and the spectrum of colors. Just as sunlight passing through a prism is dispersed into all groups of colors that make up the visual spectrum, the human species spread across the planet is dispersed into all groups of people that make up the human spectrum (humanity). As you can see in Figure 9.1, human diversity expresses itself in numerous ways, including differences in physical features, religious beliefs, mental and physical abilities, national origins, social backgrounds, gender, and sexual orientation.

Since diversity has been interpreted (and misinterpreted) in different ways by different people, we begin by defining some key terms related to diversity that should lead to a clearer understanding of its true meaning and value.

> "We are all brothers and sisters. Each face in the rainbow of color that populates our world is precious and special. Each adds to the rich treasure of humanity."
>
> —Morris Dees, civil rights leader and cofounder of the Southern Poverty Law Center

What Is Race?

A racial group (race) is a group of people who share some distinctive physical traits, such as skin color or facial characteristics. The U.S. Census Bureau (2010) identifies four races: White, Black, Asian, and American Indian or Alaska Native. However, as Anderson and Fienberg (2000) caution us, racial categories are social-political constructs (concepts) that are not based on scientific research but on classifications con-

FIGURE 9.1

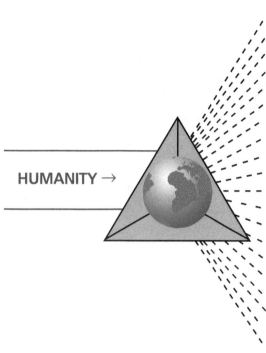

SPECTRUM
of
DIVERSITY

HUMANITY →

Gender (male-female)
Age (stage of life)
Race (e.g., White, Black, Asian)
Ethnicity (e.g., Native American, Hispanic, Irish, German)
Socioeconomic status (job status/income)
National *citizenship* (citizen of U.S. or another country)
Native (first-learned) *language*
National *origin* (nation of birth)
National *region* (e.g., raised in north/south)
Generation (historical period when people are born and live)
Political ideology (e.g., liberal/conservative)
Religious/spiritual beliefs (e.g., Christian/Buddhist/Muslim)
Family status (e.g., single-parent/two-parent family)
Marital status (single/married)
Parental status (with/without children)
Sexual orientation (heterosexual/homosexual/bisexual)
Physical ability/disability (e.g., able to hear/hearing impaired)
Mental ability/disability (e.g., mentally able/challenged)
Learning ability/disability (e.g., absence/presence of dyslexia)
Mental health/illness (e.g., absence/presence of depression)

_ _ _ _ _ _ = dimension of diversity

© Kendall Hunt

*This list represents some of the major dimensions of human diversity; it does not represent a complete list of all possible forms of human diversity. Also, disagreement exists about certain dimensions of diversity (e.g., whether certain groups should be considered races or ethnic groups).

Humanity and Diversity

structed by people. There continues to be disagreement among scholars about what groups of people constitute a human race or whether distinctive races exist (Wheelright, 2005). No identifiable set of genes distinguishes one race from another. In other words, you can't do a blood test or some type of internal genetic test to determine a person's race. Humans have simply decided to categorize people into races on the basis of certain external differences in physical appearance, particularly the color of their outer layer of skin. The U.S. Census Bureau could just as easily have divided people into categories based on such physical characteristics as eye color (blue, brown, and green) or hair texture (straight, wavy, curly, and frizzy).

Reflection 9.2

Look at the diversity spectrum in Figure 9.1 and look over the list of groups that make up the spectrum. Do you notice any groups missing from the list that should be added, either because they have distinctive backgrounds or because they've been targets of prejudice and discrimination?

The differences in skin color we now see among different human beings are largely due to biological adaptations that evolved over thousands of years among groups of humans living in different regions of the world under different climatic conditions. Darker skin tones developed among humans inhabiting and reproducing in hotter regions nearer the equator (e.g., Africans) because darker skin helped them adapt and survive by providing their bodies with better protection from the potentially damaging effects of the sun (Bridgeman, 2003). In contrast, lighter skin tones developed over time among humans inhabiting colder climates that were farther from the equator (e.g., Scandinavia) to enable their bodies to absorb greater amounts of vitamin D supplied by sunlight, which was in shorter supply in their region of the world (Jablonski & Chaplin, 2002).

While humans may display diversity in the color or tone of their outer layer of skin, the biological reality is that all members of the human species are remarkably similar. More than 98 percent of the genes that make up humans from different racial groups are exactly the same (Bridgeman, 2003; Molnar, 1991). This large amount of genetic overlap among humans accounts for the many similarities that exist, regardless of differences in skin color. For example, all people have similar external features that give them a human appearance and clearly distinguish people from other animal species, all humans have internal organs that are similar in structure and function, and regardless of the color of their outer layer of skin, when it's cut, all humans bleed in the same color.

Reflection 9.3

What race do you consider yourself to be? Would you say you identify strongly with your race, or are you rarely conscious of it?

What Is Culture?

Culture may be defined as a distinctive pattern of beliefs and values learned by a group of people who share the same social heritage and traditions. In short, culture is the whole way in which a group of people has learned to live (Peoples & Bailey, 2008): it includes their style of speaking (language), fashion, food, art, music, values, and beliefs. Cultural differences can exist within the same society (multicultural society), within a single nation (domestic diversity), or across different nations (international diversity).

A major advantage of culture is that it helps bind its members together into a supportive, tight-knit community; however, it can blind them to other cultural perspectives. Since culture shapes the way people think, it can cause groups of people to view the world solely through their own cultural lens or frame of reference (Colombo, Cullen, & Lisle, 2010). Optical illusions are a good example of how cultural perspectives can blind people, or lead them to inaccurate perceptions. For instance, compare the lengths of the two lines in Figure 9.2.

If you perceive the line on the right to be longer than the line on the left, welcome to the club. Virtually all Americans and people from Western cultures perceive the line on the right to be longer. Actually, both lines are equal in length. (If you don't believe it, take out a ruler and check it out.) Interestingly, this perceptual error isn't made by people from non-Western cultures whose architectural structures consist primarily of circular structures, rather than rectangular buildings with angled corners that have been constructed in Western cultures (Segall, Campbell, & Herskovits, 1996).

FIGURE 9.2

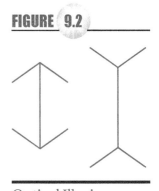

Optical Illusion

"We see what is behind our eyes."

—Chinese proverb

The key point underlying this optical illusion is that cultural experiences shape and sometimes distort perceptions of reality. People think they are seeing things objectively or as they really are, but they're really seeing things subjectively from their particular cultural vantage point. Being open to the viewpoints of diverse people who perceive the world from different cultural vantage points widens our range of perception and helps us overcome our cultural blind spots. As a result, we tend to perceive the world around us with greater clarity and accuracy.

Remember

The reality of our own culture is not the reality of other cultures. Our perceptions of the outside world are shaped (and sometime distorted) by our prior cultural experiences.

What Is an Ethnic Group?

An ethnic group (ethnicity) is a group of people who share the same culture. Thus, *culture* refers to what an ethnic group has in common and *ethnic group* refers to people who share the same culture. Unlike a racial group, whose members share physical characteristics that they are born with and that have been passed on to them biologically, an ethnic group's shared characteristics have been passed on through socialization—their common characteristics have been learned or acquired through shared social experiences.

The major cultural (ethnic) groups found within the United States include:

- Native Americans (American Indians)
  - Cherokee, Navajo, Hopi, Alaskan natives, Blackfoot, etc.
- African Americans (Blacks)
  - Americans whose cultural roots lie in the continent of Africa (e.g., Ethiopia, Kenya, Nigeria) and the Caribbean Islands (e.g., Bahamas, Cuba, Jamaica),
- Hispanic Americans (Latinos)
  - Americans with cultural roots in Mexico, Puerto Rico, Central America (e.g., El Salvador, Guatemala, Nicaragua), and South America (e.g., Brazil, Colombia, Venezuela)
- Asian Americans
  - Americans who are cultural descendants of East Asia (e.g., Japan, China, Korea), Southeast Asia (e.g., Vietnam, Thailand, Cambodia), and South Asia (e.g., India, Pakistan, Bangladesh)
- Middle Eastern Americans
  - Americans with cultural roots in Iraq, Iran, Israel, etc.
- European Americans (Whites)
  - Americans with cultural roots in Western Europe (e.g., the United Kingdom, Ireland, the Netherlands), Eastern Europe (e.g., Hungary, Romania, Bulgaria), Southern Europe (e.g., Italy, Greece, Portugal), and Northern Europe or Scandinavia (e.g., Denmark, Sweden, Norway)

Currently, European Americans are the majority ethnic group in the United States because they account for more than 50 percent of the American population. Native Americans, African Americans, Hispanic Americans, and Asian Americans are considered to be ethnic minority groups because each of these groups represents less than 50 percent of the American population.

Reflection **9.4**

Which ethnic group or groups do you belong to or identify with?

What are the most common cultural values shared by your ethnic group or groups?

Ethnic groups can be comprised of Whites or people of color. For people of color, their ethnicity is immediately visible to other people; in contrast, members of White ethnic groups have the option of choosing whether they want to identify with their ethnicity or share it with others because it is not visible to the naked eye. Members of ethnic minority groups with European ancestry can more easily "blend into" or become assimilated into the majority (dominant) culture because their minority status can't be visibly detected. Minority White immigrants of European ancestry have even changed their last names to appear to be Americans of English descent. In contrast, the immediately detectable minority status of African Americans, darker-skinned Hispanics, and Native Americans doesn't allow them the option of presenting themselves as members of an already-assimilated majority group (National Council for the Social Sciences, 1991).

As with racial grouping, classifying humans into different ethnic groups can also be very arbitrary and subject to different interpretations by different groups of people. Currently, there are three racial categories used by the U.S. Census Bureau: White, Black, and Asian. Hispanics are not defined as a race, but are classified as an ethnic group. However, among those who checked "some other race" in the 2000 census, 97 percent were Hispanic. This finding suggests that Hispanic Americans consider themselves to be a racial group, perhaps because this is how they feel they're perceived and treated by non-Hispanics (Ciancotto, 2005). Supporting the Hispanic viewpoint that others perceive them as a race, rather than an ethnic group, is the recent use of the term *racial profiling* in the American media to describe Arizona's controversial 2010 law that allows police to target people who "look" like illegal aliens from Mexico, Central America, and South America. Again, this illustrates how race and ethnicity are subjective, socially constructed concepts that depend on how society perceives and treats certain social groups, which, in turn, affect how these groups perceive themselves.

This disagreement illustrates how difficult it is to conveniently categorize groups of people into particular racial or ethnic groups. The United States will continue to struggle with this issue because the ethnic and racial diversity of its population is growing and members of different ethnic and racial groups are forming cross-ethnic and interracial families. Thus, it is becoming progressively more difficult to place people into distinct categories based on their race or ethnicity. For example, by 2050, the number of people who will identify themselves as being of two or more races is projected to more than triple, growing from 5.2 million to 16.2 million (U.S. Census Bureau, 2008).

Student Perspective

"I'm the only person from my 'race' in class."

—Hispanic student commenting on why he felt uncomfortable being the only Latino in his class on Race, Ethnicity, and Gender

"As the child of a Black man and a White woman, someone who was born in the racial melting pot of Hawaii, with a sister who's half Indonesian but who's usually mistaken for Mexican or Puerto Rican and a brother-in-law and niece of Chinese descent, with some blood relatives who resemble Margaret Thatcher and others who could pass for Bernie Mac, family get-togethers over Christmas take on the appearance of a UN General Assembly meeting. I've never had the option of restricting my loyalties on the basis of race, or measuring my worth on the basis of tribe."

—Barack Obama, 44th president of the United States

What Is Humanity?

It's important to realize that human variety and human similarity coexist and complement each other. Experiencing diversity not only enhances appreciation of the unique features of different cultures but also provides a larger perspective on the universal aspects of the human experience that are common to all humans, no matter what their particular cultural background may be. For example, despite racial and cultural differences, all people express the same emotions with the same facial expressions.

Other human characteristics that anthropologists have found to be shared by all groups of people in every corner of the world include storytelling, poetry, adornment of the body, dance, music, decoration of artifacts, families, socialization of children by elders, a sense of right and wrong, supernatural beliefs, and mourning of the dead (Pinker, 2000). Although different ethnic groups may express these shared experiences in different ways, these universal experiences are common to all humans.

"Above all nations is humanity."

—Motto of the University of Hawaii

> **Remember**
>
> *Diversity represents variations on the common theme of humanity. Although groups of humans may have different cultural backgrounds, they're still cultivated from the same soil—we're all grounded in the common experience of being human.*

Reflection 9.5

List three human experiences you think are universal—i.e., experienced by all humans in all cultures:

1.

2.

"We are all the same, and we are all unique."

—Georgia Dunston, African American biologist and research specialist in human genetics

3.

Different cultures associated with different ethnic groups may be viewed simply as variations on the same theme: being human. You may have heard the question, "We're all human, aren't we?" The answer to this important question is "yes and no." Yes, humans are all the same, but not in the same way.

A good metaphor for understanding this apparent contradiction is to visualize humanity as a quilt in which we are all joined by the common thread of humanity— by the common bond of being human. The different patches that make up the quilt represent diversity—the distinctive or unique cultures that comprise our common humanity. The quilt metaphor acknowledges the identity and beauty of all cultures. It differs from the old American "melting pot" metaphor, which viewed differences as something that should be melted down or eliminated, or the salad bowl metaphor, which suggested that America is a hodgepodge or mishmash of cultures thrown together without any common connection. In contrast, the quilt metaphor suggests that the cultures of different ethnic groups are to be recognized and celebrated, but can be woven together to create a unified whole, as in the Latin expression *E pluribus unum* ("Out of many, one")—the motto of the United States, which you'll find printed on its coins.

To appreciate diversity and its relationship to humanity is to capitalize on the power of our differences (diversity) while still preserving our collective strength through unity (humanity).

> **Remember**
>
> *When we learn about human differences (diversity), we simultaneously learn about our commonalities (humanity).*

What Is Individuality?

It's important to keep in mind that individual differences within the same racial or ethnic group are greater than the average differences between different groups. For example, differences in physical attributes (e.g., height and weight) and behavior patterns (e.g., personality characteristics) among individuals within the same racial group are greater than the average differences between racial groups (Caplan & Caplan, 2009).

As you proceed through this chapter, keep in mind the following distinctions among humanity, diversity, and individuality:

- **Diversity.** We are all members of *different groups* (e.g., different gender and ethnic groups).
- **Humanity.** We are all members of the *same group* (the human species).
- **Individuality.** We are all *unique individuals* who differ from other members of any group to which we may belong.

Major Forms or Types of Diversity in Today's World

Ethnic and Racial Diversity

America is rapidly becoming a more racially and ethnically diverse nation. In 2008, the minority population in the United States reached an all-time high of 34 percent of the total population. The population of ethnic minorities is now growing at a much faster rate than the White majority. This trend is expected to continue, and by the middle of the 21st century, the minority population will have grown from one-third of the U.S. population to more than one-half (54 percent), with more than 60 percent of the nation's children expected to be members of what we now call minority groups (U.S. Census Bureau, 2008).

By 2050, the U.S. population is projected to be more than 30 percent Hispanic (up from 15 percent in 2008), 15 percent Black (up from 13 percent), 9.6 percent Asian (up from 5.3 percent), and 2 percent Native American (up from 1.6 percent). The native Hawaiian and Pacific Islander population is expected to more than double between 2008 and 2050. During this same time period, the percentage of White Americans will drop from 66 percent (2008) to 46 percent (2050). As a result of these population trends, ethnic and racial minorities will become the new majority because they will constitute the majority of Americans by the middle of the 21st century.

"We have become not a melting pot but a beautiful mosaic."

—Jimmy Carter, 39th president of the United States and winner of the Nobel Peace Prize

"Every human is, at the same time, like all other humans, like some humans, and like no other human."

—Clyde Kluckholn, American anthropologist

Socioeconomic Diversity

Diversity also appears in the form of socioeconomic status or social class, which is typically stratified (divided) into lower, middle, and upper classes, based on level of education and income. Groups occupying lower social strata have significantly fewer economic resources and social privileges (Feagin & Feagin, 2007).

According to U.S. Census figures, the wealthiest 20 percent of the American population controls approximately 50 percent of the country's total income, and the 20 percent of Americans with the lowest income controls only 4 percent of the nation's income. Sharp discrepancies also exist in income level among different racial, ethnic, and gender groups. Poverty continues to be a problem in America; more than 12 percent of Americans (over 37 million people) live below the poverty line, making the United States one of the most impoverished of all developed countries in the world (Shah, 2008). Although all ethnic and racial groups experience poverty, minority groups experience it at significantly higher rates than the White majority.

International Diversity

Beyond our particular countries of citizenship, humans are members of a common, international world that includes multiple nations. Communication and interaction across nations are now greater than at any other time in world history, largely because of rapid advances in electronic technology (Dryden & Vos, 1999; Friedman, 2005). Economic boundaries between nations are also breaking down due to increasing international travel, international trading, and development of multinational corporations. The world of the 21st century is really a small world after all, and success in it requires an international perspective. By learning from and about different nations, you become more than a citizen of your own country: you become cosmopolitan—a citizen of the world.

Taking an international perspective allows you to appreciate the diversity of humankind. If it were possible to reduce the world's population to a village of precisely 100 people, with all existing human ratios remaining the same, the demographics of this world village would look something like this:

- 61 would be Asians, 13 Africans, 12 Europeans, 9 Latin Americans, and 5 from the United States and Canada
- 50 would be male, 50 would be female
- 75 would be non-White; 25 White
- 67 would be non-Christian; 33 would be Christian
- 80 would live in substandard housing
- 16 would be unable to read or write
- 50 would be malnourished and 1 dying of starvation
- 33 would be without access to a safe water supply
- 39 would lack access to improved sanitation
- 24 would not have any electricity (and of the 76 that do have electricity, most would only use it for light at night)
- 8 people would have access to the Internet
- 1 would have a college education
- 1 would have HIV
- 2 would be near birth; 1 near death
- 5 would control 32 percent of the entire world's wealth; all 5 would be U.S. citizens
- 48 would live on less than US$2 a day
- 20 would live on less than US$1 a day
  Source: Family Care Foundation (2012).

Reflection 9.6

What do you think is the factor that is most responsible for poverty in:

1. The United States?

2. The world?

Diversity and the College Experience

There are more than 3,000 public and private colleges in the United States. They vary in size (small to large) and location (urban, suburban, and rural), as well as in their purpose or mission (research universities, comprehensive state universities, liberal arts colleges, and community colleges). This variety makes America's higher education system the most diverse and accessible in the world. The diversity of educational opportunities in American colleges and universities reflects the freedom of opportunity in the United States as a democratic nation.

The ethnic and racial diversity of students in American colleges and universities is also rapidly rising. In 1960, Whites made up almost 95 percent of the total college population; today, it's approximately 66 percent. College students today experience more diversity on their campuses than at any other time in the history of American higher education.

Student Perspective

"I am very happy with the diversity here, but it also frightens me. I have never been in a situation where I have met people who are Jewish, Muslim, atheist, born-again, and many more."

—First-year college student (Erickson, Peters, & Strommer, 2006)

Reflection 9.7

1. What diverse groups do you see represented on your campus?

2. Are there groups on campus that you did not expect to see or to see in such large numbers?

3. Are there groups on your campus that you expected to see but do not see or see in smaller numbers than you expected?

The Benefits of Experiencing Diversity

Diversity Promotes Self-Awareness

Learning from people with diverse backgrounds and experiences sharpens our self-knowledge and self-insight by allowing us to compare and contrast our life experiences with others whose experiences differ sharply from our own. This comparative perspective gives us a reference point for viewing our own lives, placing us in a better position to see how our unique cultural backgrounds have influenced the development of our personal beliefs, values, and lifestyle. By viewing our lives in relation to the lives of others, we see more clearly what is distinctive about ourselves and how we may be uniquely advantaged or disadvantaged.

Remember

The more opportunities you create to learn from others different than yourself, the more opportunities you create to learn about yourself.

Diversity Enriches a College Education

Diversity magnifies the power of a college education by liberating students from the tunnel vision of ethnocentricity (culture-centeredness) and egocentricity (self-centeredness), enabling them to get beyond themselves and view the world from a multicultural perspective. Just as the various subjects you take in the college curriculum open your mind to multiple perspectives, so does your experience with people from varied backgrounds. A multicultural perspective helps us become aware of our "cultural blind spots" and avoid the dangers of *groupthink*—the tendency for tight-knit groups of people to think so much alike that they overlook flaws in their thinking (Baron, 2005; Janis, 1982).

Diversity Strengthens Learning and Critical Thinking

Research consistently shows that we learn more from people who are different than ourselves than we do from people similar to ourselves (Pascarella, 2001; Pascarella & Terenzini, 2005). When our brain encounters something that is unfamiliar or different from what we're accustomed to, we must stretch beyond our mental comfort zone and work harder to understand it, because doing so forces us to compare and contrast it to what is in our brains and already familiar to us (Acredolo & O'Connor, 1991; Nagda, Gurin, & Johnson, 2005). Stretching our minds to understand something that's unfamiliar to us requires extra psychological effort and energy, which produces a deeper, more powerful learning experience.

Diversity Promotes Creative Thinking

Experiences with diversity supply you with a broader base of knowledge and wider range of thinking styles that better enable you to think outside your own cultural box or boundaries. In contrast, limiting your number of cultural vantage points is akin to limiting the variety of mental tools you can use to solve new problems, thereby limiting your creativity. When like-minded people only associate with other like-minded people, they're unlikely to think outside the box.

Drawing on different ideas from people with diverse backgrounds and bouncing your ideas off them is a great way to generate energy, synergy, and serendipity—unanticipated discoveries and creative solutions. Diversity expands students' capacity for viewing issues or problems from multiple vantage points, equipping them with a wider variety of approaches to solving unfamiliar problems they may encounter in different contexts and situations.

Furthermore, ideas acquired from diverse people and diverse cultures may combine or "cross-fertilize," giving birth to new approaches for solving old problems. When ideas are generated openly and freely in groups comprised of people from diverse backgrounds, powerful "cross-stimulation" effects can occur, whereby one group member's idea can trigger different ideas from other group members (Brown, Dane, & Durham, 1998). Drawing on different ideas from people of diverse backgrounds and bouncing ideas off them serves to stimulate divergent (expansive) thinking, which can lead to synergy (idea multiplication) and serendipity (unexpected discoveries of innovative solutions).

In contrast, when different cultural perspectives are not sought out or tolerated, the variety of lenses available to students for viewing new problems is reduced, which, in turn, limits or shrinks one's capacity for creative thinking. Creativity tends to be replaced by conformity or rigidity because ideas do not flow freely and divergently (in different directions); instead, ideas tend to converge and merge into the

"When all men think alike, no one thinks very much."

—Walter Lippmann, distinguished journalist and originator of the term *stereotype*

"Research indicates the equality of men and women—socially, educationally, occupationally, and within the family—becomes more accepted by students of both sexes during the college years."

—Ernest Pascarella and Patrick Terenzini, *How College Affects Students*

"When the only tool you have is a hammer, you tend to see every problem as a nail."

—Abraham Maslow, psychologist, best known for his theory of human self-actualization

"What I look for in musicians is generosity. There is so much to learn from each other and about each other's culture. Great creativity begins with tolerance."

—Yo-Yo Ma, French-born Chinese-American virtuoso cellist, composer, and winner of multiple Grammy Awards

same cultural channel—the one shared by the homogeneous group of people doing the thinking.

Diversity Education Promotes Career Preparation for the 21st Century

Learning about and from diversity has a very practical benefit: it better prepares students for their future work roles. Whatever line of employment students may eventually pursue, they're likely to find themselves working with employers, co-workers, customers, and clients from diverse cultural backgrounds. America's workforce is now more diverse than at any other time in the nation's history and it will grow ever more diverse throughout the 21st century. By 2050, the majority of America's working-age population will be comprised of workers from minority ethnic and racial groups (U.S. Census Bureau, 2008). Thus, intercultural competence is now a highly valued skill and one that is essential for success in today's work world.

The current "global economy" also requires intercultural skills relating to international diversity. Work in today's global economy is characterized by economic interdependence among nations, international trading (imports/exports), multinational corporations, international travel, and almost instantaneous worldwide communication—due to advances in the World Wide Web (Dryden & Vos, 1999; Friedman, 2005). As a result, employers now seek job candidates with the following skills and attributes: sensitivity to human differences, ability to understand and relate to people from different cultural backgrounds, international knowledge, and ability to communicate in a second language (Fixman, 1990; National Association of Colleges & Employers, 2007; Office of Research, 1994). Thus, learning about and from diversity isn't only good education: it's also good career preparation.

> **Remember**
>
> *The wealth of diversity on college campuses today represents an unprecedented educational opportunity. You may never again be a member of a community that includes so many people from such a rich variety of backgrounds. Seize this opportunity! You're in the right place at the right time to experience the variety of people and programs that will enrich the breadth and depth of your learning.*

Stumbling Blocks and Barriers to Experiencing Diversity

Stereotypes

The word *stereotype* derives from a combination of two roots: *stereo* (to look at in a fixed way) and *type* (to categorize or group together, as in the word *typical*). Thus, stereotyping is viewing individuals of the same type (group) in the same (fixed) way.

In effect, stereotyping ignores or disregards individuality; instead, all people sharing the same group characteristic (e.g., race or gender) are viewed as having the same personal characteristics—as in the expression, "You know what they're like: they're all the same." Stereotypes involve bias, which literally means "slant." A bias can be slanted either positively or negatively. Positive bias results in a favorable stereotype (e.g., "Italians are great lovers"); negative bias produces an unfavorable stereotype (e.g., "Italians are in the Mafia"). Snapshot Summary 9.1 lists some common stereotypes.

"The benefits that accrue to college students who are exposed to racial and ethnic diversity during their education carry over in the work environment. The improved ability to think critically, to understand issues from different points of view, and to collaborate harmoniously with co-workers from a range of cultural backgrounds all enhance a graduate's ability to contribute to his or her company's growth and productivity."

—Business-Higher Education Forum, 2002

"Only a well educated, diverse work force, comprised of people who have learned to work productively and creatively with individuals from a multitude of races and ethnic, religious, and cultural backgrounds, can maintain America's competitiveness in the increasingly diverse and interconnected world economy."

—Spokesman for General Motors Corporation, quoted in Chatman (2008).

Reflection **9.8**

Have you ever been stereotyped, such as based on your appearance or group membership? If so, how did it make you feel and how did you react?

Have you ever unintentionally perceived or treated someone in terms of a group stereotype rather than as an individual? What assumptions did you make about that person? Was that person aware of, or affected by, your stereotyping?

Snapshot Summary

9.1 **Examples of Common Stereotypes**

Muslims are terrorists.

Whites can't jump (or dance).

Blacks are lazy.

Asians are brilliant in math.

Irish are alcoholics.

Gay men are feminine; lesbian women are masculine.

Jews are cheap.

Hispanic men are abusive to women.

Men are strong.

Women are weak.

Whether you are male or female, don't let gender stereotypes limit your career options.

Prejudice

If virtually all members of a stereotyped group are judged or evaluated in a negative way, the result is prejudice. (The word *prejudice* literally means to "pre-judge.") Technically, prejudice may be either positive or negative; however, the term is most often associated with a negative prejudgment that involves *stigmatizing*—associating inferior or unfavorable traits with people who belong to the same group. Thus, prejudice may be defined as a negative judgment, attitude, or belief about another person or group of people that's formed before the facts are known. Stereotyping and prejudice often go hand in hand because individuals who are placed in a negatively stereotyped group are commonly prejudged in a negative way.

Someone with a prejudice toward a group typically avoids contact with individuals from that group. This enables the prejudice to continue unchallenged because there's little chance for the prejudiced person to have positive experiences with any member of the stigmatized group that could contradict or disprove the prejudice. Thus, a vicious cycle is established in which the prejudiced person continues to avoid contact with individuals from the stigmatized group, which, in turn, continues to maintain and reinforce the prejudice.

> "Let us all hope that the dark clouds of racial prejudice will soon pass away and the deep fog of misunderstanding will be lifted from our fear-drenched communities, and in some not too distant tomorrow the radiant stars of love and brotherhood will shine over our great nation."
>
> —Martin Luther King Jr., civil rights activist and clergyman

Discrimination

Literally translated, the term *discrimination* means "division" or "separation." Whereas prejudice involves a belief or opinion, discrimination involves an action taken toward others. Technically, discrimination can be either negative or positive—for example, a discriminating eater may be careful about eating only healthy foods. However, the term is most often associated with a negative action that results in a prejudiced person treating another person, or group of people, in an unfair way. Thus, it could be said that discrimination is prejudice put into action. Hate crimes are examples of extreme discrimination because they are acts motivated solely by prejudice against members of a stigmatized group.

> "'See that man over there?'
> 'Yes.'
> 'Well, I hate him.'
> 'But you don't know him.'
> 'That's why I hate him.'"
>
> —Gordon Allport, *The Nature of Prejudice* (1954)

Other forms of discrimination are more subtle and may be practiced by society's institutional systems rather than particular individuals. These forms of *institutional racism* are less flagrant or visible, and they are rooted in societal policies and practices that discriminate against members of certain ethnic groups. For instance, *redlining*, a term coined in the late 1960s, refers to the practice of banks marking a red line on a map to indicate an area where they will not invest or lend money; many of those areas are neighborhoods in which African Americans live (Shapiro, 1993). Studies also show that compared to White patients, Black patients of the same socio-economic status are less likely to receive breast cancer screenings, eye exams if they have diabetes, and follow-up visits after hospitalization for mental illness (Schneider, Zaslavsky, & Epstein, 2002).

Thus, trying to be "race blind" and getting along with people of all colors with whom we interact on an *individual* basis is not all there is to eliminating discrimination. Racial discrimination is an issue that goes beyond individual interactions to larger institutional policies and societal systems.

Reflection **9.9**

Prejudice and discrimination can be subtle and only begin to surface when the social or emotional distance among members of different groups grows smaller. Honestly rate your level of comfort with the following situations.

Someone from another racial group:

1. Going to your school	high	moderate	low
2. Working in your place of employment	high	moderate	low
3. Living on your street as a neighbor	high	moderate	low
4. Living with you as a roommate	high	moderate	low
5. Socializing with you as a personal friend	high	moderate	low
6. Being your most intimate friend or romantic partner	high	moderate	low
7. Being your partner in marriage.	high	moderate	low

For any item you rated "low," what caused you to give it such a low rating?

Snapshot Summary 9.2 contains a summary of biased attitudes, prejudicial beliefs, and discriminatory behaviors that must be overcome if humankind is to experience the full benefits of diversity. As you read through the list, place a checkmark next to any form of prejudice that you, a family member, or friend has experienced.

Snapshot Summary

9.2 Blocks to Learning from Diversity: Biased Attitudes, Prejudicial Beliefs, and Discriminatory Behaviors

- **Stereotyping.** Viewing all (or virtually all) individuals of the same group in the same way—as having the same qualities or characteristics.
  Example: "If you're Italian, you must be in the Mafia, or have a family member who is."
- **Prejudice.** A negative pre-judgment of another group of people.
  Example: Women do not make good leaders because they're too emotional.
- **Discrimination.** Unequal and unfair treatment of a person or group of people, i.e., prejudice put into action.
  Example: People of color being paid less for performing the same job, even though they have the same level of education and job qualifications as Whites performing the same job.
- **Segregation.** A conscious decision made by a group to separate itself (socially or physically) from another group.
  Example: "White flight"—White people moving out of neighborhoods when people of color move in.
- **Racism.** A belief that one's racial group is superior to another group and expressing that belief in the form of an attitude (prejudice) or action (discrimination).

  Example: Cecil Rhodes—Englishman and empire builder of British South Africa—once claimed: "We [the British] are the finest race in the world and the more of the world we inhabit the better it is for the human race."
- **Institutional racism.** Racism rooted in organizational policies and practices that disadvantage certain racial groups.
  Example: Race-based discrimination in mortgage lending, housing, and bank loans.
- **Slavery.** Forced labor in which people are considered to be the property of others, are held against their will, and are deprived of the right to leave, to refuse to work, or to demand wages.
  Example: Enslavement of Blacks was legal in the United States until 1865.
- **"Jim Crow" laws.** Formal and informal laws created by Whites after the abolition of slavery to segregate Blacks. (The term "Jim Crow" likely derived from a song-and-dance character named "Jump Jim Crow," who was played by a White man in blackface.)
  Example: Laws in the U.S. that once required Blacks and Whites to use separate bathrooms and be educated in separate schools.

- **Apartheid.** An institutionalized system of "legal racism" supported by a nation's government. (*Apartheid* derives from a word in the Afrikaan language meaning "apartness.")
  Example: The national system of racial segregation and discrimination that existed in South Africa from 1948 to 1994.
- **Hate crimes.** Criminal action motivated solely by prejudice toward the crime victim.
  Example: Acts of vandalism or assault aimed at members of a particular ethnic group or persons with a particular sexual orientation.
- **Hate groups.** Organizations whose primary purpose is to stimulate prejudice, discrimination, or aggression toward certain groups of people based on their ethnicity, race, religion, etc.
  Example: The Ku Klux Klan, an American terrorist group that perpetrates hatred toward all non-white races.
- **Genocide.** Mass murdering of a particular ethnic or racial group by another group.
  Example: The Holocaust during World War II, in which millions of Jews were systematically murdered. Other examples include the murdering of Cambodians under the Khmer Rouge regime, the murdering of Bosnian Muslims in the former country of Yugoslavia, and the slaughter of the Tutsi minority by the Hutu majority in Rwanda.
- **Classism.** Prejudice or discrimination based on social class, particularly toward people of low socioeconomic status.
  Example: Acknowledging the contributions made by politicians and wealthy industrialists to America, while ignoring the contributions of poor immigrants, farmers, slaves, and pioneer women.
- **Religious bigotry.** Denying the fundamental human right of people to hold religious beliefs, or to hold religious beliefs that differ from one's own.
  Example: An atheist who forces non-religious (secular) beliefs on others, or a member of a religious group who believes that people who hold different religious beliefs are immoral "sinners."
- **Anti-Semitism.** Prejudice or discrimination toward Jews or people who practice the religion of Judaism.
  Example: Hating Jews because they're the ones who "killed Christ."
- **Xenophobia.** Extreme fear or hatred of foreigners, outsiders, or strangers.

- **Example:** Believing that immigrants should be banned from entering the country because they'll increase the crime rate or ruin our economy.
- **Regionalism.** Prejudice or discrimination based on the geographical region in which an individual has been born and raised.
  Example: A northerner thinking that all southerners are racists.
- **Jingoism.** Excessive interest and belief in the superiority of one's own nation without acknowledging its mistakes or weaknesses; it's often accompanied by an aggressive foreign policy that neglects the needs of other nations, or the common needs of all nations.
  Example: "Blind patriotism"—not seeing the shortcomings of one's own nation and viewing any questioning or criticism of it as disloyalty or being "unpatriotic." (As in the slogans "America: right or wrong" or "America: love it or leave it!")
- **Terrorism.** Intentional acts of violence against civilians that are motivated by political or religious prejudice.
  Example: The September 11th attacks on the United States.
- **Sexism:** Prejudice or discrimination based on sex or gender.
  Example: Believing that women should not pursue careers in fields traditionally filled only by men (e.g., engineering) because they lack the natural qualities or skills to do them.
- **Heterosexism.** Belief that heterosexuality is the only acceptable sexual orientation.
  Example: Using the word *fag* or *queer* as an insult or put-down, or believing that gays should not have the same legal rights and opportunities as heterosexuals.
- **Homophobia.** Extreme fear or hatred of homosexuals.
  Example: People who engage in "gay bashing" (acts of violence toward gays), or who create and contribute to anti-gay Web sites.
- **Ageism.** Prejudice or discrimination based on age, particularly toward the elderly.
  Example: Believing that all "old" people are bad drivers with bad memories who should not be allowed on the road.
- **Ableism.** Prejudice or discrimination toward people who are disabled or handicapped (physically, mentally, or emotionally).
  Example: Avoiding social contact or interaction with people in wheelchairs.

Have you, a family member, or a friend experienced any of the forms of prejudice in the above list? Why do you think it occurred?

Strategies for Meeting and Interacting with Students from Diverse Backgrounds

The following practices and strategies may be used to help us open up to and appreciate individuals from other groups toward whom we may hold prejudices, stereotypes, or subtle biases that bubble beneath the surface of our conscious awareness.

"Stop judging by mere appearances, and make a right judgment."
—John 7:24

"The common eye sees only the outside of things, and judges by that. But the seeing eye pierces through and reads the heart and the soul, finding there capacities which the outside didn't indicate or promise."
—Samuel Clemens, a.k.a. Mark Twain, writer, lecturer, and humorist

1. **Consciously avoid preoccupation with physical appearances.** Go deeper and get beneath the surface of appearances to judge people not in terms of how they look, but in terms of who they are and how they act. Remember the old proverb: "It's what inside that counts." Judge others by their inner qualities, not by the familiarity of their outer features.
2. **Perceive each person with whom you interact as a unique human being.** Make a conscious effort to interact with people as individuals, not as group members, and form your impressions of others on a case-by-case basis, not according to some general rule of thumb. This may seem like an obvious and easy thing to do, but research shows that humans have a natural tendency to perceive individuals from unfamiliar groups as being more alike (or all alike) than members of their own group (Taylor, Peplau, & Sears, 2006). Thus, we need to make a conscious effort to counteract this tendency.

Remember

While it's valuable to learn about different cultures and the common characteristics shared by members of the same culture, it shouldn't be done at the expense of ignoring individual differences among members of the same culture. Don't assume that all individuals who share the same cultural background share the same personal characteristics.

3. **Make an intentional attempt to interact and collaborate with members of diverse groups.** Once we've overcome our biases and begin to perceive members of diverse groups as unique individuals, we move into a position to take the next step of interacting, collaborating, and forming friendships with members of diverse groups. Interpersonal contact between diverse people takes us beyond simple awareness and acceptance, and moves us up to a higher level of diversity appreciation that involves intercultural interaction. When we take this step to cross cultural boundaries, we transform diversity appreciation from an internal attitude or personal conviction into an observable action or interpersonal commitment.

Your initial comfort level with interacting with people from diverse groups is likely to depend on how much experience you have had with diversity before college. If you've had little or no prior experience interacting with members of diverse groups, it may be more challenging for you to initiate interactions with diverse students on campus. However, the good news is that you have the most to gain from interacting and collaborating with those of other ethnic or racial groups. Research consistently shows that when we have social experiences that differ radically from our prior experiences, we gain the most in terms of learning and cognitive development (Acredolo & O'Connor, 1991; Piaget, 1985).

Reflection 9.11

Rate the amount or variety of diversity you have experienced in the following settings:

1. The high school you attended   high   moderate   low

2. The college or university you now attend   high   moderate   low

3. The neighborhood in which you grew up   high   moderate   low

4. Places where you have worked or been employed   high   moderate   low

Which setting had the *most* and the *least* diversity?

What do you think accounts for this difference?

The following strategies may be used to increase interpersonal contact and opportunities to learn with (and from) student diversity.

1. **Intentionally create opportunities for social interaction and conversation with individuals from diverse groups.** Studies show that stereotyping and prejudice can be sharply reduced if contact between members of different racial or ethnic groups is frequent enough to allow time for the development of friendships (Pettigrew, 1998). Make an intentional attempt to fight off the tendency to associate only with people who are similar to you. One way to do this is by intentionally placing yourself in situations where individuals from diverse groups are nearby so that interaction can potentially take place. Research indicates that meaningful interactions and friendships are more likely to form among people who are in physical proximity with one another (Back, Schmukle, & Egloff, 2008; Latané et al., 1995). You can create this condition in the college classroom by sitting near students from different ethnic or racial groups or by joining them if you are given the choice to select whom you will work with in class discussion groups and group projects.

2. **Take advantage of the Internet to chat with students from diverse groups.** Electronic communication can be a more convenient and more comfortable way to initially interact with members of diverse groups with whom you have had little prior experience. After you've communicated successfully *online*, you may then feel more comfortable about interacting with them *in person*. Online and in-person interaction with students from other cultures deepens your understanding of your own culture and elevates your awareness of cultural customs and values that you may have overlooked or taken for granted (Bok, 2006).

3. **Seek out the views and opinions of classmates from diverse backgrounds.** During or after class discussions, ask students from different backgrounds if there was any point made or position taken in class that they would strongly question or challenge. Seeking out divergent (diverse) viewpoints has been found to be one of the best ways to develop critical thinking skills (Inoue, 2005; Kurfiss, 1988).

4. **Join or form discussion groups with students from diverse backgrounds.** You can gain exposure to diverse perspectives by joining or forming discussion groups with students who differ from you in terms of such characteristics as gender, age, race, or ethnicity. You might begin by forming study groups with students who are different than you in one way but similar to you in other ways. For instance, you can form learning teams with students who have the same major as you, but who differ from you in terms of race, ethnicity, or age. This strategy gives the diverse members of your team some common ground for discussion (your major) and can raise your team's awareness that although you may be members of different groups, you can share similar educational goals and life plans.

• Remember

Including diversity in your learning groups not only provides social variety: it also promotes the quality of the group's work by giving its members access to diverse perspectives and life experiences of people from different backgrounds.

5. **Form collaborative learning teams.** A learning team is more than a discussion group or a study group. It moves beyond discussion to collaborative learning—its members become teammates who "co-labor" (work together) as part of a joint and mutually supportive effort to reach the same team goal. Studies show that when individuals from different ethnic and racial groups work collaboratively toward the attainment of a common goal, racial prejudice is reduced and interracial friendships are promoted (Allport, 1954; Amir, 1976; Dovidio, Eller, & Hewstone, 2011). These positive developments probably take place because individuals from diverse groups working on the same team creates a social environment in which no one is a member of an "out" group ("them"): they're all members of the same "in" group ("us") (Pratto et al., 2000; Sidanius, Levin, Liu, & Pratto, 2000). For specific strategies on how to form diverse and effective learning teams, see Do It Now! 9.1.

Summary and Conclusion

Diversity refers to differences among groups of people who, together, comprise humanity. Experiencing diversity increases appreciation of the features unique to different cultures and provides a panoramic perspective on the human experience that is shared by all people, no matter what their particular culture happens to be.

Culture is formed by the beliefs and values of a group with the same traditions and social heritage. It helps bind people into supportive, tight-knit communities. However, culture can also lead its members to view the world solely through their own cultural lens (known as ethnocentrism), which can blind them to other cultural perspectives. Ethnocentrism can contribute to stereotyping—viewing individual members of a group in the same way and seeing all of them as having the same personal characteristics.

Evaluating members of a stereotyped group negatively results in prejudice—a biased prejudgment about another person or group of people that's formed before the facts are known. Stereotyping and prejudice often go hand in hand, because if the stereotype is negative, individual members of the stereotyped group are then prejudged negatively. Discrimination takes prejudice one step further by converting the negative prejudgment into action that results in treating others unfairly. Thus, discrimination is prejudice in action.

9.1

Tips for Teamwork: Creating Diverse and Effective Learning Teams

1. **Intentionally form diverse learning teams comprised of individuals with different cultural backgrounds and life experiences.** If you team up only with friends or classmates whose lifestyles and experiences are similar to your own, it can actually impair your team's performance. Your similar experiences can cause your learning to get off track and onto topics that have nothing to do with the learning task (for example, what you did last weekend or what you are planning to do next weekend).

2. **Your team should identify and pursue a common goal.** Your team should create the same final product that represents their unified effort and accomplishment (e.g., a completed sheet of answers to questions, a list or chart of specific ideas). A collectively created end product helps individual members function as "we" rather than "me," and helps the team stay on task and moving in the same direction toward their common goal.

3. **Each teammate should have equal opportunity and assume personal responsibility for contributing to the team's final product.** For example, all team members should be equally responsible for making a specific contribution to the team's final product, such as contributing a different piece of information to the team's overall topic or project (e.g., a specific chapter from the textbook or a particular section of class notes), as if each teammate is bringing a different piece or part that's needed to complete the whole puzzle.

> "We are born for cooperation, as are the feet, the hands, the eyelids, and the upper and lower jaws."
>
> —Marcus Aurelius, Roman emperor, 161–180 AD

4. **All teammates should work interdependently—that is, they should depend on or rely upon each other to achieve their common goal.** Like members of a sports team, each member of a learning team should have a specific role to play. For instance, each teammate could assume one of the following roles:

   - Manager, whose role is to ensure that the team stays on track and moving toward their goal.
   - Moderator, whose role is to ensure that all members have equal opportunity to contribute.
   - Summarizer, whose role is to monitor the team's progress and identify what has been accomplished and what still needs to be done.
   - Recorder, whose role is to keep a written record of the team's ideas.

Teammates may also assume roles that involve contributing a particular type of thinking to the learning task (e.g., analysis, synthesis, or application) or bringing a specific perspective to the final product (e.g., cultural, national, or international).

5. **Before delving into the work task, teammates should take some social "warm-up" time to interact informally with each other.** Getting the opportunity to learn each other's names, backgrounds, and interests will enable group members to become comfortable with one another and develop a sense of team solidarity or identity, particularly if they come from diverse (and unfamiliar) cultural backgrounds. Once they get to know each other as individuals, they should become more comfortable sharing their personal thoughts and viewpoints during teamwork.

6. **Teamwork should take place in a friendly, informal setting.** The context or atmosphere in which group work takes place can influence the nature and quality of interaction among team members. People are more likely to work openly and collaboratively when they are in an environment that is conducive to relationship building. For example, a living room or a lounge area would provide a warmer and friendlier team-learning atmosphere than a sterile classroom.

7. **Learning teams should occasionally divide into smaller subgroups (e.g., pairs or trios) so that teammates get an opportunity to work with each other on a more personal level, particularly if they are from different ethnic or racial groups.** The smaller the group size, the greater the level of participation, involvement, and interaction between group members. For example, it's much easier not to participate in a group of six than in a group of two. If opportunities are created for different team members to work together, everyone gets at least one opportunity to work closely with every other member of the team. This can promote diversity appreciation by allowing each team member to experience working at a personal level with an individual from a minority group that's not represented in large numbers at your school.

When contact among people from diverse groups takes place under the above conditions, it has the greatest potential for having positive impact on learning and diversity appreciation. A win-win scenario is created: Learning is strengthened, and at the same time, prejudice is weakened.

References: Allport (1979); Amir (1969); Aronson, Wilson, & Akert (2009); Brown & Hewstone (2005); Cook (1984); Sherif, Harvey, White, Hood, & Sherif (1961).

Once stereotyping and prejudice are overcome, we are positioned to experience diversity and reap its multiple benefits, which include sharper self-awareness, broadened personal perspectives, deeper learning, higher-level thinking, and career success.

The increasing diversity of students on campus, combined with the wealth of diversity-related educational experiences found in the college curriculum and cocurriculum, presents you with an unprecedented opportunity to infuse diversity into your college experience. Seize this opportunity and capitalize on the power of diversity to increase the quality of your college education and your prospects for success in the 21st century.

Learning More through the World Wide Web

Internet-Based Resources for Further Information on Diversity

For additional information related to the ideas discussed in this chapter, we recommend the following Web sites:

www.tolerance.org

www.amnesty.org

www.intercultural.org

9.1 Gaining Awareness of Multi-Group Identities

We can be members of multiple groups at the same time, and our membership in these overlapping groups can influence our personal development and self-identity. In the figure that follows, consider the shaded center circle to be yourself and the six non-shaded circles to be six groups you belong to that you think have influenced your personal development or personal identity.

© Kendall Hunt

Fill in the non-shaded circles with the names of groups to which you belong that have had the most influence on your personal development. You can use the diversity spectrum that appears on the second page of this chapter to help you identify different groups. You don't have to come up with six groups and fill all six circles. What's important is to identify those groups that have had a major influence on your development and identity.

Self-Assessment Questions

1. Which one of the groups you identified has had the greatest influence on your personal identity? Why?

2. Have you ever felt limited or disadvantaged by being a member of any particular group or groups?

3. Have you ever felt that you experienced advantages or privileges because of your membership in any group or groups?

9.2 Intercultural Interview

Find a student, faculty member, or administrator on campus whose cultural background differs from your own and ask if you can interview that person about his or her culture. Use the following questions in your interview:

1. How is "family" defined in your culture, and what are the traditional roles and responsibilities of different family members?

2. What are the traditional gender (male vs. female) roles associated with your culture? Are they changing?

3. What is your culture's approach to time? Is there an emphasis on punctuality? Is moving quickly and getting things done rapidly valued more than reflection and deliberation?

4. What are your culture's staple foods and favorite beverages?

5. What cultural traditions or rituals are highly valued and commonly practiced?

6. What special holidays are celebrated?

9.3 Hidden Bias Test

Go to www.tolerance.org/activity/test-yourself-hidden-bias and take one or more of the hidden bias tests on the Web site. These tests assess subtle bias with respect to gender, age, Native Americans, African Americans, Asian Americans, religious denominations, sexual orientations, disabilities, and body weight. The site allows you to assess whether you have a bias toward any of these groups.

Self-Assessment Questions

1. Did the results reveal any bias that you were unaware of?

2. Did you think the assessment results were accurate or valid?

3. What do you think best accounts for or explains your results?

4. If your closest family member and best friend took the test, how do you think their results would compare with yours?

Hate Crime: A Racially Motivated Murder

Jasper County, Texas, has a population of approximately 31,000 people. In this county, 80 percent of the people are White, 18 percent are Black, and 2 percent are of other races. The county's poverty rate is considerably higher than the national average, and its average household income is significantly lower. In 1998, the mayor, the president of the chamber of commerce, and two councilmen were Black. From the outside, Jasper appeared to be a town with racial harmony, and its Black and White leaders were quick to state that there was no racial tension in Jasper.

However, on June 7, 1998, James Byrd Jr., a 49-year-old African American man, was walking home along a road one evening and was offered a ride by three White men. Rather than taking Byrd home, Lawrence Brewer (age 31), John King (age 23), and Shawn Berry (age 23), three individuals linked to White supremacist groups, took Byrd to an isolated area and began beating him. They dropped his pants to his ankles, painted his face black, chained Byrd to their truck, and dragged him for approximately three miles. The truck was driven in a zigzag fashion to inflict maximum pain on the victim. Byrd was decapitated after his body collided with a culvert in a ditch alongside the road. His skin, arms, genitalia, and other body parts were strewn along the road, while his torso was found dumped in front of a Black cemetery. Medical examiners testified that Byrd was alive for much of the dragging incident.

While in prison awaiting trial, Brewer wrote letters to King and other inmates. In one letter, Brewer wrote: "Well, I did it and am no longer a virgin. It was a rush and I'm still licking my lips for more." Once the trials were completed, Brewer and King were sentenced to death. Both Brewer and King, whose bodies were covered with racist tattoos, had been on parole before the incident, and they had previously been cellmates. King had spent an extensive amount of time in prison, where he began to associate with White males in an environment in which each race was pitted against the other.

As a result of the murder, Byrd's family created the James Byrd Foundation for Racial Healing in 1998. On January 20, 1999, a wrought iron fence that separated Black and White graves for more than 150 years in Jasper Cemetery was removed in a special unity service. Members of the racist Ku Klux Klan have since visited the gravesite of Byrd several times, leaving racist stickers and other marks that have angered the Jasper community and Byrd's family.

Sources: *Houston Chronicle* (June 14, 1998); *San Antonio Express News* (September 17, 1999); *Louisiana Weekly* (February 3, 2003).

Reflection and Discussion Questions

1. What factors do you think were responsible for causing this incident to take place?

2. Could this incident have been prevented? If yes, how? If no, why not?

3. How likely do you think it is that an incident like this could take place in your hometown or near your college campus?

4. If this event took place in your hometown, how would you and members of your family and community react?

Test-Taking Skills and Strategies 10

What to Do before, during, and after Exams

LEARNING GOAL

To strengthen your performance on college exams and tests for admission to professional and graduate programs.

1. On which of the following types of activities do you tend to perform best? (Circle one.) On which do you perform the worst? (Circle one.)

   Taking multiple-choice tests

   Taking essay tests

   Writing papers

   Making oral presentations

2. What do you think accounts for the fact that you perform better on one of these types than the others?

Test-Taking Strategies

Academic learning in college involves three stages: acquiring information from lectures and readings; studying that information and storing it in your brain as knowledge; and demonstrating that knowledge on exams. What follows is a series of strategies related to stage three of this process: test taking. The strategies are divided into three categories:

- Strategies to use in advance of the test,
- Strategies to use during the test, and
- Strategies to use after test results are returned.

Pre-Test Strategies: What to Do in Advance of the Test

Your ability to remember what you've studied depends not only on how much and how well you studied, but also on how you will be tested (Stein, 1978). You may be able to remember what you've studied if you are tested in one format (e.g., multiple-choice questions) but may not remember the material as well if the test is in a different format (e.g., essay questions). You need to be aware of the type of test you'll be taking and adjust your study strategies accordingly.

College test questions fall into two major categories: (1) recognition questions, and (2) recall questions. Each of these types of questions requires a different type of memory and a different study strategy.

1. **Recognition test questions.** Recognition questions ask you to select or choose the correct answer from choices that are provided for you. Falling into this category are multiple-choice, true-false, and matching questions. These test questions don't require you to supply or produce the correct answer on your own: instead, you're asked to recognize or pick out the correct answer—similar to picking out the "correct" criminal from a lineup of potential suspects.

2. **Recall test questions.** Recall questions require you to retrieve information you've studied and reproduce it on your own at test time. As the word *recall* implies, you have to "call back" to mind the information you need and supply it yourself, rather than selecting it or picking it out from information that's supplied for you. Recall test questions include essay and short-answer questions, which require a written response.

Since recognition test questions ask you to recognize or identify the correct answer from among answers that are provided for you, repeatedly reading over your class and textbook notes to identify important concepts may be an effective study strategy for multiple-choice and true-false test questions. Doing so matches the type of mental activity you'll be asked to perform on the exam—read over and identify correct answers.

On the other hand, recall test questions, such as essay questions, require you to retrieve information and generate answers on your own. Studying for essay tests by looking over your class notes and highlighted reading will not prepare you to recall information because it does not simulate what you'll be doing on the test itself. However, when you study for essay tests, if you retrieve information without looking at it and write out your answers to questions, you will ensure that your practice (study) sessions match your performance (test) situation because you are rehearsing what you'll be expected to do on the test—write essays.

Two strategies that are particularly effective for practicing the type of memory retrieval you will need to perform on essay tests are recitation and creation of retrieval cues. Each of these strategies is described below.

Recitation

Recitation involves saying the information you need to recall without looking at it. Research indicates that memory for information is significantly strengthened when students study by trying to generate that information on their own, rather than simply looking it over or rereading it (Roediger & Karpicke, 2006). Reciting strengthens recall memory in three ways:

1. Recitation forces you to actively retrieve information, which is what you will have to do on the test, instead of passively reviewing information that's in front of you and in full view, which is not what you will do on the test.

2. Recitation gives you clear feedback on whether you can recall the information you're studying. If you can't retrieve and recite it without looking at it, you know for sure that you won't be able to recall it at test time and that you need to study it further. One way to provide yourself with this feedback is to put the question on one side of an index card and the answer on the flip side. If you find yourself flipping over the index card to look at the answer in order to remember it, you clearly cannot retrieve the information on your own and need to study it further.

3. Recitation encourages you to use your own words; this gives you feedback on whether you can paraphrase it. If you can paraphrase it (rephrase it in your own words), it's a good indication that you really understand it, and if you really understand it, you're more likely to recall it at test time.

Recitation can be done silently, by speaking aloud, or by writing out what you're saying. We recommend speaking aloud or writing out what you're reciting because these strategies involve physical action, which keeps you actively involved in the learning process.

Creation of Retrieval Cues

Suppose you're trying to remember the name of a person you know but just cannot recall it. If a friend gives you a clue (e.g., the first letter of the person's name or a name that rhymes with it), it's likely to suddenly trigger your memory of that person's name. What your friend did was provide you with a retrieval cue. A *retrieval cue* is a type of memory reminder (like a string tied around your finger) that brings back to your mind what you've temporarily forgotten. Since human memories are stored as parts in an interconnected network, if you're able to recall one piece or segment of the network (the retrieval cue), it can trigger recall of the other pieces of information linked to it in the same organizational network (Willingham, 2001).

Reflection 10.2

Think of material in a course you're taking this term that could be easily grouped into categories to help you remember that material. What is the course?

What categories could you use to organize information that's been covered in the course?

Studies show that students who can't remember previously studied information are better able to recall that information if they are given a retrieval cue. If you take information that you need to recall on an essay test and organize it into categories, you can use the category names as retrieval cues at test time. Another strategy for creating retrieval cues is to come up with your own catchwords or catchphrases that you can use to "catch" or batch together all related ideas you're trying to remember. For instance, an acronym can serve as a catchword, with each letter acting as a retrieval cue for a batch of related ideas. Suppose you're studying for an essay test in abnormal psychology that will include questions testing your knowledge of different forms of mental illness. You could create the acronym SCOT as a retrieval cue to help you remember to include each of the following elements of mental illness in your essay answers: symptoms (S), causes (C), outcomes (O), and therapies (T). See Do It Now! 10.1 for ideas on how to create your own memory-retrieval cues.

Remember

On multiple-choice questions, you're given a list of answers and you pick out the right one. On essay questions, you have a blank sheet of paper and you have to dig out the answer on your own, which means you have to recite (rehearse) your answers before the test and use memory-retrieval cues during the test to dig up the information you need to remember.

10.1   DO IT **NOW**

Key Questions to Guide Creation of Your Own Retrieval Cues

1. Can you relate or associate what you're trying to remember with something you already know, or can you create a short meaningful story out of it? (Meaningful Association)
2. Can you remember it by visualizing an image of it, or by visually associating the pieces of information you

want to recall with familiar places or sites? (Visualization)
3. Can you represent each piece of information you're trying to recall as a letter and string the letters together to form a single word or short phrase? (Acronym)
4. Can you rhyme what you're trying to remember with a word or expression you know well, or can you create a little poem, jingle, or melody out of it that contains the information? (Rhythm and Rhyme)

Strategies to Use Immediately before a Test

1. **Before the exam, try to take a brisk walk.** Physical activity increases mental alertness by increasing oxygen flow to the brain; it also decreases tension by increasing the brain's production of emotionally "mellowing" brain chemicals (e.g., serotonin and endorphins).
2. **Come fully armed with all the test-taking tools you need.** In addition to the required supplies (e.g., No. 2 pencil, pen, blue book, Scantron, calculator, etc.), bring backup equipment in case you experience equipment failure (e.g., an extra pen in case your first one runs out of ink or extra pencils in case your original one breaks).
3. **Try to get to the classroom a few minutes early.** Arriving at the test ahead of time gives you a chance to review any formulas and equations you may have struggled to remember and any memory-retrieval cues you've created (e.g., acronyms). You want to be sure that you have this information in your working memory when you receive the exam so that you can get it down on paper before you forget it. Arriving early also allows you to take a few minutes to get into a relaxed pre-test state of mind by thinking positive thoughts, taking slow, deep breaths, and stretching your muscles. Also, avoid last-second discussions with unprepared classmates about the test just before the test is handed out; their hurried and harried questions can often cause confusion and elevate your level of test anxiety.
4. **Sit in the same seat that you normally occupy in class.** Research indicates that memory is improved when information is recalled in the same place where it was originally received or reviewed (Sprenger, 1999). Thus, taking the test in the same seat you normally occupy during lectures should improve your test performance because it puts you in the same place where you originally heard much of the information that is going to appear on the test. Studies show that when students take a test in the same environment that they studied in, they tend to remember more of that information at test time than do students who study in one place and take the test in a different place (Smith, Glenberg, & Bjork, 1978). While it is unlikely that you'll be able to do all your studying in the same room that you will take your test in, it may be possible to do your final review in your classroom or in an empty classroom with similar features. This could strengthen your memory for the information you studied, because the features of the room

in which you studied the information may become associated with the information, and seeing these features again at test time may help trigger memory of the information (Tulving, 1983).

5. **If you feel you need an energy boost immediately before an exam, eat a piece of fruit rather than a candy bar.** Candy bars are processed sweets that can offer a short burst of energy provided by synthetic sugar. Unfortunately, this short-term rise in blood sugar and quick jolt of energy are typically accompanied by increased bodily tension followed by a sudden drop in energy and a feeling of sluggishness. The key is to find a food that can produce a state of elevated energy without elevating tension and maintain that state of energy at an even level. The best nutritional option for producing a sustained, steady state of energy is the natural sugar contained in a piece of fruit, not processed sugar that's artificially slipped into a candy bar.

6. **Avoid consuming caffeine before an exam.** Even though caffeine is a stimulant that increases alertness, it also qualifies as a legal drug that can significantly increase bodily tension and nervousness; these are feelings you don't want to experience during a test, particularly if you're prone to test anxiety. Also, caffeine is a diuretic, which means it will increase your urge to urinate. This is a distracting urge you certainly want to avoid during an exam when you're confined to a classroom for an extended period of time, sitting on your butt (and bladder).

Consuming large doses of caffeine or other stimulants before exams may increase your alertness, but may also increase your level of stress and test anxiety.

Strategies to Use during the Test

1. **As soon as you receive a copy of the test, write down key information you need to remember.** In particular, write down any hard-to-remember terms, formulas, and equations and any memory-retrieval cues you may have created as soon as you start the exam to ensure that you don't forget this information after you begin answering specific test questions.

2. **Answer the easier test questions first.** As soon as you receive the test, before launching into answering the first question listed, check out the layout of the test. Note the questions that are worth the most points and the questions that you know well. You can do this by first surveying the test and putting a checkmark next to questions whose answers you're unsure of; come back to these questions later after you've answered the questions you're sure of, to ensure all their points are added into your final test score.

Reflection **10.3**

During tests, if I experience memory block, I usually . . .

I am most likely to experience memory block in the following subject areas:

3. **If you tend to experience memory block for information that you know is stored in your brain, use the following strategies:**

    -   Mentally put yourself back in the environment or situation in which you studied the information. Recreate the steps in which you learned the information that you've temporarily forgotten by mentally picturing the place where you first heard or saw it and where you studied it, including sights, sounds, smells, and time of day. This memory-improvement strategy is referred to as *guided retrieval*, and research supports its effectiveness for recalling information, including information recalled by eyewitnesses to a crime (Glenberg, 1997; Glenberg, Bradley, Kraus, & Renzaglia, 1983).

    -   Think of any idea or piece of information that may be related to the information you can't remember. Studies show that when students experience temporary forgetting, they're more likely to suddenly recall that information if they first recall a piece or portion of that information that relates to it in some way (Reed, 1996). This related piece of information can trigger your memory for the forgotten information because related pieces of information are typically stored within the same neural network of cells in the brain.

    -   Take your mind off the question and turn to another question. This may allow your subconscious to focus on the forgotten information, which may trigger your conscious memory of it. Also, you may find some information included in other test questions that can help you remember an answer to a previous test question.

    -   Before turning in your test, carefully review and double-check your answers. This is the critical last step in the process of effective test taking. Sometimes the rush and anxiety of taking a test can cause test takers to overlook details, misread instructions, unintentionally skip questions, or make absentminded mistakes. When you're done, take time to look over your answers to be sure you didn't make any mindless mistakes. Avoid the temptation to immediately cut out because you're pooped out, or to take off on an ego trip by being among the first and fastest students in class to finish the test. Instead, take the full amount of test time available to you. When you think about the amount of time and effort you put into preparing for the exam, it's foolish not to take a little more time on the exam itself.

Strategies for Answering Multiple-Choice Questions

Multiple-choice questions are commonly used on college tests, on certification or licensing exams to practice in particular professions (e.g., nursing and teaching), and on admissions tests for graduate school (e.g., master's and doctoral degree programs) or professional school (e.g., law school and medical school). Since you're likely to encounter multiple-choice tests frequently in college and beyond, this section of the text is devoted to a detailed discussion of strategies for answering such test questions. These strategies are also applicable to true-false tests, which are really multiple-choice tests that involve two choices (true or false).

Reflection **10.4**

How would you rate your general level of test anxiety during most exams? (Circle one.)

high   moderate   low

What types of tests or subjects tend to produce the most test stress or test anxiety for you?

Why?

1. **Read all choices listed and use a *process-of-elimination* approach.** You can find an answer by eliminating choices that are clearly wrong and continue to do so until you're left with one answer that is the most accurate option. Keep in mind that the correct answer is often the one that has the highest probability or likelihood of being true; it doesn't have to be absolutely true—just truer than the other choices listed.

2. **Use *test-wise* strategies when you don't know the correct answer.** Your first strategy on any multiple-choice question should be to choose an answer based on your knowledge of the material, rather than trying to outsmart the test or the test maker by guessing the correct answer based on how the question is worded. However, if you've relied on your knowledge and used the process-of-elimination strategy to eliminate clearly wrong choices but you're still left with two or more answers that appear to be correct, then you should turn to being *test wise*, which refers to your ability to use the characteristics of the test question itself (such as its wording or format) to increase your chances of selecting the correct answer (Flippo & Caverly, 2009). Listed here are three test-wise strategies for multiple-choice questions whose answers you don't know or can't remember:

A *process-of-elimination* approach is an effective test-taking strategy to use when answering difficult multiple-choice questions.

- **Pick an answer that contains qualifying words.** Look for words such as *usually*, *probably*, *likely*, *sometimes*, *perhaps*, or *may*. Knowledge often doesn't come neatly wrapped in the form of absolute truths, so choices that are stated as broad generalizations are more likely to be false. For example, answers containing words such as *always*, *never*, *only*, *must*, and *completely* are more likely to be false than true.
- **Pick the longest answer.** True statements often require more words to make them true.
- **Pick a middle answer rather than the first or last answer.** For example, on a question with four choices, if you've narrowed down the correct answer to a "b" or "c" versus an "a" or "d" choice, go with the "b" or "c" choice. Studies show that instructors have a tendency to place correct answers as middle choices rather than as the first or last choice (Linn & Gronlund, 1995), perhaps because they think the correct answer will be too obvious or stand out if it's listed at the beginning or end.

3. **Check to be sure that your answers are aligned with the right questions.** When looking over your test before turning it in, search carefully for questions you may have skipped and intended to go back to later. Sometimes you may skip a test question on a multiple-choice test and forget to skip the number of that question on the answer form, which will throw off all your other answers by one space or line. On a computer-scored test, this means that you may get multiple items marked wrong because your answers are misaligned, resulting in a "domino effect" of wrong answers, which can do major damage to your test score. As a damage-prevention measure, check all of your answers to be sure there are no blank lines or spaces on your answer sheet to set off this damaging domino effect.

4. **Don't feel that you must remain locked in to your first answer.** When checking your answers on multiple-choice and true-false tests, don't be afraid to change an answer after you've given it more thought. There have been numerous studies on the topic of changing answers on multiple-choice and true-false tests dating back to 1928 (Kuhn, 1988). These studies consistently show that most changed test answers go from being incorrect to correct, resulting in improved test scores (Bauer, Kopp, & Fischer, 2007; Benjamin, Cavell, & Shallenberger, 1984; Prinsell, Ramsey, & Ramsey, 1994). These findings probably reflect the fact that students often catch mistakes when they read the question again or when they find some information later in the test that causes them to reconsider their first answer.

Don't buy into the common belief that your first answer is always your best answer. If you have good reason to think a change should be made, don't be afraid to make it. The only exception to this general rule is when you find yourself changing many of your original answers; this is an indication that you were not well prepared for the exam and are just doing a lot of random second-guessing.

Reflection **10.5**

On exams, do you ever change your original answers?

If you do change answers, what's the usual reason you make changes?

Strategies for Answering Essay Questions

Along with multiple-choice questions, essay questions are among the most commonly used forms on college exams. Listed below are strategies that will help you achieve peak levels of performance on essay questions.

1. **Focus on main ideas first.** Before you begin answering the question by writing full sentences, make a brief outline or list of bullet points to represent the main ideas you will include in your answers. Outlines are effective for several reasons:

   - **An outline helps you remember the major points.** It prevents you from becoming so wrapped up in the details of constructing sentences and choosing words for your answers that you lose the big picture and forget the most important points you need to make.

   - **An outline improves your answer's organization.** In addition to reminding you of the points you intend to make, an outline gives you a plan for sequencing your ideas in an order that ensures they flow smoothly. One factor that instructors consider when awarding points for an answer to an essay question is how well that answer is organized. An outline makes your answer's organization clearer by calling your attention to its major categories and subcategories.

   - **Having an advanced idea of what you will write reduces your test anxiety.** An outline takes care of the answer's organization beforehand so you don't have the added stress of worrying about how to organize your answer at the same time you're writing and explaining your answer.

   - **An outline can add points to an incomplete answer's score.** If you run out of test time before writing out your full answer to an essay question, an outline allows your instructor to see what you planned to include in your written answer. Your outline itself is likely to earn you points because it demonstrates your knowledge of the major points called for by the question. In contrast, if you skip an outline and just start writing answers to test questions one at a time, you run the risk of not getting to questions you know well before your time is up; you'll then have nothing on your test to show what you know about those unfinished questions.

Exhibit 1

Identical twins
Adoption
Parents/family tree

6/6

1. There are several different studies that scientists conduct, but one study that they conduct is to find out how genetics can influence human behavior in _identical twins_. Since they are identical, they will most likely end up very similar in behavior because of their identical genetic makeup. Although environment has some impact, genetics are still a huge factor and they will, more likely than not, behave similarly. Another type of study is with _parents and their family trees_. Looking at a subject's family tree will explain why a certain person is bipolar or depressed. It is most likely caused by a gene in the family tree, even if it was last seen decades ago. Lastly, another study is with adopted children. If an _adopted child_ acts a certain way that is unique to that child, and researchers find the parents' family tree, they will most likely see similar behavior in the parents and siblings as well.

No freewill
No afterlife

6/6

2. The monistic view of the mind-brain relationship is so strongly opposed and criticized because there is a belief or assumption that _free will_ is taken away from people. For example, if a person commits a horrendous crime, it can be argued "monistically" that the chemicals in the brain were the reason, and that a person cannot think for themselves to act otherwise. This view limits responsibility.

    Another reason that this view is opposed is because it has been said that _there is no afterlife_. If the mind and brain are one and the same, and there is _NO_ difference, then once the brain is dead and is no longer functioning, so is the mind. Thus, it cannot continue to live beyond what we know today as life. _And_ this goes against many religions, which is why this reason, in particular, is heavily opposed.

Written answers to two short essay questions given by a college sophomore, which demonstrate effective use of bulleted lists or short outlines (in the side margin) to ensure recall of most important points.

2. **Get directly to the point on each essay question.** Avoid elaborate introductions that take up your test time (and your instructor's grading time) but don't earn you any points. For example, an answer that begins with the statement "This is an interesting question that we had a great discussion on in class . . ." is pointless because it will not add points to your test score. The time available to you on essay tests is often limited, so you can't afford flowery introductions that waste valuable test time and don't contribute anything to your overall test score.

    One effective way to get directly to the point on essay questions is to include part of the question in the first sentence of your answer. For example, suppose the test question asks you to "Argue for or against capital punishment by explaining how it will or will not reduce the nation's murder rate." Your first sentence could be, "Capital punishment will not reduce the murder rate for the following reasons . . ." Thus, your first sentence becomes your thesis statement, which immediately points you directly to the major points you're going to make in your answer and earns immediate points for your answer.

3. **Answer all essay questions with as much detail as possible.** Don't assume that your instructor already knows what you're talking about or will be bored by details. Instead, take the approach that you're writing to someone who knows little or nothing about the subject—as if you're an expert teacher and the reader is a clueless student.

Remember

As a rule, it's better to overexplain than underexplain your answers to essay questions.

4. **Support your points with evidence—facts, statistics, quotes, or examples.** When taking essay tests, take on the role of a lawyer making a case by presenting concrete evidence (exhibit A, exhibit B, etc.). Since timed essay tests can often press you for time, be sure to prioritize and cite your most powerful points and persuasive evidence. If you have time later, you can return to add other points worth mentioning.

Do It Now! 10.2 contains a list of thinking verbs that you're likely to see in college writing assignments and the type of mental action typically called for by each of these verbs. As you read the list, make a short note after each mental action indicating whether or not you've been asked to use such thinking on any assignments you completed before college.

10.2   DO IT NOW

Ten Mental-Action Verbs Commonly Found in Essay-Test Questions

1. **Analyze.** Break the topic down into its key parts and evaluate the parts in terms of their accuracy, strengths, and weaknesses.
2. **Compare.** Identify the similarities and differences between major ideas.
3. **Contrast.** Identify the differences between ideas, particularly sharp differences and opposing viewpoints.
4. **Describe.** Provide details (e.g., who, what, where, and when).
5. **Discuss.** Analyze (break apart) and evaluate the parts (e.g., strengths and weaknesses).
6. **Document.** Support your judgment and conclusions with references or information sources.
7. **Explain.** Provide reasons that answer the questions "Why?" and "How?"
8. **Illustrate.** Supply concrete examples or specific instances.
9. **Interpret.** Draw your own conclusion about something, and explain why you came to that conclusion.
10. **Support.** Back up your ideas with research findings, factual evidence, or logical arguments.

"I keep six honest serving men. They taught me all I knew. Their names are what and why and how and when and where and who."

—Rudyard Kipling, "The Elephant's Child," *Just So Stories*

Reflection 10.6

Which of the mental actions in the list in Do It Now! 10.3 was most often required on your high school writing assignments?

Which was least often (or never) required?

5. **Leave space between your answers to each essay question.** This strategy will enable you to easily add information to your original answer if you have time or if you recall something later in the test that you forgot initially.
6. **Proofread your answers for spelling and grammar.** Before turning in your test, proofread what you've written and correct any obvious spelling or grammatical errors you find. Eliminating them is likely to improve your test score. Even if

your instructor doesn't explicitly state that grammar and spelling will be counted in determining your grade, these mechanical mistakes are still likely to influence your professor's overall evaluation of your written work.

7. **Neatness counts.** Studies show that neatly written essays tend to be scored higher than sloppy ones, even if the answers are essentially the same (Huck & Bounds, 1972; Klein & Hart, 1968; Hughes, Keeling, & Tuck, 1983; Pai, Sanji, Pai, & Kotian, 2010). These findings are understandable when you consider that grading essay answers is a time-consuming task that requires your instructor to plod through multiple styles of handwriting whose readability may range from crystal-clear to cryptic. Make an earnest attempt to write as clearly as possible, and if you finish the test with time to spare, clean up your work by rewriting any sloppily written words or sentences.

Reflection 10.7

Rate yourself in terms of how frequently you use these test-taking strategies according to the following scale:

4 = always,   3 = sometimes,   2 = rarely,   1 = never

1. I take tests in the same seat that I usually sit in to take class notes. 4 3 2 1

2. I answer easier test questions first. 4 3 2 1

3. I use a process-of-elimination approach on multiple-choice tests to eliminate choices until I find one that is correct or appears to be the most accurate option. 4 3 2 1

4. On essay questions, I outline or map out my ideas before I begin to write the answer. 4 3 2 1

5. I look for information included on the test that may help me answer difficult questions or that may help me remember information I've forgotten. 4 3 2 1

6. I leave extra space between my answers to essay questions in case I want to come back and add more information later. 4 3 2 1

7. I carefully review my work, double-checking for errors and skipped questions before turning in my tests. 4 3 2 1

Post-Test Strategies: What to Do after Receiving Test Results

1. **Use your test results as feedback to improve your future performance.** Your test score is not just an end result: it can be used as a means to an end—a higher score on your next test performance and a higher course grade. When you get tests back, examine them carefully and make special note of any written comments your instructor may have made. If your test results are disappointing, don't get bitter, get better. Use the results as feedback to diagnose where you went wrong so that you can avoid making the same mistakes again. If your test results were positive, see where you went right so you can do it right again.

2. **Seek additional feedback.** In addition to using your own test results as a source of feedback, ask for feedback from others whose judgment you trust and value. Three social resources you can use to obtain feedback on how to improve your performance are your instructors, professionals in your Learning or Academic Support Center, and your peers.

    Make appointments with your instructors to visit them during office hours and get their feedback on how you might be able to improve your test performance. You'll likely find it easier to see your instructors after a test than before it, because most students don't realize that it's just as valuable to seek feedback from instructors following an exam as it is to get last-minute help before an exam.

    Tutors and other learning support professionals on your campus can also be excellent sources of feedback about what adjustments to make in your study habits or test-taking strategies to improve your future performance. Also, be alert and open to receiving feedback from trusted peers. While feedback from experienced professionals is valuable, don't overlook your peers as another source of information on how to improve your performance. You can review your test with other students in class, particularly with students who did exceptionally well. Their tests can provide you with models of what type of work your instructor expects on exams. You might also consider asking successful students what they did to be successful—for example, what they did to prepare for the test and what they did during the test.

    Whatever you do, don't let a bad test grade get you mad, sad, or down, particularly if it occurs early in the course when you're still learning the rules of the game. Look at mistakes in terms of what they can do *for* you, rather than to you. A poor test performance can be turned into a valuable learning experience by using test results as a source of feedback and as an error detector to pinpoint the source of your mistakes. Look back at your mistakes so you can move forward and progress toward future success.

> "People can't learn without feedback. It's not teaching that causes learning. Attempts by the learner to perform cause learning, dependent upon the quality of the feedback and opportunities to use it."
> —Grant Wiggins, author of *Feedback: How Learning Occurs*

> "When you make a mistake, there are only three things you should do about it: admit it; learn from it; and don't repeat it."
> —Paul "Bear" Bryant, legendary college football coach

> Failure is not fatal, but failure to change might be."
> —John Wooden, legendary college basketball coach

> **Remember**
> *Your past mistakes should be neither ignored nor neglected: they should be detected and corrected so that you don't replay them on future tests. Just as you learn before tests by preparing for your performance, you can learn after tests by reviewing your performance.*

Strategies for Pinpointing the Source of Lost Points on Exams

On test questions where you lost points, identify the stage in the learning process where the breakdown occurred by asking yourself the following questions.

1. **Did you have the information you needed to answer the question correctly?** If you didn't have the information, what was the source of the missing information? Was it information presented in class that didn't get into your notes? If so,

look at our strategies for improving listening and note-taking habits. (See p. 96.) If the missing information was contained in your assigned reading, check whether you're using effective reading strategies. (See p. 103.)

2. **Did you have the information but not study it because you didn't think it was important?** If you didn't realize the information would be on the test, review the study strategies for finding and focusing on the most important information in class lectures and reading assignments. (See p. 109.)

3. **Did you study it, but not retain it?** Not remembering information you studied may mean one of three things:
   - You didn't store the information adequately in your brain, so your memory trace wasn't strong enough to recall. This suggests that more study time needs to be spent on recitation or rehearsal. (See p. 124.)
   - You may have tried to cram in too much information too quickly just before the exam and may have not given your brain time enough to "digest" (consolidate) it and store it in long-term memory. The solution would be to distribute your study time more evenly in advance of the next exam and take advantage of the part-to-whole study method. (See p. 113.)
   - You put in enough study time and you didn't cram, but you didn't study effectively or strategically. For example, you may have studied for essay questions by just reading over your class notes and reading highlights rather than rehearsing and reciting them. The solution would be to adjust your study strategy so that it better matches or aligns with the type of test you're taking. (See p. 135.)

4. **Did you study the material but not really understand it or learn it deeply?** This suggests you may need to self-monitor your comprehension more carefully while studying to track whether you truly understand the material at a deeper level. (See p. 135.)

5. **Did you know the information but find yourself unable to retrieve it during the exam?** If you had the information on the "tip of your tongue" during the exam, this indicates that you did retain it and it was stored (saved) in your brain, but you couldn't get at it and get it out (retrieve it) when you needed it. This error may be corrected by making better use of memory-retrieval cues. (See p. 118.)

6. **Did you know the answer but just make a careless test-taking mistake?** If your mistake was careless, the solution may be simply to take more time to review your test once you've completed it and check for absentminded errors before turning it in. Or, your careless errors may be the result of test anxiety that's interfering with your ability to concentrate during exams.

Strategies for Reducing Test Anxiety

1. **Understand what test anxiety is and what it's not.** Don't confuse anxiety with stress. Stress is a physical reaction that prepares your body for action by arousing and energizing it; this heightened arousal and energy can be used productively to strengthen your performance. In fact, if you're totally stress-free during an exam, it may mean that you're too "laid back" and couldn't care less about how well you're doing. Stress is something that cannot and should not be completely eliminated when you're trying to reach peak levels of performance, whether academic or athletic. Instead of trying to block out stress altogether, your goal should be to control it, contain it, and maintain it at a level that maximizes the

quality of your performance. The key is to keep stress at a moderate level, thereby capitalizing on its capacity to help you get psyched up or pumped up, but preventing it from reaching such a high level that you become psyched out or stressed out.

If you experience the following symptoms during tests, your stress level may be at a level high enough to be accurately called test anxiety.

- You feel physical symptoms of tension during the test, such as a pounding heartbeat, a rapid pulse, muscle tension, sweating, or an upset stomach.
- Negative thoughts and feelings rush through your head—for example, fear of failure or self-defeating putdowns such as "I always mess up on exams."
- You rush through the test just to get it over with (probably because you want to get rid of the anxiety you're experiencing).
- You have difficulty concentrating or focusing your attention while answering test questions.
- Even though you studied and know the material, you go blank during the exam and forget what you studied. (However, you're able to remember the information after you turn in your test and leave the test situation.)

To minimize test anxiety, consider the following practices and strategies.

2. **Avoid cramming for exams.** Research indicates that college students who display greater amounts of procrastination experience higher levels of test anxiety (Rothblum, Solomon, & Murakami, 1986). High levels of pre-test tension associated with rushing and late-night cramming are likely to carry over to the test itself, resulting in higher levels of test-taking tension. Furthermore, loss of sleep caused by previous-night cramming results in lost dream (REM) sleep, which, in turn, elevates anxiety levels the following day—test day.

3. **Use effective test-preparation strategies prior to the exam.** Test-anxiety research indicates that college students who prepare well for exams not only achieve higher test scores, but also experience lower levels of test anxiety (Zohar, 1998). Other research findings demonstrate that using effective study strategies prior to the exam—such as those discussed in Chapter 5—reduces test anxiety during the exam (Benjamin, McKeachie, Lin, & Holinger, 1981; Jones & Petruzzi, 1995; Zeidner, 1995).

4. **During the exam, concentrate on the here and now.** Devote your attention fully to answering the test question that you're currently working on; don't spend time thinking (and worrying) about the test's outcome and what your grade will be.

5. **Stay focused on the test in front of you, not the students around you.** Don't spend valuable test time looking at what others are doing and wondering whether they're doing better than you are. If you came to the test well prepared and still find the test difficult, it's very likely that other students are finding it difficult too. If you happen to notice that other students are finishing before you do, don't assume they breezed through the test or that they're smarter than you. Their faster finish may simply reflect the fact that they didn't know many of the answers and decided to give up and get out, rather than prolong the agony.

6. **Don't spend a lot of time focusing on the amount of time left in the exam.** Repeatedly checking the time during the test can disrupt the flow of your thought process and increase your stress level. Although it's important that you remain aware of how much time remains to complete the exam, only check the time periodically, and do your time-checking after you've completed answering a question so you don't disrupt or derail your train of thought.

7. **Control your thoughts by focusing on what you're getting right, rather than worrying about what answers you don't know and how many points you're losing.** Our thoughts influence our emotions (Ellis, 1995), and positive emotions, such as those associated with optimism and a sense of accomplishment, can improve mental performance by enhancing the brain's ability to process, store, and retrieve information (Rosenfield, 1988). Keep in mind that college exams are often designed to be more difficult than high school tests, so it's less likely that students will get 90 to 100 percent of the total points. You can still achieve a good grade on a college exam without having to achieve a near-perfect test score.

8. **Remember that if you're experiencing a *moderate* amount of stress during the exam, this isn't abnormal or an indication that you're suffering from test anxiety.** If you're experiencing moderate levels of tension, it indicates that you're motivated and want to do well. In fact, research shows that experiencing *moderate* levels of tension during tests and other performance-evaluation situations serves to maximize alertness, concentration, and memory (Sapolsky, 2004).

9. **Don't forget that it's just a test: it's not a measure of your ability or character.** An exam is not a measure of your overall intelligence, your overall academic ability, or your quality as a person. In fact, a test grade may be less of an indication of your effort or ability than of the complexity of the particular content covered by the test material or the nature of the test itself. Furthermore, one low grade on one particular test doesn't mean you're not capable of doing good work and are going to end up with a poor grade in the course, particularly if you use the results as feedback to improve your next test performance. (See p. 135.)

One final note on the topic of test anxiety: if you continue to experience test anxiety after implementing the above strategies, don't hesitate to seek assistance from a professional in your Learning (Academic Support) Center or Personal Counseling Office.

Summary and Conclusion

Improving performance on college exams involves strategies used in advance of the test, during the test, and after test results are returned. Good test performance begins with good test preparation and adjustment of your study strategy to the type of test you'll be taking (e.g., multiple-choice or essay test).

You can learn and improve your grades not only by preparing for tests, but also by reviewing your tests and using them as feedback to apply as you continue in the course. Past mistakes shouldn't be ignored or neglected: they should be detected and corrected so that they're not replayed on future tests.

Learning More through the World Wide Web

Internet-Based Resources for Further Information on Test-Taking Skills

For additional information related to ideas discussed in this chapter, we recommend the following Web sites:

Test-Taking Strategies:

www.muskingum.edu/~cal/database/general/testtaking.html

Overcoming Test Anxiety:

www.studygs.net/tstprp8.htm

www.swccd.edu/~asc/lrnglinks/test_anxiety.html

10.1 Midterm Self-Evaluation

Since you are near the midpoint of this textbook, you may be near the midpoint of your first term in college. At this time of the term, you are likely to experience the midterm crunch—a wave of midterm exams and due dates for certain papers and projects. This may be a good time to step back and assess your academic progress thus far.

Use the form that follows to list the courses you're taking this term and the grades you are currently receiving in each of these courses. If you do not know what your grade is, take a few minutes to check your syllabus for your instructor's grading policy and add up your scores on completed tests and assignments; this should give you at least a rough idea of where you stand in your courses. If you're having difficulty determining your grade in any course, even after checking your course syllabus and returned tests or assignments, then ask your instructor how you could estimate your current grade.

Course No.	Course Title	Instructor	Grade
1.			
2.			
3.			
4.			
5.			

Self-Assessment Questions

1. Were these the grades you were hoping for? Are you pleased or disappointed by them?
2. Were these the grades you expected to get? If not, were they better or worse than expected?
3. Do you see any patterns in your performance that suggest things you are doing well or things that you need to improve?
4. If you had to pinpoint one action you could immediately take to improve your lowest course grades, what would it be?

10.2 Calculating Your Midterm Grade Point Average

Use the information in the Snapshot Summary 10.2 to calculate what your grade point average (GPA) would be if these grades turn out to be your final course grades for the term.

Snapshot Summary

10.1 How to Compute Your Grade Point Average (GPA)

Most colleges and universities use a grading scale that ranges from 0 to 4.0 to calculate a student's grade point average (GPA) or quality point average (QPA). Some schools use letter grades only, while other institutions use letter grades with pluses and minuses.

Grading System Using Letters Only

Grade = Point Value

A = 4
B = 3
C = 2
D = 1
F = 0

GRADE POINTS Earned Per Course = Course Grade Multiplied by the Number of Course Credits (Units)

$$\text{GRADE POINT AVERAGE (GPA)} = \frac{\text{Total Number of Grade Points for All Courses}}{\text{Divided by Total Number of Course Units}}$$

SAMPLE/EXAMPLE

Course	Units	×	Grade	=	Grade Points
Roots of Rock 'n' Roll	3	×	C (2)	=	6
Daydreaming Analysis	3	×	A (4)	=	12
Surfing Strategies	1	×	A (4)	=	4
Wilderness Survival	4	×	B (3)	=	12
Sitcom Analysis	2	×	D (1)	=	2
Love and Romance	3	×	A (4)	=	12
	16				48

$$\text{GPA} = \frac{48}{16} = 3.0$$

1. What is your overall GPA at this point in the term?
2. At the start of this term, what GPA were you hoping to attain?
3. Do you think your actual GPA at the end of the term will be higher or lower than it is now? Why?

Notes: It's normal for GPAs to be lower in college than they were in high school, particularly during the first year of college. Here are the results of one study that compared students' high school GPAs with their GPAs after their first year of college:

- 29 percent of beginning college students had GPAs of 3.75 or higher in high school, but only 17 percent had GPAs that high at the end of their first year of college.
- 46 percent had high school GPAs between 3.25 and 3.74, but only 32 percent had GPAs that high after the first year of college (National Resource Center for the First-Year Experience and Students in Transition, 2004).

10.3 Preparing an Oral Presentation on Student Success

1. Scan this textbook and identify a chapter topic or chapter section that you find most interesting or think is most important to you.

2. Create an introduction for a class presentation on this topic that:
   a. Provides an overview or sneak preview of what you will cover in your presentation;
   b. Grabs the attention of your audience (your classmates); and
   c. Demonstrates the topic's relevance or importance for your audience.

3. Create a conclusion to your presentation that:
   a. Relates back to your introduction;
   b. Highlights your most important point or points; and
   c. Leaves a memorable last impression.

Bad Feedback: Shocking Midterm Grades

Joe Frosh has enjoyed his first weeks on campus. He has met lots of interesting people and feels that he fits in socially. He's also very pleased to discover that his college schedule doesn't require him to be in class for five to six hours per day, like it did in high school. This is the good news. The bad news is that unlike in high school, where his grades were all As and Bs, his first midterm grades in college are three Cs, one D, and one F. He's stunned and a bit depressed by his midterm grades because he thought he was doing well. Since he never received grades this low in high school, he's beginning to think that he's not college material and may flunk out.

Reflection and Discussion Questions

1. What factors may have caused or contributed to Joe's bad start?

2. What are Joe's options at this point?

3. What do you recommend Joe do right now to get his grades up and avoid being placed on academic probation?

4. What might Joe do in the future to prevent this midterm setback from happening again?

Finding a Path to Your Future Profession

11

Career Exploration, Preparation, and Development

ACTIVATE YOUR THINKING *Reflection* **11.1**

LEARNING GOAL

To acquire strategies you can use now and throughout the remaining years of your college experience for effective career exploration, preparation, and development.

Before you start to dig into this chapter, take a moment to answer the following questions:

1. Have you decided on a career, or are you leaning strongly toward one?

2. If yes, why have you chosen this career? (Was your decision strongly influenced by anybody or anything?)

3. If no, what careers are you considering as possibilities?

The Importance of Career Planning

Once you enter the workforce full time, most of the remaining waking hours of your life will be spent working. The only other single activity you'll spend more time on in your entire life is sleeping. When you consider that such a sizable portion of life is spent working, it's understandable how your career can have such a strong influence on your personal identity and self-esteem. Given the importance of career choice, the process of career exploration and planning should begin now—during the first year of your college experience.

Even if you've decided on a career that you've been dreaming about since you were a preschooler, you still need to engage in the process of career exploration and planning because you still need to decide on what specialization within that career you'll pursue. For example, if you're interested in pursuing a career in law, you'll need to eventually decide what branch of law you wish to practice (e.g., criminal law, corporate law, or family law). You'll also need to decide what employment sector or type of industry you would like to work in, such as nonprofit, for-profit, education, or government. Thus, no matter how certain or uncertain you are about your career path, you still need to explore career options and start taking your first steps toward formulating a career development plan.

Remember

- *When you're doing career planning, you're doing life planning because you're planning how you will spend most of the waking hours of your future life.*

Becoming a 21st-Century Graduate

Although graduation seems to be in the far and distant future, it's never too soon to plan for the demands that will await you once you have your degree in hand. What will those demands be specifically? Well, that may be hard to anticipate right now when you think about how quickly our world is changing. When you consider the list of jobs in Snapshot Summary 11.1 that didn't exist 10 years ago, you can see how these careers express the global changes that have occurred in the past decade. While planning for the future seems to be full of uncertainties, you can work now with your advisor and the Career Development Center on identifying your abilities, interests, and values and then factor this information into your educational plan, as discussed in Chapter 11. Be sure to take full advantage of the curricular and co-curricular opportunities that align with the components of your plan. In doing so, you will prepare yourself to become a 21st-century graduate who is ready for an ever-changing world.

Snapshot Summary

11.1   Jobs That Didn't Exist 10 Years Ago

1. **App developer.** When you hear "there's an app for that," that's because a career track emerged for programmers who expanded their professional knowledge and skills into the world of mobile devices.
2. **Market research data miner.** Ever wonder how retailers know how to market to you? Market research data miners collect data on consumer behaviors and predict trends for advertisers to use to develop marketing strategies.
3. **Educational or admissions consultant.** Some parents take extra steps to make sure their children are accepted into the "right" schools (from preschool to college). Educational or admissions consultants are hired to guide families through the application and interview process.
4. **Millennial generation expert.** It's very common to find members of different generations who are working together in the same organization. Millennial generation experts help employers maximize the potential of their staff by providing advice on working with their youngest employees and how to mentor them for future success.
5. **Social media manager.** The business world has made great use of social media to market and advertise their products and services. Social media managers target their marketing to the users of the various social media sites.
6. **Chief listening officer.** Similar to a social media manager, a chief listening officer uses social media to monitor consumer discussions and shares this information with marketing agents so they can design strategies that appeal to various segments of the population.
7. **Cloud computing services.** Most Web sites used every day by consumers store incredibly large amounts of data. These computer engineers, who have an expertise in data management, store and index tremendous volumes of bytes for companies (in the area of a quadrillion!).
8. **Elder care.** As life expectancy in the U.S. has increased, so has the need for individuals who have the knowledge, abilities, and compassion to serve the elderly, their families, and the agencies and companies that assist them.
9. **Sustainability expert.** For environmental and economic reasons, companies are seeking ways to minimize their carbon footprints. Sustainability experts have an expertise in the science of sustainability and the know-how to develop "green" business practices that are also cost-effective.
10. **User experience designer.** User experience designers do exactly what their titles suggest—they create experiences for consumers through technology. These designers bring to life color, sound, and images using HTML, Photoshop, and CSS.

Source: Casserly (2012)

Strategies for Career Exploration and Preparation

Reaching an effective decision about a career involves the same four steps involved in setting and reaching any personal goal:

1. **Awareness of yourself.** Your abilities, interests, needs, and values.
2. **Awareness of your options.** The variety of career fields available to you.
3. **Awareness of what options provide the best "fit" for you.** What career best matches your personal abilities, interests, needs, and values.
4. **Awareness of the process.** How to prepare for and gain entry into the career of your choice.

Step 1. Self-Awareness

The more you know about yourself, the more effective your personal choices and decisions will be. Self-awareness is a particularly important step to take when making career decisions because your career choice says a lot about who you are and what you want from life. Your career choice should be based on and built around your personal identity and life goals, not the other way around.

One way to gain greater self-awareness of where your career interests may lie is by taking psychological tests or assessments. There are assessment instruments that allow you to see how your interests in certain career fields compare with those of other students and professionals who've experienced career satisfaction and success in particular careers. These comparative perspectives provide you with an important reference point for assessing whether your level of interest in a career is high, average, or low relative to other students and working professionals. You can find these career interest tests, as well as other instruments for assessing your career-related abilities and values, in the Career Development Center on your campus.

When making choices about a career, in addition to your interests, abilities, and values, you should also be aware of your personal needs. A *need* may be described as something stronger than an interest. When you do something that satisfies a personal need, you're doing something that makes your life more personally satisfying and fulfilling (Melton, 1995). Psychologists have identified several important human needs that vary in strength or intensity from person to person. Listed in Do It Now! 11.1 are personal needs that are especially important to consider when making a career choice.

> "Don't expect a recluse to be motivated to sell, a creative thinker to be motivated to be a good proofreader day in and day out, or a sow's ear to be happy in the role of a silk purse."
>
> —Pierce Howard, *The Owner's Manual for the Brain* (2000)

Reflection **11.2**

Which of the five needs in Do It Now! 11.1 did you indicate as being strong personal needs?

What career or careers do you think would best match your strongest needs?

In summary, four key personal characteristics should be considered when exploring and choosing a career: abilities, interests, values, and needs. As illustrated in Figure 11.1, these core characteristics are the pillars that provide foundational support for making effective career choices and decisions. You want to choose a career that you're good at, interested in, and passionate about and that fulfills your personal needs.

Student Perspective

> "I believe following my passion is more crucial than earning money. I think that would come itself eventually."
>
> —College sophomore responding to the question "What are you looking for in a career?"

11.1

Personal Needs to Consider When Making Career Choices

As you read the needs in this box, make a note after each one indicating how strong the need is for you (high, moderate, or low).

1. **Autonomy.** Need for working independently without close supervision or control. Individuals with a high need for autonomy would experience greater fulfillment working in careers that allow them to be their own bosses, make their own decisions, and control their own work schedules. Individuals low in this need may experience greater satisfaction working in careers that are more structured and involve working with a supervisor who provides direction, assistance, and frequent feedback.

2. **Affiliation.** Need for social interaction, a sense of belonging, and the opportunity to collaborate with others. Individuals with a high need for affiliation would experience greater fulfillment working in careers that involve frequent interpersonal interaction and teamwork with colleagues or co-workers. Individuals low in this need are more likely to be satisfied working alone or in competition with others.

Student
Perspective

"To me, an important characteristic of a career is being able to meet new, smart, interesting people."

—First-year student

3. **Achievement.** Need to experience challenge and a sense of personal accomplishment. Individuals with high achievement needs would feel a stronger sense of fulfillment working in careers that push them to solve problems, generate creative ideas, and continually learn new information or master new skills. Individuals with a low need for achievement are likely to be more satisfied with careers that don't continually test their abilities and don't repeatedly challenge them to

stretch their skills with new tasks and different responsibilities.

Student
Perspective

"I want to be able to enjoy my job and be challenged by it at the same time. I hope that my job will not be monotonous and that I will have the opportunity to learn new things often."

—First-year student

4. **Recognition.** Need for prestige, status, and respect from others. Individuals with high recognition needs are likely to feel satisfied working in careers that are perceived by family, friends, and society to be prestigious or high-ranking. Individuals with a low need for recognition would feel comfortable working in careers that they find satisfying, regardless of how impressive or enviable their careers appear to others.

5. **Sensory stimulation.** Need for experiencing variety, change, and risk. Individuals with a high need for sensory stimulation are more likely to be satisfied working in careers that involve frequent changes of pace and place (e.g., travel), unpredictable events (e.g., work tasks that vary considerably), and moderate stress (e.g., working under pressure of competition or deadlines). Individuals with a low need for sensory stimulation may feel more comfortable working in careers that involve regular routines, predictable situations, and minimal amounts of risk or stress.

Student
Perspective

"For me, a good career is very unpredictable and interest-fulfilling. I would love to do something that allows me to be spontaneous."

—First-year student

Sources: Baumeister & Leary (1995); Chua & Koestner (2008); Deci & Ryan (2002); Ryan (1995)

Lastly, since a career choice is a long-range decision that involves life beyond college, self-awareness should involve not only reflection on who you are now but also self-projection—reflecting on how you see yourself in the future. When you engage in the process of self-projection, you begin to see a connection between where you are now and where you want or hope to be.

FIGURE 11.1

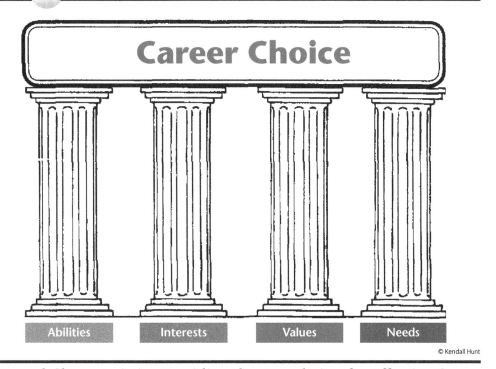

Personal Characteristics Providing the Foundation for Effective Career Choice

Ideally, your choice of a career should be one that leads to the best-case future scenario in which your typical day goes something like this: You wake up in the morning and hop out of bed enthusiastically, eagerly looking forward to what you'll be doing at work that day. When you're at work, time flies by; before you know it, the day's over. When you go to bed at night and reflect on your day, you feel good about what you did and how well you did it. In order for this ideal scenario to have any chance of becoming (or even approaching) reality, you should make every attempt to select a career path that's true to yourself and leads you to a career that's "in sync" with your abilities (what you do well), your interests (what you like to do), your values (what you feel good about doing), and your needs (what provides you with a sense of satisfaction and personal fulfillment).

Step 2. Awareness of Your Options

In addition to self-awareness and knowledge about yourself, making an effective decision about your career path also requires knowledge about the nature of different careers and the realities of the work world. The first place to go for information on and help with career exploration and planning is the Career Development Center. Besides helping you explore your personal career interests and abilities, this is your campus resource for learning about the nature of different careers and for strategies on locating career-related work experiences.

"To love what you do and feel that it matters—how could anything be more fun?"

—Katharine Graham, former CEO of the *Washington Post* and Pulitzer Prize-winning author

"Make your vocation your vacation."

—Mark Twain

Reflection 11.3

Project yourself 10 years into the future and visualize your ideal career and your ideal life.

1. What are you spending most of your time doing during your typical workday?

2. Where and with whom are you working?

3. How many hours are you working per week?

4. Where are you living?

5. Are you married? Do you have children?

6. How does your work influence your home life?

If you were to ask people to name as many careers as they could, they wouldn't come close to naming the 900 career titles listed by the federal government in its Occupational Information Network. Many of these careers you may have never heard of, yet some of them may be good career choices for you. You can learn more about the multitude of careers available to you in the following ways:

*   Reading about careers (in books or online)
*   Becoming involved in co-curricular programs on campus related to career development
*   Taking career development courses
*   Interviewing people in different career fields
*   Observing (shadowing) people at work in different careers
*   Volunteering or service learning
*   Part-time work (on or off campus)
*   Internships (paid or unpaid)
*   Co-op programs

There are many more career choices in today's work world than there were for our early ancestors.

Resources on Careers

Your Career Development Center and your College Library are campus resources where you can find a wealth of reading material on careers, either in print or online. Listed below are some of the best sources of written information on careers.

Dictionary of Occupational Titles (DOT) (www.occupationalinfo.org). This is the largest printed resource on careers; it contains concise definitions of more than 17,000 jobs. It also includes information on:

*   Work tasks typically performed by people in different careers
*   Background experiences of people working in different careers that qualified them for their positions
*   Types of knowledge, skills, and abilities that are required for different careers
*   Interests, values, and needs of individuals who find working in particular careers to be personally rewarding

Occupational Outlook Handbook (OOH) (www.bls.gov/oco). This is one of the most widely available and used resources on careers. It contains descriptions of approximately 250 positions, including information on the nature of work, work conditions, places of employment, training or education required for career entry and advancement, salaries, careers in related fields, and additional sources of information about particular careers (e.g., professional organizations and governmental agencies). A distinctive feature of this resource is that it contains information about the *future employment outlook* for different careers.

Encyclopedia of Careers and Vocational Guidance (Chicago: Ferguson Press). As the name suggests, this is an encyclopedia of information on qualifications, salaries, and advancement opportunities for a wide variety of careers.

Occupational Information Network (O*NET) Online (www.online.onetcenter. org). This is America's most comprehensive source of online information about careers. It contains an up-to-date set of descriptions for almost 1,000 careers, plus lots of other information similar to what you would find in print in the *Dictionary of Occupational Titles*.

In addition to these general sources of information, your Career Development Center and College Library should have other books and published materials related to specific careers or occupations (e.g., careers for English majors). You can also learn a lot about careers by simply reading advertisements for position openings in your local newspaper or online at such sites as www.careerbuilder.com and college. monster.com. When reading position descriptions, make special note of the tasks, duties, or responsibilities they involve and ask yourself whether these positions are compatible with your personal abilities, interests, needs, and values.

Career Planning and Development Programs

Periodically during the academic year, co-curricular programs devoted to career exploration and career preparation are likely to be offered on your campus. For example, the Career Development Center may sponsor career exploration or career planning workshops that you can attend for free. Research conducted on career development workshops indicates that they're effective in helping students plan for and choose careers (Brown & Krane, 2000; Hildenbrand & Gore, 2005). Your Career Center may also organize career fairs, at which professionals working in different career fields are given booths on campus where you can visit with them and ask questions about their careers.

Career Development Courses

Many colleges offer career development courses for elective credit. These courses typically include self-assessment of your career interests, information about different careers, and strategies for career preparation. You need to do career planning while you're enrolled in college, so why not do it by enrolling in a career development course that rewards you with college credit for doing it? Studies show that students who participate in career development courses benefit significantly from them (Pascarella & Terenzini, 2005).

It might also be possible for you to take an independent study course that will give you the opportunity to investigate issues in a career field you're considering. An independent study is a project that you work out with a faculty member, which usually involves writing a paper or detailed report. It allows you to receive academic credit for an in-depth study of a topic of your choice without having to enroll with other students in a traditional course that has regularly scheduled classroom meetings. You could use this independent study option to choose a project related to a career. To see whether this independent study option is available at your campus, check the college catalog or consult with an academic advisor.

You may be able to explore a career of interest to you in a writing or speech course that allows you to choose the topic that you'll write or speak about. If you can choose to research any topic, consider researching a career that interests you and make that the topic of your paper or presentation.

Information Interviews

One of the best and most overlooked ways to get accurate information about a career is to interview professionals working in that career. Career development specialists refer to this strategy as information interviewing. Don't assume that working professionals aren't interested in taking time to speak with a student; most are open to being interviewed and many report that they enjoy it (Crosby, 2002).

Information interviews provide you inside, realistic information about what careers are like because you're getting that information directly from the horse's mouth. The interview process also helps you gain experience and confidence in interview situations, which may help you prepare for future job interviews. Furthermore, if you make a good impression during information interviews, the people you interview may suggest that you contact them again after graduation to see if there are position openings. If there is an opening, you might find yourself being the interviewee instead of the interviewer (and you might find yourself a job).

Because interviews are a valuable source of information about careers and provide possible contacts for future employment, we strongly recommend that you complete the information interview assignment included at the end of this chapter.

Career Observation (Shadowing)

In addition to learning about careers from reading and interviews, you can experience careers more directly by placing yourself in workplace situations and work environments that allow you to observe workers performing their daily duties. Two college-sponsored programs may be available on your campus that will allow you to observe working professionals:

- **Job shadowing programs.** These programs enable you to follow (shadow) and observe a professional during a typical workday.
- **Externship programs.** These programs are basically an extended version of job shadowing that lasts for a longer time period (e.g., two or three days).

Visit your Career Development Center to learn about what job shadowing or externship programs may be available on your college campus. If you're unable to find any in a career field that interests you, consider finding one on your own by using strategies similar to those we recommend for information interviews at the end of this chapter. It's basically the same process; the only difference is that instead of asking the person for an interview, you're asking if you can observe that person at work. In fact, the same person who granted you an information interview may also be willing to be observed at work. Just one or two days of observation can give you some great information about a career.

Reflection **11.4**

If you were to observe or interview a working professional in a career that interests you, what position would that person hold?

Information interviewing, job shadowing, and externships can supply great information about a career. However, information is not experience. To get career-related work *experience*, you've got four major options:

- Internships
- Cooperative education programs
- Volunteer work or service learning
- Part-time work

Each of these options for gaining work experience is discussed below.

Internships

In contrast to job shadowing or externships, where you observe someone at work, an internship actively involves you in the work itself and gives you the opportunity to perform career-related work duties. A distinguishing feature of internships is that you can receive academic credit and sometimes financial compensation for the work you do. An internship usually totals 120 to 150 work hours, which may be completed at the same time you're enrolled in a full schedule of classes or when you're not taking classes (e.g., during summer term). A major advantage of internships is that they enable college students to avoid the classic catch-22 situation they often run into when interviewing for their first career positions after graduation. The interview scenario usually goes something like this: The potential employer asks the college graduate, "What work experience have you had in this field?" The recent graduate replies, "I haven't had any work experience because I've been a full-time student." You can avoid this scenario by completing an internship during your college experience. We strongly encourage you to participate in at least one internship while you're enrolled in college so you can beat the "no experience" rap after graduation and distinguish yourself from many other college graduates. Surveys show that more than three of every four employers prefer candidates with internships (National Association of Colleges & Employers, 2010), and students who have internships while in college are more likely to develop career-relevant work skills and find employment immediately after college graduation (Pascarella & Terenzini, 2005; Peter D. Hart Research Associates, 2006).

Internships are typically available to college students during their junior or senior year; however, some campuses offer internships for first- and second-year students. Check with your Career Center if this option may be available to you. You can also pursue internships on your own by consulting published guides that describe various career-related internships, along with information on how to apply for them (e.g., *Peterson's Internships* and the *Vault Guide to Top Internships*). Consider searching for internships on the Web as well (for example, go to www.internships.com or www.vaultreports.com). Information on internships may also be available from the local chamber of commerce in the town or city where your college is located or in your hometown.

"Give me a history major who has done internships and a business major who hasn't, and I'll hire the history major every time."

—William Ardery, senior vice president, Investor Communications Company

Cooperative Education (Co-op) Programs

A co-op program is similar to an internship but involves work experience that lasts longer than one academic term and often requires students to stop their coursework temporarily to participate in the program. However, some co-op programs allow you to continue to take classes while working part time at a co-op position; these are sometimes referred to as "parallel co-ops." Students are paid for participating in co-op programs but don't receive academic credit; however, their co-op experience is officially noted on their college transcript (Smith, 2005).

Typically, co-ops are only available to juniors or seniors, but you can begin now to explore co-op programs by reviewing your college catalog and visiting your Career Development Center to see whether your school offers co-op programs in career areas that may interest you. If you find one, build it into your long-range educational plan because it can provide you with authentic and extensive career-related work experience.

The value of co-ops and internships is strongly supported by research, which indicates that students who have these experiences during college are more likely to:

- Receive higher evaluations from employers who recruit them on campus
- Have less difficulty finding an initial position after graduation
- Be more satisfied with their first career position after college
- Report that their college education was relevant to their career (Gardner, 1991; Knouse, Tanner, & Harris, 1999; Pascarella & Terenzini, 1991, 2005).

In surveys that ask employers to rank various factors they considered important when hiring new college graduates, internships or cooperative education programs typically receive the highest ranking (National Association of Colleges & Employers, 2012a). Furthermore, employers report that when full-time positions open up in their organization or company, they usually turn first to their own interns and co-op students (National Association of Colleges & Employers, 2003).

Volunteer Work or Service Learning

Volunteering not only provides a service to your community: it also serves you by giving you the opportunity to explore different work environments and gain work experience in career fields that relate to your area of service. For example, volunteer work performed for different age groups (e.g., children, adolescents, or the elderly) and in different work environments (e.g., hospital, school, or laboratory) provides you with firsthand work experience and simultaneously allows you to test your interest in careers related to these age groups and work environments (To get an idea of the wide range of service opportunities that may be available to you, go to www.serve.gov).

Volunteer work also enables you to network with professionals outside of college who may serve as excellent references and resources for letters of recommendation for you. Furthermore, if these professionals are impressed with your volunteer work, they may become interested in hiring you part-time while you're still in college or full-time when you graduate.

It may be possible to do volunteer work on campus by serving as an informal teaching assistant or research assistant to a faculty member. Such experiences are particularly valuable for students intending to go to graduate school. If you have a good relationship with any faculty members who are working in an academic field that interests you, consider asking them whether they would like some assistance with their teaching or research responsibilities. You might also check out your professors' Web pages to find out what types of research projects they're working on; if any of these projects interest you or relate to a career path you're considering, contact the professor and offer your help. Volunteer work for a college professor could lead to making a presentation with your professor at a professional conference or even result in your name being included as a coauthor on an article published by the professor.

Volunteer work may also be available to you through college courses. Some courses may integrate volunteer service into the course as a required or optional assignment, where you participate in the volunteer experience and then reflect on it in a written paper or class presentation. When volunteer work is integrated into an academic course and involves reflection on the volunteer experience through writing or speaking, it's referred to as *service learning*.

Another course-integrated option for gaining work experience that may be available to you is to enroll in courses that include a *practicum* or *field work*. For instance, if you're interested in working with children, courses in child psychology or early childhood education may offer experiential learning opportunities in a preschool or daycare center on campus. Similarly, you could take a course in a field you may want to pursue as a career to enable you to get work experience in that field. For instance, taking a class in child psychology may help you get a part-time or summer job that involves working with children.

Reflection 11.5

Have you done volunteer work? If you have, did you learn anything about yourself or anything from your volunteer work that might help you identify careers that best match your interests, talents, and values?

Part-Time Work

Jobs that you hold during the academic year or during summer break should not be overlooked as potential sources of career information and as resume-building experience. Part-time work can provide opportunities to learn or develop skills that may be relevant to your future career, such as organizational skills, communication skills, and ability to work effectively with co-workers from diverse backgrounds and cultures.

It's also possible that work in a part-time position may eventually turn into a full-time career.

It might also be possible for you to obtain part-time work experience on campus through your school's work-study program. Work-study jobs can be done in a variety of campus settings (e.g., Financial Aid Office, Library, Public Relations Office, or Computer Services Center) and they typically allow you to build your employment schedule around your course schedule. On-campus work can provide you with valuable career exploration and resume-building experiences, and the professionals for whom you work can also serve as excellent references for letters of recommendation to future employers. To see whether you are eligible for your school's work-study program, visit the Financial Aid Office on your campus. If you're not eligible for work-study jobs, ask about other campus jobs that are not funded through the work-study program.

Learning about careers through firsthand experience in actual work settings (e.g., shadowing, internships, volunteer services, and part-time work) is critical to successful career exploration and preparation. You can take a career-interest test, or you can test your career interest through actual work experiences. There is simply no substitute for direct, hands-on experience for gaining knowledge about careers. These firsthand experiences represent the ultimate career reality test. They allow you direct access to information about what careers are like, as opposed to how they are portrayed on TV or in the movies, which often paint an inaccurate or unrealistic picture of careers and make them appear more exciting or glamorous than they are.

> **Remember**
>
> *One key characteristic of effective goal setting is to create goals that are realistic. In the case of careers, getting firsthand experience in actual work settings (e.g., shadowing, internships, volunteer services, and part-time work) allows you to get a much more realistic view of what work is like in certain careers, as opposed to the idealized or fantasized way they are portrayed on TV and in the movies.*

In summary, firsthand experiences in actual work settings equip you with five powerful career advantages that enable you to:

- Learn about what work is like in a particular field.
- Test your interest and skills for certain types of work.
- Strengthen your resume by adding experiential learning to academic (classroom) learning.
- Acquire contacts who may serve as personal references and sources for letters of recommendation.
- Network with employers who may hire you or refer you for a position after graduation.

Furthermore, gaining firsthand work experience early in college not only promotes your job prospects after graduation, but also makes you a more competitive candidate for internships and part-time positions that you may apply for during college.

Be sure to use your campus resources (e.g., the Career Development Center and Financial Aid Office), local resources (e.g., Chamber of Commerce), and your personal contacts (e.g., family and friends) to locate and participate in work experiences that relate to your career interests. When you land a work experience, work hard at it, learn as much as you can from it, and build relationships with as many people there as possible, because these are the people who can provide you with future contacts, references, and referrals. Research indicates that as many as 75 percent of all jobs are obtained through interpersonal relationships, i.e., "networking" (Brooks, 2009).

Step 3. Awareness of What Best Fits You

Effective decision making requires identifying all relevant factors that need to be considered and determining how much weight (influence) each of these factors should carry. As we've emphasized throughout this chapter, the factor that should carry the greatest weight in career decision making is the match between your career choice and your personal abilities, interests, needs, and values.

Reflection **11.6**

1. Have you had firsthand work experiences that may influence your future career plans?

2. If you could get firsthand work experience in any career field right now, what would it be?

A good career decision should involve more than salary and should take into consideration how the career will affect different dimensions of yourself (social, emotional, physical, etc.) at different stages of your future life: young adulthood, middle age, and late adulthood. It's almost inevitable that your career will affect your identity, the type of person you become, how you balance the demands of work and family, and how well you serve others beyond yourself. An effective career decision-making process requires you to make tough and thoughtful decisions about what matters most to you.

> **Remember**
>
> *A good career choice should bring you more than just personal wealth: it should also provide you with personal fulfillment.*

Reflection 11.7

Answer the following questions about a career you're considering or have chosen:

1. What attracted you to this career? (What led or caused you to become interested in it?)

2. Would you say that your interest in this career is characterized primarily by *intrinsic* motivation—something "inside" of you, such as your personal abilities, interests, needs, and values? Or, would you say that your interest in the career is driven by *extrinsic* motivation—something "outside" of you, such as starting salary, pleasing parents, or meeting expectations of your gender (i.e., an expected career role for a male or female)?

3. If money wasn't an issue and you could earn a comfortable living working in any career, would you choose the same career that you're currently considering?

Step 4. Awareness of the Process

Whether you're keeping your career options open or you think you've already decided on a particular career, you can start taking early steps for successful entry into any career by using the following strategies.

Self-Monitoring: Watching and Tracking Your Personal Skills and Positive Qualities

Don't forget that the learning skills you acquire in college become the earning skills in your career after college. It may appear that you're just developing *academic* skills, but you're also developing *career* skills. When you're engaged in the process of completing academic tasks (such as note-taking, reading, writing papers and taking tests), you're strengthening career-relevant skills (such as analysis, synthesis, communication, and problem solving).

The general education skills and qualities developed by the liberal arts component of your college education are critical to *career advancement* (your ability to move up the career ladder) and *career mobility* (your ability to move into different career paths). General educational skills enable workers to move into and take on different positions, which is important in today's work world. On average, Americans now change jobs 10 times by the time they're 40 years old (AAC&U, 2007). Specific technical skills are important for getting you into a particular career, but general educational skills enable you to move into different career and move up the career

"If you want to earn more, learn more."

—Tom Hopkins, internationally acclaimed trainer of business and sales professionals ladder. These skills are growing more important for college graduates entering the workforce in the 21st century because the demand for upper-level positions in management and leadership will exceed the supply of workers available to fill these positions (Herman, 2000). The courses you take as part of your general education will prepare you for advanced career positions, not just your first one (Boyer, 1987; Miller, 2003).

Students often think it's the final product (a college diploma) that provides them with the passport to a good job and career success (AAC&U, 2007; Sullivan, 1993). However, for most employers of college graduates, what matters much more than the credential are the skills and personal qualities the job applicant brings to the job (Education Commission of the States, 1995; Figler & Bolles, 2007). You can start building these skills and qualities through effective *self-monitoring*—by monitoring (watching) yourself and keeping track of the skills you're using and developing during your college experience. Skills are mental habits, and like all other habits that are repeatedly practiced, their development can be so gradual that you may not even notice how much growth is taking place—perhaps somewhat like watching grass grow. Thus, career development specialists recommend that you consciously reflect on the skills you're using so that you remain aware of them and are ready to "sell" them to potential employers (Lock, 2004).

The key to discovering career-relevant skills and positive personal qualities is to get in the habit of stepping back from your academic and out-of-class experiences to reflect on what skills and qualities these experiences involved and then get them down in writing before they slip your mind. One strategy you can use to track your developing skills is to keep a *career development journal* in which you note academic tasks and assignments you've completed, along with the skills you used to complete them. Also, don't forget to record skills in your journal that you've developed in non-academic situations, such as skills used while performing part-time jobs, personal hobbies, co-curricular activities, and volunteer services. Since skills are actions, it's best to record them as action verbs in your career development journal. You're likely to find that many personal skills you develop in college will be the same ones that employers will seek in the workforce. Do It Now! 11.2 contains a sample of important, action-oriented career skills that you're likely to develop during your college experience.

11.2   DO IT NOW

Personal Skills Relevant to Successful Career Performance

The following behaviors represent a sample of useful skills that are relevant to success in various careers (Figler & Bolles, 2007; Bolles, 1998). As you read these skills, underline or highlight any of them that you have performed, either inside or outside of school.

advising	creating	initiating	operating	resolving
assembling	delegating	measuring	planning	sorting
calculating	designing	mediating	presenting	summarizing
coaching	evaluating	motivating	producing	supervising
coordinating	explaining	negotiating	researching	synthesizing

In addition to tracking your developing skills, track the positive traits, attitudes, and attributes you may be developing. In contrast to skills, which are best recorded in a career journal as action verbs because they represent actions that you can perform for anyone who hires you, personal attributes are best recorded as adjectives because they describe who you are and what positive qualities you can bring to the job. Do It Now! 11.3 supplies an assortment of personal traits and qualities that are relevant to successful performance in any career.

11.3 DO IT NOW

Personal Traits and Qualities Relevant to Successful Career Performance

The following personal attributes are important for success in any career. As you read these traits, underline or highlight any of them that you feel you possess or will soon possess.

conscientious	energetic	loyal	positive	reflective
considerate	enthusiastic	observant	precise	sincere
courteous	ethical	open-minded	prepared	tactful
curious	flexible	outgoing	productive	team player
dependable	imaginative	patient	prudent	thorough
determined	industrious	persuasive	punctual	thoughtful

Reflection 11.8

Look back at the personal skills and traits listed in Do It Now! 11.2 and 11.3 that you noted you possess or will soon possess.

1. Are your personal skills and traits relevant to the career(s) that you're considering?

2. Do you see your skills and traits as being relevant to any other career(s) that you haven't yet considered?

Remember

Keeping track of your developing skills and positive qualities is as important to your successful entry into a future career as completing courses and compiling credits.

Self-Marketing: Packaging and Presenting Your Personal Strengths and Achievements

One way to help convert your college degree into gainful employment is to view yourself (a college graduate) as a product and future employers as customers who may be interested in purchasing your product (your skills and attributes). As a first-year student, it could be said that you're in the early stages of developing your product. Begin the process now of developing and packaging your skills and attributes so that by the time you graduate, you've developed into a high-quality product that potential employers will notice and be interested in purchasing.

An effective self-marketing plan is one that gives employers a clear idea of what you can bring to the table and do for them. You can effectively market or advertise your personal skills, qualities, and achievements to future employers through the following channels.

Course Transcript

Your course transcript is a listing of all courses you enrolled in and the grades you received in those courses. Two pieces of information included on your college transcript can strongly influence employers' hiring decisions or admissions committee decisions about your acceptance to a graduate or professional school: (1) the grades you earned in your courses and (2) the types of courses you completed.

Simply stated, the better grades you earn in college, the better are your employment prospects after college. Research on college graduates indicates that higher grades improve the following:

- The prestige of their first job
- Their total earnings (salary and fringe benefits)
- Their job mobility (ability to change jobs or positions).

This relationship between higher college grades and greater career success exists for students at all types of colleges and universities, regardless of the reputation or prestige of the institution they attend (Pascarella & Terenzini, 1991, 2005).

Co-curricular Experiences

Participation in student clubs, campus organizations, and other types of co-curricular activities is a valuable source of experiential learning that can complement classroom-based learning and contribute to your career preparation and development. A sizable body of research supports the power of co-curricular experiences for career success (Astin, 1993; Kuh, 1993; Pascarella & Terenzini, 1991, 2005; Peter D. Hart Research Associates, 2006). Get involved with co-curricular experiences on your campus, especially those that:

- Allow you to develop leadership and helping skills—e.g., leadership retreats, student government, college committees, peer counseling, or peer tutoring.
- Enable you to interact with others from diverse ethnic and racial groups—e.g., multicultural or international clubs and organizations.
- Provide you with out-of-class experiences related to your academic major or career interests—e.g., student clubs in your college major or intended career field.

Keep in mind that co-curricular experiences are also resume-building experiences that provide solid evidence of your commitment to the college community outside the classroom. Be sure to showcase these experiences to prospective employers. Also, don't forget that the campus professionals with whom you may interact while participating in co-curricular activities (e.g., the director of student activities or dean of students) can serve as valuable references for letters of recommendation to future employers or graduate and professional schools.

Personal Portfolio

You may have heard the word *portfolio* in reference to a collection of artwork that professional artists put together to showcase or advertise their artistic talents. However, a portfolio can be a collection of any materials or products that illustrate skills and talents or demonstrate educational and personal development. For example, a portfolio could include such items as:

- Outstanding papers, exam performances, research projects, or lab reports
- Artwork and photos from study abroad, service learning, or internship experiences
- Video footage of oral presentations or theatrical performances
- Recordings of musical performances
- Assessments from employers or coaches
- Letters of recognition or commendation

You can start the process of portfolio development right now by saving your best work and performances. Store them in a traditional portfolio folder, or save them on a computer disc to create an electronic portfolio. Another option would be to create a Web site and upload your materials there. Eventually, you'll be able to build a well-stocked portfolio that documents your skills and demonstrates your development to future employers or future schools. You can start to develop an electronic portfolio now by completing Exercise 11.2 at the end of this chapter.

Reflection 11.9

What do you predict will be your best work products in college—those that you're most likely to include in a portfolio?

Why?

The high school ritual of burning completed coursework is not recommended in college. Instead, save your best work, and include it in a personal portfolio.

Personal Resume

Unlike a portfolio, which contains actual products or samples of your work, a resume may be described as a listed summary of your most important accomplishments, skills, and credentials. If you have just graduated from high school, you may not have accumulated enough experiences to construct a fully developed resume. However, you can start to build a skeletal resume that contains major categories or headings (the skeleton) under which you'll eventually include your experiences and accomplishments, as well as skills you developed and problems you solved. (See Do It Now! 11.4 for a sample skeletal resume.) As you acquire experiences, you can flesh

11.4   DO IT NOW

Constructing a Resume

Use this skeletal resume as an outline or template for beginning construction of your own resume and for setting your future goals. (If you have already created a resume, use this template to identify and add categories that may be missing from your current one.)

NAME
(First, Middle, Last)

Current Addresses: Permanent Addresses:
Postal address   Postal address
E-mail address   E-mail address (be sure it's professional)
Phone number   Phone number

EDUCATION: Name of College or University, City, State
Degree Name (e.g., Bachelor of Science)
College Major (e.g., Accounting)
Graduation Date
GPA

RELATED WORK   Position Title, City, State   Start and stop dates
EXPERIENCES: (Begin the list with the most recent position
dates held.)

(List skills you used or developed.)

VOLUNTEER (COMMUNITY SERVICE) EXPERIENCES:
(List skills you used or developed.)

NOTABLE COURSEWORK
(e.g., leadership, interdisciplinary, or intercultural courses; study abroad experiences)

CO-CURRICULAR EXPERIENCES:
(e.g., student government or peer leadership)
(List skills you used or developed.)

PERSONAL SKILLS AND POSITIVE QUALITIES:
(List as bullets; be sure to include those that are especially relevant to the position for which you're applying.)

HONORS AND AWARDS:
(In addition to those received in college, you may include those received in high school.)

PERSONAL INTERESTS:
(Include special hobbies or talents that may not be directly tied to school or work experiences.)

out the resume's skeleton by gradually filling in its general categories with your skills, accomplishments, and credentials.

Letters of Recommendation (Letters of Reference)

Letters of recommendation can serve to support and document your skills and strengths. To maximize the power of your personal recommendations, give careful thought to (1) who should serve as your references, (2) how to approach them, and (3) what to provide them. Strategies for improving the quality of your letters of recommendation are suggested in Do It Now! 11.5.

11.5   DO IT **NOW**

The Art and Science of Requesting Letters of Recommendation: Effective Strategies and Common Courtesies

1. **Select recommendations from people who know you well.** Think about individuals with whom you've had an ongoing relationship, who know you by name, and who know about your personal strengths and skills (e.g., an instructor you've had for more than one class, an academic advisor whom you see often, or an employer with whom you've worked for an extended period).

2. **Seek a balanced blend of letters from people who have observed your performance in different settings or situations.** The following are settings in which you may have performed well and people who may have observed your performance in these settings:
   - The classroom—a professor who can speak to your academic performance
   - On campus—a student life professional who can comment on your contributions outside the classroom
   - Off campus—a professional for whom you've performed volunteer service, part-time work, or an internship

3. **Pick the right time and place to make your request.** Be sure to request your letter well in advance of the letter's deadline date (e.g., at least two weeks). First, ask the person if he or she is willing to write the letter, and come back at a later time with forms and envelopes. Don't approach the person with these materials in hand, because it may send the message that you've already assumed or presumed the person will automatically say "yes." This isn't the most socially sensitive message to send someone whom you're about to ask for a favor.

Also, pick a place and time where the person can give full attention to your request. For instance, make a personal visit to the person's office, rather than making the request in a busy hallway or in front of a classroom full of students.

4. **Waive your right to see the letter.** If the school or organization to which you're applying has a reference-letter form that asks whether or not you want to waive (give up) your right to see the letter, waive your right—as long as you feel reasonably certain that you will be receiving a good letter of recommendation. By waiving your right to see your letter of recommendation, you show confidence that the letter to be written about you will be positive, and you assure the person who reads the letter that you didn't inspect or screen it to make sure it was a good one before sending it.

5. **Provide your references with a fact sheet about yourself.** Include your experiences and achievements—both inside and outside the classroom. This will help make your references' job a little easier by providing points to focus on. More importantly, it will help you because your letter becomes more powerful when it contains concrete examples or illustrations of your positive qualities and accomplishments. On your fact sheet, be sure to include any exceptionally high grades you may have earned in certain courses, as well as volunteer services, leadership experiences, special awards or forms of recognition, and special interests or talents relevant to your academic major and career choice. Your fact sheet is the place and time for you to "toot your own horn," so don't be afraid of coming across as a braggart or egotist. You're not being conceited; you're just showcasing your strengths.

6. **Provide your references with a stamped, addressed envelope.** This is a simple courtesy that makes their job a little easier and demonstrates your social sensitivity.

(continued)

7. **Follow up with a thank-you note.** Send this note at about the time your letter of recommendation should be sent. This is the right thing to do because it shows your appreciation; it's also the smart thing to do, because if the letter hasn't been written yet, the thank-you note serves as a gentle reminder for your reference to write the letter.

8. **Let your references know the outcome of your application.** If you've been offered the position or been admitted to the school to which you applied, let those know who wrote letters on your behalf. This is the socially sensitive thing to do, and your references are likely to remember your social sensitivity, which is likely to strengthen the quality of future letters of recommendation they may write for you.

Reflection 11.10

Have you met a faculty member or other professional on campus who knows you well enough to write a letter of recommendation for you?

If yes, who is this person, and what position does he or she hold on campus?

Summary and Conclusion

In national surveys, employers rank attitude of the job applicant as the number one factor in making hiring decisions. They rate this higher in importance than such factors as reputation of the applicant's school, previous work experience, and recommendations of former employers (Education Commission of the States, 1995; Institute for Research on Higher Education, 1995; National Association of Colleges & Employers, 2012b). However, many college students think that it's the degree itself—the credential or piece of paper—that will get them the career they want (AAC&U, 2007).

Graduating from college with a diploma in hand may make you a more competitive job candidate, but you still have to compete by documenting and selling your strengths and skills. Your diploma doesn't work like a merit badge or passport that you flash to gain automatic access to your dream job. Your college experience opens career doors for you, but it's your attitude, initiative, and effort that enable you to step through those doors and into a successful career.

Your career success *after* college depends on what you do *during* college. Touching all the bases that lead to *college* success will also lead to *career* success:

1. **Get actively involved in the college experience**—get good grades in your classes and get work-related experiences outside the classroom.
2. **Use your campus resources**—capitalize on the career preparation and development opportunities that your Career Development Center has to offer.
3. **Interact and collaborate with others**—network with students in your major, college alumni, and career professionals.
4. **Take time for self-awareness and personal reflection**—deepen your self-awareness so that you choose a career path that's compatible with your personal interests, talents, values, and needs, and maintain awareness of your developing skills and personal qualities so that you can successfully "sell yourself" to future employers.

"Life just doesn't hand you things. You have to get out here and make things happen."

—Emeril Lagasse, award-winning American chef, cookbook author, and TV celebrity

Learning More through the World Wide Web

Internet-Based Resources for Further Information on Careers

For additional information related to the ideas discussed in this chapter, we recommend the following Web sites:

Assessing Your Strengths, Talents, and Values:

www.authentichappiness.sas.upenn.edu

www.viacharacter.org

Developing a Personalized Career Plan:

www.mappingyourfuture.org

Navigating the Job Market:

www.youmajoredinwhat.com

Career Descriptions and Future Employment Outlook:

www.bls.gov

Internships:

www.internships.com

www.vaultreports.com

Position Openings and Opportunities:

www.rileyguide.com

www.monster.com

Resume and Interview Resources:

www.quintcareers.com

11.1 Conducting an Information Interview

One of the best ways to acquire accurate information about a career that interests you is to interview a working professional in that career. This career exploration strategy is known as an *information interview*. An information interview enables you to (1) get an insider's view of what the career is really like, (2) network with a professional in the field, and (3) gain confidence in interview situations that prepares you for later future job interviews.

Steps in the Information Interview Process

1. Select a career that you may be interested in pursuing. Even if you're currently keeping your career options open, pick a career that might be a possibility. You can use the resources cited on pp. 284–285 in this chapter to help you identify a career that may be most appealing to you.

2. Find someone who is working in the career you selected and set up an information interview with that person. To locate possible interview candidates, consider members of your family, friends of your family members, and family members of your friends. Any of these people may be working in the career you selected and may be good interview candidates, or they may know others who could be good candidates. The Career Development Center on your campus and the Alumni Association (or the Rotaract Club) may also be able to connect you with graduates of your college, or professionals working in the local community near your college, who are willing to talk about their careers with students.

    The Yellow Pages or the Internet may also be used to locate names and contact information for interview candidates. Send candidates a short letter or e-mail asking about the possibility of scheduling a short interview, and mention that you would be willing to conduct the interview in person or by phone, whichever would be more convenient for them. If you don't hear back within a reasonable period (e.g., within a couple of weeks), send a follow-up message. If you don't receive a response to the follow-up message, then consider contacting someone else.

3. Conduct an information interview with the professional who has agreed to speak with you. Consider using the following suggested strategies.

Tips for Conducting Information Interviews

*   **Thank the person for taking the time to speak with you.** This should be the first thing you do after meeting the person—before you officially begin the interview.
*   **Prepare your interview questions in advance.** Here are some questions that you might consider asking:

1. During a typical day's work, what do you spend most of your time doing?

2. What do you like most about your career?

3. What are the most difficult or frustrating aspects of your career?

4. What personal skills or qualities do you see as being critical for success in your career?

5. How did you decide on your career?

6. What personal qualifications or prior experiences enabled you to enter your career?

7. How does someone find out about openings in your field?

8. What steps did you take to find your current position?

9. What advice would you give first-year students about what they might do at this stage of their college experience to help prepare them to enter your career?

10. How does someone advance in your career?

11. Are there any moral issues or ethical challenges that tend to arise in your career?

12. Are members of diverse groups likely to be found in your career? (This is an especially important question to ask if you're a member of an ethnic, racial, or gender group that is underrepresented in the career field.)

13. What impact does your career have on your home life or personal life outside of work?

14. **If you had to do it all over again, would you choose the same career?**

15. Would you recommend that I speak with anyone else to obtain additional information or a different perspective on this career field? (If the answer is "Yes," you may follow up by asking, "May I mention that you referred me?") It's always a good idea to obtain more than one person's perspective before making an important choice, especially one that can have a major influence on your life, such as your career choice.

• Take notes during the interview. This not only benefits you by helping you remember what was said, but also sends a positive message to the persons you interview because it shows them that their ideas are important and worth writing down.

Final Note: If the interview goes well, you might ask whether you could observe or shadow your interviewee during a day at work.

Self-Assessment Questions

After completing your interview, take a moment to reflect on it and answer the following questions:

1. What information did you receive that impressed you about this career?
2. What information did you receive that distressed (or depressed) you about this career?
3. **What was the most useful thing you learned from conducting this interview?**
4. Knowing what you know now, would you still be interested in pursuing this career? (If yes, why?) (If no, why not?)

11.2 Creating a Skeletal Resume

Review the headings of a skeletal resume described on p. 296.

1. Under each heading, list any experiences or skills that you've already acquired.

2. Return to each heading and add (in a different color) any experiences or skills you plan to acquire during your college experience.

3. Review your entries under each heading and identify any experiences or skills that may result in work products or artifacts that you can include in a personal portfolio. (See p. 295 for samples of work products that could be included in a portfolio.)

Career Choice: Conflict and Confusion

Josh is a first-year student whose family has made a great financial sacrifice to send him to college. He deeply appreciates the tremendous commitment his family members have made to his education and wants to pay them back as soon as possible. Consequently, he has been looking into careers that offer the highest starting salaries to college students immediately after graduation. Unfortunately, none of these careers seem to match Josh's natural abilities and personal interests, so he's conflicted, confused, and starting to get stressed out. He knows he'll have to make a decision soon because the careers with high starting salaries involve majors that have many course requirements, and if he expects to graduate in a reasonable period, he'll have to start taking some of these courses during his first year.

Reflection and Discussion Questions

1. If you were Josh, what would you do?

2. Do you see any way that Josh might balance his desire to pay back his family as soon as possible with his desire to pursue a career that's compatible with his interests and talents?

3. What other questions or factors do you think Josh should consider before making his decision?

Health and Wellness

Body, Mind, and Spirit

ACTIVATE YOUR THINKING   *Reflection* **12.1**

LEARNING GOAL

To acquire strategies for physical wellness that can be applied to promote success during the first year of college and beyond.

What would you say are the three most important things that college students could do to maintain their health and promote peak performance?

1.

2.

3.

What Is Wellness?

Wellness may be described as a state of high-quality health and personal well-being that promotes peak physical and mental performance.

There's still some debate about the exact number and nature of the components that define or comprise wellness (Miller & Foster, 2010; President's Council on Physical Fitness and Sports, 2001). However, the following key dimensions of holistic (whole-person) development provide a comprehensive foundation for achieving total wellness.

- **Physical.** Applying knowledge about how the human body functions to prevent disease, maintain wellness, and promote peak performance.
- **Intellectual (mental).** Acquiring knowledge; learning how to learn and how to think deeply and positively.
- **Social development.** Enhancing the quality and depth of interpersonal relationships.
- **Emotional development.** Strengthening skills for coping with, controlling, and expressing emotions.
- **Vocational (occupational) development.** Exploring career options, making career choices wisely, and developing skills needed for lifelong career success.
- **Ethical (character) development.** Acquiring a clear value system for guiding life choices and personal decisions, and developing consistency between moral convictions (beliefs) and moral commitments (actions).
- **Spiritual development.** Developing an appreciation for introspection and contemplation about the meaning or purpose of life and death, and a capacity for exploring ideas that transcend human life and the physical or material world.
- **Personal development.** Developing a coherent self-concept, personal identity, self-direction, and self-determination.

"To keep the body in good health is a duty, otherwise we shall not be able to keep our mind strong and clear."

—Buddha, founder of Buddhism

"Everyone is a house with four rooms: a physical, a mental, an emotional, and a spiritual. Most of us tend to live in one room most of the time but unless we go into every room every day, even if only to keep it aired, we are not complete."

—Native American proverb

As can be seen in Figure 12.1, these elements of self join together to form the spokes of the "wellness wheel." Development of all these elements is a primary goal of wellness and being a well-rounded person.

FIGURE 12.1

© Kendall Hunt

Components of the Wellness Wheel

The physical component of wellness is the primary focus of this chapter. It could be said that physical health is a necessary precondition or prerequisite that enables all other elements of wellness to be experienced. For instance, it's hard to develop intellectually and socially if you're not well physically, and it's hard to become wealthy and wise unless you're first healthy.

Physical wellness means more than simply avoiding illness or disease, nor is it something done in response or reaction to illness (e.g., getting well after being sick); instead, it's engaging in health-promoting behavior proactively to prevent illness from happening in the first place (Corbin, Pangrazi, & Franks, 2000). Wellness puts into practice two classic proverbs: "Prevention is the best medicine" and "An ounce of prevention is worth a pound of cure."

As depicted in Figure 12.2, there are three potential interception points for preventing illness, maintaining health, and promoting peak performance that range from the reactive (after illness) to proactive (before illness). Wellness goes beyond merely maintaining physical health to attaining a high quality of life that includes personal satisfaction, happiness, vitality (energy and vigor), and longevity (a longer life span).

FIGURE 12.2

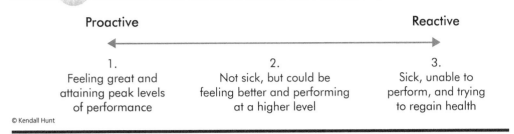

Proactive		Reactive

1.
Feeling great and
attaining peak levels
of performance

2.
Not sick, but could be
feeling better and performing
at a higher level

3.
Sick, unable to
perform, and trying
to regain health

© Kendall Hunt

Potential Points for Preventing Illness, Preserving Health, and Promoting Peak Performance

The Relevance of Wellness for Today's College Students

When students move directly from high school to college, and when they move from life at home to life on campus, they're moving toward taking personal responsibility for their wellness. Mom, Dad, and other family members are no longer around to monitor their health habits and to remind them about what to eat, what hours to keep, or when to go to sleep.

In addition to receiving less parental guidance and supervision, new college students are making a major life transition. When anyone undergoes significant change or experiences a major life transition, stress tends to increase. Unhealthy habits, such as eating poorly, further increase stress and moodiness (Khoshaba & Maddi, 2005). In contrast, maintaining good health habits is an effective stress-management strategy.

In the introduction to this book, we noted research that pointed to the advantages of the college experience. Among the advantages experienced by college graduates are that they lead physically healthier and longer lives and experience higher levels of psychological well-being (mental health) and personal happiness (life satisfaction). These findings show that students are learning something about wellness and how to promote it by the time they graduate from college. This chapter is designed to help you learn more about wellness at the very start of your college experience, so you can experience its benefits immediately and continually throughout your college years.

Reflection **12.2**

If you could single out one thing about your physical health that you'd like to improve or learn more about, what would it be?

Elements of Physical Wellness

A healthy physical lifestyle includes four elements:

1. Supplying the body with effective fuel (nutrition)
2. Transforming the fuel we consume into bodily energy (exercise)

3. Giving the body adequate rest (sleep) so that it can recover and replenish the energy it has expended
4. Avoiding risky substances (alcohol and drugs) and risky behaviors that can threaten our health and safety

Nutrition

Your body needs nutrients to replenish its natural biochemicals and repair its tissues. The food you put into your body supplies it with energy much like fuel does for a car. Just as high-quality gasoline can improve how well and how long your car runs, so can high-quality (nutritious) food improve the performance of your body and mind, allowing them to function at peak capacity. Unfortunately, however, people often pay more attention to the quality of fuel they put in their cars than to the quality of food they put into their bodies. Humans often eat without any intentional planning about what they eat. They eat at places where they can get access to food fast, where they can pick up food conveniently while they're on the go, and where they can consume it without having to step out of their cars (or get off their butts) to consume it. America has become a "fast-food nation," accustomed to consuming food that can be accessed quickly, conveniently, cheaply, and in large (super-sized) portions (Schlosser, 2005).

Studies show that the least nutritious and healthy foods are the very ones that receive the most media advertising, and the most frequently advertised food items that people are consuming in the largest quantities tend to be junk food—i.e., the food with the least nutrients, the most calories, and the highest health risks (Caroli, Argentieri, Cardone, & Masi, 2004; Hill, 2002). The advertising, availability, and convenience of high-calorie, low-cost food contribute to the fact that Americans today are heavier and have higher rates of obesity than at any other time in our nation's history.

National surveys of first-year college students indicate that less than 40 percent report that they maintain a healthy diet (Sax, Lindholm, Astin, Korn, & Mahoney, 2004). The phrase "freshman 15" is a popular term used to describe the 15-pound weight gain that some students experience during their first year of college. Research indicates that the average weight gain among first-year students is not nearly that high, but they still do put on weight during their first college year (Brody, 2003; Levitsky, Nussbaum, Halbmaier, & Mrdjenovic, 2003). Their weight gain may be temporary and is likely due to the initial transition to the college eating lifestyle (e.g., all-you-can-eat dining halls, late-night pizzas, and junk-food snacks). However, for other students, it may signal the start of a longer-lasting pattern of gaining and carrying excess weight. The disadvantage of being overweight isn't merely a matter of appearance: it's also a matter of health and survival because excess weight increases susceptibility to the leading life-threatening diseases, such as diabetes, heart disease, and certain forms of cancer.

Reflection **12.3**

Have your eating habits changed since you've begun college? If yes, in what ways have they changed?

We should eat in a thoughtful, nutritionally conscious way, rather than solely out of convenience, habit, or pursuit of what's most pleasant to our taste buds. We should also "eat to win" by eating the types of food that will best equip us to defeat disease and allow us to reach peak levels of physical and mental performance.

"May the sun bring you new energy by day; may the moon restore you by night. May the rain wash away your worries; may the breeze blow strength into your being. May you walk gently through the world and know its beauty all the days of your life."

—Apache Indian blessing

"Tell me what you eat and I'll tell you what you are."

—Anthelme Brillat-Savarin, French lawyer, gastronomist, and founder of the low-carbohydrate diet

"If we are what we eat, then I'm cheap, fast, and easy."

—Steven Wright, award-winning comedian

Chi mangia bene, vive bene. ("Who eats well, lives well.")

—Italian proverb

Snapshot Summary

12.1

Eating Disorders

While some students experience the "freshman 15," others experience eating disorders related to weight loss and loss of control of their eating habits. The disorders described in this box are more common among females largely because Western cultures place more emphasis and pressure on females than males to maintain lighter body weight and body size.

What follows is a short summary of the major eating disorders experienced by college students. These disorders are often accompanied by emotional issues (e.g., depression and anxiety) that are serious enough to require professional treatment. The earlier these disorders are identified and treated, the better the prognosis or probability of complete and permanent recovery. The Counseling Center and Student Health Center are the key campus resources where students can seek help and treatment for any of the following eating disorders.

Anorexia Nervosa

The self-esteem of people who experience anorexia nervosa disorder is often tied closely to their body weight or shape. They see themselves as overweight and have an intense fear of gaining weight, even though they're dangerously thin. Anorexics typically deny that they're severely underweight, and even if their weight drops to the point where they may look like walking skeletons, they may continue to be obsessed with losing weight, eating infrequently, and eating in extremely small portions. Anorexics may also use other methods to lose weight, such as compulsive exercise, diet pills, laxatives, diuretics, or enemas.

Bulimia Nervosa

The eating disorder known as bulimia nervosa is characterized by repeated episodes of binge eating—consuming excessive amounts of food within a limited period of time. Bulimics tend to lose all sense of self-control during their binges, then try to compensate for overeating by

engaging in behavior to purge their guilt and prevent weight gain. For example, they may purge by self-induced vomiting, consuming excessive amounts of laxatives or diuretics, using enemas, and fasting. The binge-purge pattern typically takes place at least twice a week and continues for three or more months.

Unlike anorexia, bulimia is harder to detect because bulimics' binges and purges take place secretly and their body weight looks about normal for their age and height. However, similar to anorexics, bulimics fear gaining weight, aren't happy with their bodies, and have an intense desire to lose weight.

Binge-Eating Disorder

Like bulimia, binge-eating disorder involves repeated, out-of-control binging on large quantities of food. However, unlike bulimics, binge eaters don't purge after binging episodes. For someone to be diagnosed as suffering from binge-eating disorder, that person must demonstrate at least three of the following symptoms, two or more times per week, for several months:

1. Eating more rapidly than normal
2. Eating until becoming uncomfortably full
3. Eating large amounts of food when not physically hungry
4. Eating alone because of embarrassment about others seeing how much they eat
5. Feeling guilty, disgusted, or depressed after overeating

Since individuals suffering from these eating disorders usually don't recognize or admit their illness, friends and family members play a key role in helping them receive help before the disorder progresses to a life-threatening level. If someone you know is experiencing an eating disorder, consult with a professional at the Student Health Center or Counseling Center about strategies for approaching and encouraging this person to seek help.

Student
Perspective

"I've had a friend who took pride in her ability to lose 30 lbs. in one summer because of not eating and working out excessively. I know girls that find pleasure in getting so ill that they throw up and can't eat because the illness causes them to lose weight."

—Comments written in a first-year student's journal

Nutrition-Management Strategies

The following nutrition-management strategies may be used to enhance your body's ability to stay well and perform well.

1. **Develop a nutrition management plan to ensure your diet has variety and balance.** Planning what you eat is essential to ensure you eat what's best for preserving health and promoting wellness. If you don't plan ahead to acquire the

food you should eat, you're more likely to eat food that can be accessed conveniently and doesn't require advanced preparation. Unfortunately, the types of foods that are readily available, easily accessible, and immediately consumable are usually fast food and packaged food, which are the least healthy foods. If you're serious about eating in a way that's best for your health and performance, you need to do some nutritional planning in advance.

Figure 12.3 depicts the MyPlate chart, which is the new version of the former Food Guide Pyramid and created by the United States Department of Agriculture (USDA). Since foods vary in terms of the nutrients they provide (carbohydrates, protein, and fat), no single food group can supply all the nutrients your body needs. Therefore, your diet should be balanced and include all of these food groups, but you should include them in different proportions or percentages. To find the daily amount of food you should be consuming from each of these major food groups (e.g., for your age and gender), go to www.choosemyplate.gov or www.cnpp.usda.gov/dietaryguidelines.htm. You can use these guidelines to create a dietary plan that ensures you consume each of these food groups every day, resulting in a balanced diet that minimizes your risk of experiencing any nutritional deficits or deficiencies. If this guide to nutrition is followed, there should be no need for you to take vitamins or dietary supplements.

FIGURE 12.3

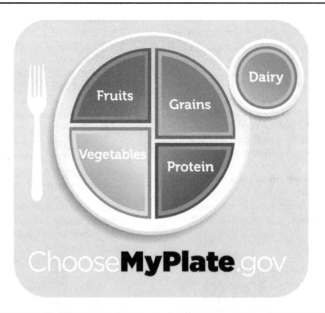

Source: USDA

MyPlate

 **12.4**

What types of junk food (if any) do you currently eat? Why?

If you do eat junk food, what's the likelihood that you'll continue to do so? Why?

2. **Maintain self-awareness of your eating habits.** A key step toward effective nutrition management is to become fully aware of your current eating habits. People often make decisions about what to eat without giving it much thought or

even without conscious awareness. You can increase awareness of your eating habits by simply taking a little time to read the labels on the food products before you put them into your shopping cart and into your body. Keeping a nutritional log or journal of what you eat in a typical week to track its nutrients and caloric content is also an effective way to become self-aware of your eating habits.

Another thing to be aware of is your family history. Are there members of your immediate and extended family who have shown tendencies toward heart disease, diabetes, or cancer? If so, intentionally adopt a diet that reduces your risk for developing the types of illnesses that you may have the genetic potential to develop. (For regularly updated information on dietary strategies for reducing the risk of common diseases, see the following Web site: fnic.nal.usda.gov/diet-and-disease.)

Reflection 12.5

Are you aware of any disease or illness that tends to run in your family?

If yes, are you aware of how you may decrease your risk of experiencing this disease or illness through your diet?

Exercise and Fitness

Wellness depends not only on fueling the body but also on moving it. The benefits of physical exercise for improving the longevity and quality of human life are simply extraordinary. Physical activity was something that our early ancestors did daily to stay alive. They had no motorized vehicles to move them from point A to point B, and no one sold or served them food. Exercise was part of their daily survival routine of roaming and rummaging for fruit, nuts, and vegetables, as well as running after and tracking down animals for meat to eat. Just as eating natural (unprocessed) food is better for your health because it's long been part of human history and has contributed to the survival of the human species, so too is exercise a "natural" health-promoting activity that has contributed to the survival of our species (Booth & Vyas, 2001). If done regularly, exercise may well be the most effective "medicine" available to humans for preventing disease and preserving lifelong health.

"If exercise could be packaged into a pill, it would be the single most widely prescribed and beneficial medicine in the nation."

—Robert N. Butler, former director of the National Institute of Aging

Benefits of Exercise for the Body

1. **Exercise promotes cardiovascular health.** Exercise makes for a healthy heart. The heart is a muscle, and like any other muscle in the body, its size and strength are increased by exercise. A bigger and stronger heart pumps more blood per beat, reducing the risk for heart disease and stroke (loss of oxygen to the brain) by increasing circulation of oxygen-carrying blood throughout the body and by increasing the body's ability to dissolve blood clots (Khoshaba & Maddi, 2005). Exercise further reduces the risk of cardiovascular disease by decreasing the level of triglycerides (clot-forming fats) in the blood, increasing the levels of "good" cholesterol (high-density lipoproteins), and preventing "bad" cholesterol (low-density lipoproteins) from sticking to and clogging up blood vessels.

2. **Exercise stimulates the immune system.** Exercise improves the functioning of the immune system, enabling you to better fight off infectious diseases (e.g., colds and the flu) for the following reasons:

- Exercise reduces stress, which normally weakens the immune system.
- Exercise increases breathing rate and blood flow throughout the body, which helps flush out germs from your system by increasing the circulation of antibodies carried through the bloodstream.
- Exercise increases body temperature, which helps kill germs—similar to how a low-grade fever kills germs when you're sick.

3. **Exercise strengthens muscles and bones.** Exercise reduces muscle tension, which helps prevent muscle strain and pain. For example, strengthening abdominal muscles reduces the risk of developing lower back pain. Exercise also maintains bone density and reduces the risk of osteoporosis (brittle bones that bend and break easily). It's noteworthy that bone density before age 20 affects a person's bone density for the remainder of life. Thus, engaging in regular exercise early in life pays long-term dividends by preventing bone deterioration throughout life.

Reflection **12.6**

Have your exercise habits changed (for better or worse) since you've begun college?

If yes, why do you think this change has taken place?

4. **Exercising promotes weight loss and weight management.** The increasing national trend toward weight gain is due not only to Americans consuming more calories but also to reduced levels of physical activity. Much of this reduction in physical activity results from the emergence of modern technological conveniences that have made it easier for humans to go about their daily business without exerting themselves in the slightest. For example, almost all TVs now come with remote controls so that you don't have to move to change channels, change volume, or turn the TV on and off. We now have video games galore that are played virtually so that we can have fun playing without getting up, running around, or jumping up and down. Consequently, people today are playing double jeopardy with their health by eating more and moving less.

Exercise is superior to dieting in one major respect: it raises the body's rate of metabolism (i.e., the rate at which consumed calories are burned as energy rather than stored as fat). In contrast, low-calorie dieting lowers the body's rate of metabolism (Leibel, Rosenbaum, & Hirsch, 1995) and the rate at which calories are burned. After two to three weeks of low-calorie dieting without exercising, the body saves more of the limited calories it's getting by storing them as fat. This happens because long-term low-calorie dieting makes the body "think" it's starving; therefore, it tries to compensate and increase its chances of survival by conserving more calories as fat so that they can be used for future energy (Bennet & Gurin, 1983). In contrast, exercise speeds up basal metabolism—the body's rate of metabolism when it's resting. So, in addition to burning fat directly while exercising, exercise burns fat by continuing to keep the body's metabolic rate higher after you stop exercising and move on to do more sedentary things.

Student
Perspective

"I'm less active now than before college because I'm having trouble learning how to manage my time."

—First-year student

Benefits of Exercise for the Mind

In addition to the multiple benefits of exercise for the body, it has numerous benefits for the mind. What follows is a summary of the powerful benefits of physical exercise for mental health and mental performance.

1. **Exercise increases mental energy and improves mental performance.** Have you ever noticed how red your face gets when you engage in strenuous physical activity? This rosy complexion occurs because physical activity pumps enormous amounts of blood into your head region, resulting in more oxygen reaching your brain. Exercise increases the heart's ability to pump blood throughout the body, and since the brain needs more oxygen to function at peak capacity than any other part of the body, it's the bodily organ that benefits most from exercise. Moreover, aerobic exercise, i.e., exercise that increases respiratory rate and circulates oxygen throughout the body, has been found to (1) enlarge the frontal lobe, the part of the brain responsible for higher-level thinking (Colcombe et al., 2006; Kramer & Erickson, 2007), and (2) increase the production of chemicals in the brain that create neurological connections between brain cells (Howard, 2000; Ratey, 2008). As noted in Chapter 5, these are the connections that provide the biological basis of learning and memory. Furthermore, exercise is a stimulant—it stimulates both the mind and the body. In fact, its stimulating effects are similar to those provided by popular energy drinks (e.g., Red Bull, Full Throttle, and Monster) but without the sugar, caffeine, and negative side effects, such as nervousness, irritability, increased blood pressure, and a crash (sharp drop in energy) after the stimulating effects of these drinks wear off (Malinauskas, Aeby, Overton, Carpenter-Aeby, & Barber-Heidal, 2007).

2. **Exercise elevates mood.** Exercise increases the release of endorphins (morphine-like chemicals found in the brain that produce a natural high) and serotonin (a mellowing brain chemical that reduces feelings of tension, anxiety, and depression). It is for these reasons that psychotherapists prescribe exercise for patients who are experiencing mild cases of anxiety and depression (Johnsgard, 2004). Studies show that people who exercise regularly report feeling happier (Myers, 1993).

3. **Exercise strengthens self-esteem.** Exercise can improve self-esteem by giving us a sense of personal achievement or accomplishment and by improving our physical self-image (e.g., improved weight control, body tone, and skin tone).

4. **Exercise deepens and enriches the quality of sleep.** Research on the effects of exercise on sleep indicates that exercise at least three hours before bedtime helps us fall asleep, stay asleep, and sleep more deeply (Singh, Clements, & Fiatarone, 1997). This is the reason why exercise is a common component of treatment programs for people seeking help with insomnia (Dement & Vaughan, 2000).

"It is exercise alone that supports the spirits, and keeps the mind in vigor."

—Marcus Cicero, ancient Roman orator and philosopher

Guidelines and Strategies for Maximizing the Effectiveness of Exercises

Specific types of exercises benefit the body and mind in different ways. Nevertheless, there are general guidelines and strategies that can be applied to improve the positive impact of any exercise routine or personal fitness program, such as those discussed below.

1. **Warm up before exercising and cool down after exercising.** Start with a 10-minute warm-up of low-intensity movements similar to the ones you'll be

using in the actual exercise. This increases circulation of blood to the muscles that you'll be exercising and reduces muscle soreness and your risk of muscle pulls. End your exercise routine with a 10-minute cool-down, during which you stretch the muscles that were strenuously used while exercising. Stretch the muscle until it burns a little bit, and then release it. Cooling down after exercise improves circulation to the exercised muscles and enables them to return more gradually to a tension-free state, which will minimize the risk of muscle tightness, cramps, pulls, or tears.

2. **Engage in cross-training to attain total body fitness.** A balanced, comprehensive fitness program is one that involves cross-training—a combination of different exercises to achieve overall bodily fitness. For instance, you can combine exercises that promote:
   - Endurance and weight control (e.g., running, cycling, or swimming);
   - Muscle strength and tone (e.g., weight training, push-ups, or sit-ups); and
   - Flexibility (e.g., yoga, Pilates, or tai chi).

   A total fitness plan also includes exercising various muscle groups on a rotational basis (e.g., upper-body muscles one day, lower-body muscles the next). This gives different sets of muscle tissue extra time to rest, repair, and recover before they're exercised again.

3. **Exercising with regularity and consistency is as important as exercising with intensity.** Doing exercise regularly, and allowing strength and stamina to increase gradually, is the key to attaining fitness and avoiding injury. One strategy you can use to be sure that you're training your body, rather than straining or overextending it, is to see whether you can talk while you're exercising. If you can't continue speaking without having to catch your breath, you may be overdoing it. Drop the intensity level and allow your body to adapt or adjust to a less strenuous level. After continuing at this lower level awhile, try again at the higher level while trying to talk simultaneously. If you can do both, then you're ready to continue at that level for some time. By continuing to use this strategy, you can gradually increase the intensity, frequency, or duration of your exercise routine to a level that produces maximum benefits with minimal post-exercise strain or pain.

4. **Take advantage of exercise and fitness resources on your campus.** You paid for use of the campus gym or recreation center with your college tuition, so take advantage of this and other exercise resources on campus. Also, consider taking physical education courses offered by your college. They count toward your college degree, and typically they carry one unit of credit so that they can be easily added to your course schedule. If exercise-related groups or clubs meet on campus, consider joining them; they can provide motivational support and convert your exercise routine from one that's done in isolation to one done in conjunction with others. (This is also a good way to meet and form friendships with other people.)

5. **Take advantage of natural opportunities for physical activity that present themselves during the day.** Exercise can take place outside a gym or fitness center and outside scheduled workout times. Opportunities for exercise often occur naturally as you go about your daily activities. For example, if you can walk or ride your bike to class, do that instead of driving a car or riding a bus. If you can climb some stairs instead of taking an elevator, take the route that requires more bodily activity and generates the most physical exercise.

Reflection 12.7

Do you have a regular exercise routine?

1. If not, why not?

2. If yes, what do you do and how often do you do it?

What more could you do to improve your:

1. Endurance?

2. Strength?

3. Flexibility?

Rest and Sleep

Sleep experts agree that humans in today's information-loaded, multitasking world aren't getting the quantity and quality of sleep needed to perform at peak levels (Mitler, Dinges, & Dement, 1994). We often underestimate the power of sleep and think we can cheat on sleep without compromising the quality of our lives. As discussed below, sleep has multiple benefits for the body and mind, which strongly suggest that good sleep habits are necessary for ensuring our physical and mental well-being.

The Value and Purpose of Sleep

Resting and reenergizing the body are the most obvious purposes of sleep (Dement & Vaughan, 1999). However, other benefits of sleep are less well known but equally important for physical and mental health (Dement & Vaughan, 2000; Horne, 1988). Some of these equally important, but less apparent benefits of sleep are described below.

1. **Sleep restores and preserves the power of the immune system.** Studies show that when humans and other animals lose sleep, it lowers their production of disease-fighting antibodies and make them more susceptible to illness, such as common colds and the flu.
2. **Sleep helps you cope with daily stress.** Sleep research shows that the amount of time we spend in dream sleep increases when we're experiencing stress. When we lose dream sleep, emotional problems such as anxiety and depression worsen (Voelker, 2004). It's thought that the biochemical changes that take place in our brain during dream sleep help to restore imbalances in brain chemistry that occur when we experience anxiety or depression. Getting quality sleep, especially dream sleep, is essential for recovering and maintaining our emotional stability and keeping us in a positive frame of mind. Indeed, research reveals that people who sleep better report feeling happier (Myers, 1993).
3. **Sleep helps the brain form and store memories.** Studies show that loss of dream sleep at night results in poorer memory for information learned earlier in the day (Peigneux, Laureys, Delbeuck, & Maquet, 2001). For instance, it's been found that adolescents who get minimal sleep have more difficulty retaining new information learned in school (Horne, 1988).

"Sleep deprivation is a major epidemic in our society. Americans spend so much time and energy chasing the American dream that they don't have much time left for actual dreaming."

—William Dement, pioneering sleep researcher and founder of the American Sleep Disorders Association

The Importance of Sleep for College Students

College students, in particular, tend to have poor sleep habits and experience more sleep problems. Heavier academic workloads, more opportunities for late-night socializing, and more frequent late-night (or all-night) study sessions often lead to more irregular sleep schedules and more sleep deprivation among college students.

How much sleep do you need and should you get? The answer lies in your genes and varies from person to person. On average, adults need seven to eight hours of sleep each day and teenagers need slightly more—about nine hours (Roffwarg, Muzio, & Dement, 1966). Studies show that college students get an average of less than seven hours of sleep each night (Hicks, as cited in Zimbardo, Johnson, & Weber, 2006), which means that they're not getting the amount of sleep needed for optimal academic performance.

Attempting to train your body to sleep less is likely to be an exercise in futility because you're trying to force your body to do something that it's not naturally (genetically) inclined or "wired up" to do. When your body is deprived of the amount of sleep it's genetically designed to receive, it accumulates "sleep debt," which, like financial debt, must be eventually paid back to your body at a later time (Dement & Vaughan, 1999). If your sleep debt isn't repaid, it catches up with you and you pay the price with lower energy, lower mood, poorer health, and poorer performance (Van Dongen, Maislin, Mullington, & Dinges, 2003). For example, the effects of sleep loss on automobile-driving performance are similar to the effects of drinking alcohol (Arnedt, Wilde, Munt, & MacLean, 2001; Fletcher, Lamond, Van Den Heuvel, & Dawson, 2003), and sleep-deprived students' academic performance is poorer than that of students who get sufficient sleep (Spinweber, as cited in Zimbardo et al., 2006).

Strategies for Improving Sleep Quality

Since sleep has powerful benefits for both the body and the mind, if you can improve the quality of your sleep, you can improve your physical and mental well-being. Listed here is a series of strategies for improving sleep quality that should also improve your health and performance.

Reflection 12.8

How much sleep per night do you think you need to perform at peak level?

How many nights per week do you typically get this amount of sleep?

If you're not getting this optimal amount of sleep each night, what's preventing you from getting it?

1. **Increase awareness of your sleep habits by keeping a sleep log or sleep journal.** Make note of what you did before going to bed on nights when you slept well or poorly. Tracking your sleep experiences in a journal may enable you to detect patterns that reveal relationships between certain things you do (or don't do) during the day and sleeping well at night. If you find such a pattern, you may have found yourself a routine you can follow to ensure that you consistently get a good night's sleep.

2. **Try to get into a regular sleep schedule by going to sleep and getting up at about the same time each day.** Irregular sleep schedules can disrupt the quality of sleep. This is what happens to people who experience jet lag. Traveling to a new time zone often requires travelers to change their sleep schedule to accommodate the time shift, which can disrupt the quality of their sleep. Your body likes to work on a biological rhythm of set cycles; if you can get your body on a regular sleep schedule, you're more likely to establish a biological rhythm that makes it easier for you to fall asleep, stay asleep, and wake up naturally from sleep according to your internal alarm clock.

   Establishing a stable sleep schedule is particularly important around midterms and finals. Unfortunately, these are the times during the term when students often disrupt their normal sleep patterns by cramming in last-minute studying, staying up later, getting up earlier, or not going to sleep at all. Sleep research shows that if you want to be at your physical and mental best for upcoming exams, you should get yourself on a regular sleep schedule of going to bed at about the same time and getting up at about the same time for at least one week before your exams (Dement & Vaughan, 1999).

3. **Attempt to get into a relaxing bedtime ritual each night.** Taking a hot bath or shower, consuming a hot (non-caffeinated) beverage, or listening to relaxing music are bedtime rituals that can get you into a worry-free state and help you fall asleep sooner. Making a list of things you intend to do the next day before going to bed may help you relax and fall asleep because you can go to bed with the peace of mind that comes from being organized and ready to handle the following day's tasks.

   Light reading or reviewing notes at bedtime might also be a good ritual to adopt because sleep helps you retain what you experienced just before going to sleep. Many years of studies show that the best thing you can do after attempting to learn something is to sleep on it, probably because your brain can then focus on processing it without interference from outside distractions (Jenkins & Dallenbach, 1924).

Student
Perspective

"I 'binge' sleep. I don't sleep often and then I hibernate for like a day or two."
—First-year student

Student
Perspective

"Something I noticed when playing guitar: I would play a song better the first time I tried to in the morning than the last time I played it before I went to bed. This made me think that my brain must be strengthening what I'd been learning while I was asleep."
—College sophomore

Reflection **12.9**

What do you do on most nights immediately before going to bed? Do you think this helps or hinders the quality of your sleep?

4. **Make sure the temperature of your sleep room is not too warm (no higher than 70 degrees Fahrenheit).** Warm temperatures often make people feel sleepy, but they usually don't help them stay asleep or sleep deeply. This is why people have trouble sleeping on hot summer evenings. High-quality, uninterrupted sleep is more likely to take place at cooler, more comfortable room temperatures (Coates, 1977).

5. **Avoid intense mental activity just before going to sleep.** Light mental work may serve as a relaxing pre-sleep ritual, but cramming intensely for a difficult exam or doing intensive writing before bedtime is likely to generate a state of mental arousal, which can interfere with your ability to wind down and fall asleep.

6. **Avoid intense physical exercise before going to sleep.** Physical exercise generates an increase in muscle tension and mental energy (by increasing oxygen flow to the brain), which energizes you and keeps you from falling asleep. If you're

going to exercise in the evening, it should be done at least three hours before bedtime (Hauri & Linde, 1996).

7. **Avoid consuming sleep-interfering foods, beverages, or drugs in the late afternoon or evening.** In particular, avoid the following substances near bedtime:

- **Caffeine.** It works as a stimulant drug for most people, so it's likely to stimulate your nervous system and keep you awake.
- **Nicotine.** This is a stimulant drug that's also likely to reduce the depth and quality of your sleep. (Note: Smoking hookah through a water pipe delivers the same amount of nicotine as a cigarette.)
- **Alcohol.** It's a drug that will make you feel sleepy in larger doses, but smaller doses can have a stimulating effect. Furthermore, alcohol in all doses disrupts the quality of sleep by reducing the amount of time you spend in dream-stage sleep. (Marijuana does the same.)
- **High-fat foods.** Eating anything right before bedtime isn't a good idea because the internal activity your body engages in to digest the food is likely to interfere with the quality of your sleep, but particularly peanuts, beans, fruits, raw vegetables, and high-fat snacks should be avoided because your stomach has to work hard to digest them; this extra internal and combustion (and noise) can interrupt or disrupt your sleep.

Remember

Substances that make you feel sleepy or cause you to fall asleep (e.g., alcohol and marijuana) reduce the overall quality of your sleep by interfering with dream sleep.

Wellness is built on a balanced foundation of nutrition, exercise, and rest.

Alcohol, Drugs, and Risky Behavior

In addition to putting healthy nutrients into your body, exercising it, and resting it, two other elements can help you maintain physical wellness: (1) keeping risky substances out of your body, and (2) keeping away from risky behaviors that jeopardize your body. New college students are often confronted with new choices to make about what risks to take, or not to take, during their first year of college.

Alcohol Use among College Students

In the United States, alcohol is a legal beverage (drug) for people 21 years of age and older. However, whether you're of legal age or not, it's likely that alcohol has already been available to you and will continue to be available to you when you're in college. Since it's a substance commonly accessible at college parties and social gatherings, you'll be confronted with two sets of decisions about alcohol:

1. To drink or not to drink,
2. To drink responsibly or irresponsibly—i.e., drinking to get drunk or escape problems.

If you decide to drink, here are some quick tips for drinking responsibly:

- Don't drink with the intention of getting intoxicated; set a limit about how much you will drink. (Use alcohol as a beverage, not as a mind-altering drug.)
- Drink slowly. (Sip, don't gulp, and avoid "shotgunning" or "chug-a-lugging" drinks.)
- Space out your drinks over time. (This gives your body time to metabolize the alcohol and keeps your blood alcohol level manageable.)
- Eat well before you drink and snack while you're drinking. (This will lower the peak blood alcohol level in your bloodstream.)

Naturally, the best way to avoid irresponsible drinking is to not to drink at all. This is the safest option, particularly if your family has a history of alcohol abuse. If you choose to drink, make sure that it's *your* choice, not a choice imposed on you through social pressure or the need to conform. Research indicates that first-year college students drink more than they did in high school and that alcohol abuse is higher among first-year college students than students at more advanced stages of their college experience (Bergen-Cico, 2000). The most common reason why first-year students drink is to "fit in" or to feel socially accepted (Meilman & Presley, 2005). However, college students overestimate the number of their peers who drink and the total amount they drink; this overestimation can lead them to believe that if they don't conform to this "norm," they're not "normal" (DeJong & Linkenback, 1999). Student beliefs that college partying and college drinking go hand in hand may also be exaggerated by media portrayals of college students as wild party animals. Popular magazines rank the "top party schools," television shows and movies depict female college students who've "gone wild," and popular movies have been made whose entire plots revolve around the drunken escapades of college students (*Animal House, Spring Break I, II,* etc.).

College students' expectations that they should drink (and drink to excess) account, at least in part, for the fact that the number one drug problem on college campuses is *binge drinking*—periodic drinking episodes during which a large amount of alcohol (four or five drinks) is consumed in a short period of time, resulting in an

FIGURE 12.4

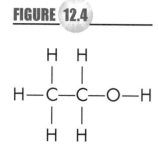

Ethyl Alcohol: The Mind-Altering Ingredient Contained in Alcohol

"If you drink, don't park. Accidents cause people."

—Steven Wright, American comedian

acute state of intoxication—i.e., a drunken state (Marczinski, Estee, & Grant, 2009). Although alcohol is a legal substance (if you're 21 or older) and it's consumed as a beverage rather than injected, smoked, or snorted, alcohol is still a mind-altering substance when consumed in large quantities (doses). Just as THC is the mind-altering ingredient in marijuana, ethyl alcohol is the mind-altering ingredient in beer, wine, and hard liquor (see Figure 12.4).

Also, like any other drug, alcohol abuse is a form of drug abuse. Approximately 7 to 8 percent of people who drink develop alcohol addiction or dependency, i.e., alcoholism (Julien, 2004). Although binge drinking may not be alcoholism, it's still a form of alcohol abuse because it has direct, negative effects on the drinker's:

- Behavior—e.g., drunk driving accidents and deaths,
- Body—e.g., acute alcohol withdrawal syndrome, better known as a hangover, and
- Mind—e.g., memory loss ("blackouts").

Research indicates that repeatedly getting drunk can reduce the size and effectiveness of the part of the brain involved with memory formation (Brown, Tapert, Granholm, & Delis, 2000), which has led some researchers to the conclusion that the more often a person gets drunk, the dumber that person gets (Weschsler & Wuethrich, 2002).

Furthermore, binge drinking can have indirect negative effects on health and safety by reducing the drinker's inhibitions about engaging in risk-taking behavior, which, in turn, increases the risk of personal accidents, injuries, and illnesses. Arguably, no other drug reduces a person's inhibitions as dramatically as alcohol. After consuming a significant amount of alcohol, people can become much less cautious about doing things they normally wouldn't do. This chemically induced sense of courage (sometimes referred to as "liquid courage") can override the process of logical thinking and decision making, increasing the drinker's willingness to engage in irrational risk-taking behavior. Typically, binge drinkers become less inhibited about engaging in reckless driving, increasing the risk of accidental injury or death, and less cautious about engaging in reckless (unprotected) sex, increasing the risk of accidental pregnancy or contracting sexually transmitted infections (STIs). It could be said that binge drinkers think they've become invincible, immortal, and infertile.

It's noteworthy that the legal age for consuming alcohol was once lowered to 18 years; it was raised back to 21 because the number of drunk-driving accidents and deaths among teenage drinkers increased dramatically when the legal age was lowered. Traffic accidents still account for more deaths of Americans between the ages of 15 and 24 than any other single cause.

When teenagers gain independence and acquire their first taste of new freedoms, they often take the newfound freedom beyond moderation and push it to the outer limits—for example, driving as fast as they can and drinking as much as they can—perhaps to prove to themselves and others how much freedom they now have. It's as if the more risks they take with their new freedom, the more of it they think they have. In the case of freedom to drink and freedom to drive, they can be a dangerous (or deadly) combination.

Since alcohol is a depressant drug, it depresses (slows) the nervous system. This can increase the probability of aggressive and sexual behavior by slowing signals normally sent from the upper, front part of the brain (the "human brain") that's responsible for rational thinking and inhibits or controls the lower, middle part of the brain (the "animal brain") that is responsible for basic animal drives, such as sex and aggression (see Figure 12.5). When the upper (rational) brain's messages are slowed by alcohol, the animal brain is freed from the signals that normally restrain or inhibit it, allowing its basic drives to be released or expressed. Thus, the less inhibited drinker is more likely to engage in aggressive or sexual behavior.

Reflection 12.10

During the Prohibition years (1920–1933), laws were passed in America that made alcohol illegal for anyone to consume at any age.

Why do you think prohibition laws were passed?

Why do you think alcohol still continued to be produced illegally during the Prohibition era (as bootleg liquor) and that prohibition laws were eventually eliminated?

FIGURE 12.5

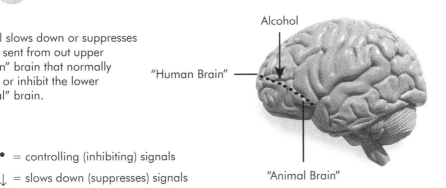

Alcohol slows down or suppresses signals sent from out upper "human" brain that normally control or inhibit the lower "animal" brain.

Alcohol

"Human Brain"

"Animal Brain"

•••••• = controlling (inhibiting) signals

↓ = slows down (suppresses) signals

Modified brain image © David Huntley, 2013. Under license from Shutterstock, Inc

How Alcohol Works in the Brain to Reduce Personal Inhibitions

The Connection between Alcohol and Aggressive Behaviors

This is the underlying biological reason why excessive alcohol use increases the risk of aggressive behaviors, such as fighting, damaging property, sexual harassment, assault, and abuse (Abbey, 2002; Bushman & Cooper, 1990).

Unhealthy Relationships

When a relationship becomes unhealthy, there are often clear warning signs telling you it's time to end things for your own well-being. If you are feeling disrespected or controlled, or you are concerned for your safety, it's essential that you acknowledge and act upon these signals. Relationship violence—whether emotional, psychological, physical, or sexual—is *never* appropriate or acceptable. Neither is it an effective means for dealing with a dating conflict. If you are in such a situation, or you have a friend who is, addressing the violence immediately is of primary importance. (See Snapshot Summary 12.2 for a list of the major types of sexual abuse and violence.)

Sometimes victims and perpetrators don't recognize that they are in fact in a violent relationship because they don't identify the behaviors as abusive. Behaviors that characterize relationship violence include, but are not limited to, degrading language, dominating or dictating a partner's actions, and physical and/or sexual assault. Without such recognition, victims and perpetrators are likely to remain in their current relationships or have relationships that are more violent in the future (Miller, 2011).

Unfortunately, this type of violence is highly common among college-aged women and men. In fact, recent studies have reported that 13 to 42 percent of college students have experienced and/or perpetrated physical relationship violence (Beyers, Leonard, Mays, & Rosen, 2000; Luthra & Gidycz, 2006; Miller, 2011; Perry & Fromuth, 2005; Shook, Gerrity, Jurich, & Segrist, 2000). In another study, 88 percent of females and 81 percent of males reported being victims and/or perpetrators of psychological and/or emotional relationship violence (White & Koss, 1991). Also important to note is that relationship violence occurs among all segments of the college-aged population. When looking at the demographics of victims and perpetrators, studies show comparable rates among men and women and among members of all races, ethnicities, and socioeconomic groups (Malik, Sorenson, & Aneshensel, 1997). Comparable levels of occurrence have also been found among victims and perpetrators who are gay, bisexual, and straight (Freedner, Freed, Yang, & Austin, 2002). Taken together, these data highlight the unfortunate fact that relationship violence is all too common. Furthermore, they emphasize the need for such cases to be stopped before they escalate to even more dangerous levels.

Since victims of relationship violence often experience distress, and perhaps even trauma, it is critical that they seek help. Victims tend to be reluctant to do so, however, for fear of embarrassment or retribution. If you find yourself in a violent relationship, it is important that you tell someone what is going on and get support. Don't let fear immobilize you. Talking to a trusted friend who has your health and safety in mind is a good place to start. Also, connecting with your college's Counseling Center is especially helpful so that you can get the trained assistance you might need. Counseling Centers are often staffed with professionals who have experience working with victims—and perpetrators—of relationship violence and will explain to you your rights as a victim. If the center on your campus is not staffed with such experienced professionals, they are likely to help connect you to a center in your community that is.

Snapshot Summary

12.2   Sexual Abuse and Violence

This list explains various forms of abuse and violence experienced by both men and women. Note that these examples are not just physical or sexual in nature—emotional and psychological violence can be just as harmful to victims.

Sexual Harassment

Sexual harassment in college includes any unwanted and unwelcome sexual behavior that significantly interferes with a student's access to education opportunities, whether it's committed by a peer or an employee of the college. Harassment can take the following forms:

1. Verbal—e.g., making sexual comments about someone's body or clothes, sexual jokes, or teasing (which includes spreading sexual rumors about a person's sexual activity or orientation, or requesting sexual favors in exchange for a better grade, job, or promotion)

2. Nonverbal—e.g., staring or glaring at someone's body; making erotic or obscene gestures at the person; sending unsolicited pornographic material or obscene messages

3. Physical—e.g., contact by touching, grabbing, pinching, or brushing up against someone's body

Recommendations for dealing with sexual harassment:

- Make your objections clear and firm. Tell the harasser directly that you are offended by the unwanted behavior and you know it constitutes sexual harassment.
- Keep a written record of any harassment. Record the date, place, and specific details about the harassing behavior.
- Become aware of the sexual harassment policy at your school. (Your school's policy is likely to be found in the *Student Handbook* or may be available from the Office of Human Resources on campus.)
- If you're unsure about whether you are experiencing sexual harassment, or what to do about it, seek help from the Counseling Center or Office of Human Resources.

Sexual Assault (a.k.a. Sexual Violence)

Sexual assault refers to nonconsensual (unwanted or unwilling) sexual contact, which includes rape, attempted rape, and any other type of sexual contact that a person forces on another person without their consent. *Rape* is an extreme form of sexual assault or sexual violence that involves forced sexual penetration (intercourse), which takes place through physical force, by threat of bodily harm, or when the victim is incapable of giving consent due to alcohol or drug intoxication. Rape takes place in two major forms:

1. Stranger rape—when a total stranger
2. forces sexual intercourse on the victim.

Acquaintance rape or date rape—when the victim knows, or is dating, the person who forces unwanted sexual intercourse. It's estimated that about 85 percent of reported rapes are committed by an acquaintance. Alcohol is frequently associated with acquaintance rapes because it lowers rapists' inhibitions and reduces victims' ability to judge whether they are in a potentially dangerous situation. Since the victim is familiar with the offender, she or he may feel at fault or conclude that what happened is not sexual assault. The bottom line: Even though the partners know each other, acquaintance rape is still rape and still a crime because it's nonconsensual sex.

Recommendations for women to reduce the risk of experiencing sexual assault:

- Don't drink to excess or associate with others who drink to excess.

- Go to parties with at least one friend so you can keep an eye out for each other.
- Clearly and assertively communicate your sexual limits. Use "I messages" to firmly resist unwanted sexual advances by rejecting the behavior rather than the person (e.g., "I'm not comfortable with your touching me like that").
- Remain mindful of the difference between lust and love. If you just met someone who makes sexual advances toward you, that person lusts for you but doesn't love you.
- Take a self-defense class.
- Carry Mace or pepper spray.

Recommendations for men for reducing the risk of committing sexual assault:

- Don't assume a woman wants to have sex just because she's:
    a. Very friendly or flirtatious,
    b. Dressed in a provocative way, or
    c. Drinking alcohol.
- If a woman says no, don't interpret that to mean she's really saying yes.
- Don't think that just because you're "the man," you have to be the sexual initiator or aggressor.
- Don't interpret sexual rejection as personal rejection or a blow to masculinity.

Note: Title IX of the Education Amendment of 1972 is a federal civil rights law that prohibits discrimination on the basis of sex, which includes sexual harassment, rape, and sexual assault. A college or university may be held legally responsible when it knows about and ignores sexual harassment or assault in its programs or activities, whether the harassment is committed by a faculty member, staff, or a student. If you have been sexually harassed and believe that your campus has not responded effectively to your concern, you can contact or file a complaint with the Department of Education's Office of Civil Rights (http://www2.ed.gov/about/offices/list/ocr/complaintprocess.html).

Abusive Relationships

An abusive relationship may be defined as one in which one partner abuses the other—physically, verbally, or emotionally. Abusers are often dependent on their partners for their sense of self-worth; they commonly have low self-esteem and fear their partners will abandon them, so they attempt to prevent this abandonment by over-controlling their partners. Frequently, abusers feel powerless or weak in other areas of their lives and overcompensate by attempting to gain and exert power and personal strength over their partners.

Potential Signs of Abuse	Strategies for Avoiding or Escaping Abusive Relationships
• Abuser is possessive and tries to dominate or control all aspects of the partner's life (e.g., discourages the partner from having contact with friends or family members) • Abuser frequently yells, shouts, intimidates, or makes physical threats toward the partner • Abuser constantly puts down the partner and damages the partner's self-esteem • Abuser displays intense and irrational jealousy (e.g., accusing the partner of infidelity without evidence) • Abuser demands affection or sex when the partner is not interested • Abuser often appears charming to others in public settings, but is abusive toward the partner in private • The abused partner behaves differently and is more inhibited when the abuser is around • The abused partner fears the abuser	• Avoid relationship isolation by continuing to maintain social ties with friends outside of the relationship • Don't make excuses for or rationalize the abuser's behavior (e.g., he was under stress or he was drinking) • Get an objective third-party perspective by asking close friends for their views on your relationship (love can be "blind," so it's possible to be in denial about an abusive relationship and not see what's really going on) • Speak with a professional counselor on campus to help you see your relationships more objectively and help you cope or escape from any relationship that you sense is becoming abusive

Illegal Drugs

In addition to alcohol, other substances are likely to be encountered on college campuses that are illegal for anyone to use at any age. Among the most commonly used illegal drugs are the following:

- **Marijuana (weed, pot).** Primarily a depressant or sedative drug that slows the nervous system and produces a mellow feeling of relaxation
- **Ecstasy (X).** A stimulant typically taken in pill form that speeds up the nervous system and reduces social inhibitions
- **Cocaine (coke, crack).** A stimulant that's typically snorted or smoked and produces a strong rush of euphoria
- **Amphetamines (speed, meth).** A strong stimulant that increases energy and general arousal; it is usually taken in pill form but may also be smoked or injected
- **Hallucinogens (psychedelics).** Drugs that alter or distort perception and are typically swallowed—e.g., LSD or acid and hallucinogenic mushrooms ("shrooms")
- **Narcotics (e.g., heroin and prescription pain pills).** Depressant or sedative drugs that slow the nervous system and produce feelings of relaxation (heroin is a particularly powerful narcotic that can be injected or smoked and produces an intense rush of euphoria)
- **Date-rape drugs.** Depressant (sedative) drugs that induce sleepiness, memory loss, and possible loss of consciousness, of which the most common are Rohypnol ("roofies") and GHB ("liquid E"); they are typically colorless, tasteless, and odorless, so they can be easily mixed into a drink without the drinker noticing and render the drinker vulnerable to rape or other forms of sexual assault

All of these drugs are potentially habit-forming, especially if they're injected in-travenously (directly into a vein) or smoked (inhaled through the lungs). These routes of drug delivery are particularly dangerous because they allow the drug to reach the brain faster and with more intense impact, resulting in the drug's effect being experienced more rapidly and at a higher peak effect. However, this is followed by a rapid and sharp drop (crash) after the drug's peak effect has been experienced (see Figure 12.6). This peak-to-valley, roller-coaster effect creates a greater risk for craving and desire to use the drug again, thereby increasing the user's risk of depen-dency (addiction).

When a drug is smoked (or injected), it reaches the brain faster and produces a higher peak effect, followed by a sharper drop or "crash," which increases the risk of addiction.

FIGURE 12.6

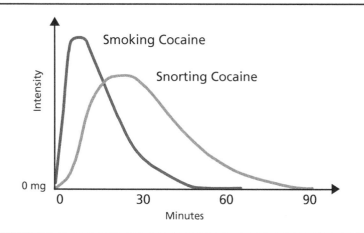

Drugs Smoked Produce a Higher and More Rapid Peak Effect

Listed here are common signs that use of any drug (including alcohol) is moving in the direction of *dependency* (*addiction*):

- Steadily using more of the drug and/or using it more often
- Difficulty cutting back (e.g., unable to use the drug less frequently or in smaller amounts)
- Difficulty controlling or limiting the amount taken after starting
- Keeping a steady supply of the drug on hand
- Spending more on the drug than you can afford
- Using the drug alone
- Hiding or hoarding the drug
- Lying about your drug use to family and friends
- Reacting angrily or defensively when questioned about drug use
- Being in denial about abusing the drug (e.g., "I don't have a problem")
- Rationalizing drug abuse (e.g., "It's no big deal; it's just part of the college experience")
- Continuing to use the drug matters more to you than the personal and interper-sonal problems caused by its use

Addiction is one major motive for repeated use of any drug. However, there are other motives underlying the desire to do drugs. A summary of the major motives for drug use is provided in Snapshot Summary 12.3.

Snapshot Summary

12.3   Drug Use among College Students: Common Causes and Major Motives

1. **Social pressure.** To fit in or be socially accepted (e.g., smoking marijuana because lots of college students seem to be doing it).
2. **Recreational (party) use.** For fun, stimulation, or pleasure (e.g., drinking alcohol at parties to loosen inhibitions and to have a good time).
3. **Experimental use.** Doing drugs out of curiosity—to test out their effects (e.g., experimenting with LSD to see what it's like to have a psychedelic or hallucinogenic experience).
4. **Therapeutic use.** Using prescription or over-the-counter drugs for medical purposes (e.g., taking Prozac for depression or Ritalin to treat attention deficit disorder).
5. **Performance enhancement.** To improve physical or mental performance (e.g., taking steroids to improve athletic performance or stimulants to stay awake all night and cram for an exam).
6. **Escapism.** To temporarily escape a personal problem or an unpleasant emotional state (e.g., taking ecstasy to escape depression or boredom).
7. **Addiction.** Physical or psychological dependence resulting from habitual use of a drug (e.g., continuing to use nicotine or cocaine because stopping will result in withdrawal symptoms such as anxiety or depression).

Student Perspective

"For fun." "To party." "To fit in." "To become more talkative, outgoing, and flirtatious."

"To try anything once." "To become numb." "To forget problems." "Being bored."

—Responses of freshmen and sophomores to the question "Why do college students take drugs?"

Reflection 12.11

What drugs (if any) have you seen being used on your campus?

How would the types and frequency of drug use on your campus compare to what you saw in high school?

What motives for drug use listed in Snapshot Summary 12.3 would you say are the most common reasons for drug use on your campus?

Strategies for Minimizing or Eliminating the Negative Effects of Alcohol and Other Drugs

1. **Don't let yourself be pressured into drinking.** Keep in mind that college students tend to overestimate how much their peers drink, so don't feel you're uncool, unusual, or abnormal if you prefer not to drink.

2. **If you drink, maintain awareness of how much you're drinking while you're drinking by monitoring your physical and mental state.** Don't continue to drink after you've reached a state of moderate relaxation or a mild loss of inhibition. Drinking to the point where you're drunk or bordering on intoxication doesn't improve your physical health or your social life. You're not exactly the life of the party if you're slurring your speech, vomiting in the restroom, nodding out, or on the verge of falling sound asleep.

   The key to drinking responsibly and in moderation is to have a plan for managing your drinking. Your plan should include strategies such as:
   - Drinking slowly,
   - Eating while drinking,
   - Alternating between drinking alcoholic and nonalcoholic beverages, and
   - Tapering off your drinking after the first hour of a party or social gathering.

   Lastly, don't forget that alcohol is costly, both in money and in calories. Thus, reducing or eliminating your drinking is not only a good way to manage your health, but also a good money-management and weight-management strategy.

3. **If you're a woman who drinks, or who frequents places where others drink, remain aware of the possibility of date-rape drugs being dropped into your drink.** Drugs such as gamma-hydroxybutyric acid (a.k.a. GHB or G) and Rohypnol (a.k.a. roofies or roaches) induce sleep and memory loss, and their effects are particularly powerful when taken with alcohol. To guard against this risk, don't let others give you drinks, and hold onto your drink at all times (e.g., don't leave it, go to the restroom, and come back to drink it again).

4. **If you find yourself in a situation where an illegal drug is available to you, our bottom-line recommendation is this: If you're in doubt, keep it out—don't put anything into your body that you're unsure about.** We acknowledge that the college years are a time for exploring and experimenting with different ideas,

There are safer and more productive ways to blow your mind than using mind-altering substances.

experiences, feelings, and states of consciousness. However, doing illegal drugs just isn't worth the risk. Even if you're aware of how an illegal drug affects people in general, you don't know how it will affect you in particular, because each individual has a unique genetic makeup. Furthermore, unlike legal drugs that have to pass through rigorous testing by the Food and Drug Administration before they're approved for public consumption, you can't be sure how an illegal drug has been produced and packaged from one time to the next, and you don't know if it may have been "cut" (mixed) with other substances during the production process. Thus, you're not just taking a criminal risk by using a drug that's illegal: you're also taking a health risk by consuming an unregulated substance whose effects on your body and mind are likely to be more unpredictable and potentially detrimental.

Minimize Your Risk of Contracting Sexually Transmitted Infections (STIs)

STIs are a group of contagious infections that are spread through sexual contact. Latex condoms provide the best protection against STIs (Holmes, Levine, & Weaver, 2004). You can also reduce your risk of contracting an STI by having sex with fewer partners. Naturally, not engaging in sexual intercourse is the most foolproof way to eliminate the risk of an STI (and unwanted pregnancy). When it comes to sexual intercourse, you've got three basic options: do it recklessly, do it safely, or just don't do it. If you choose the last option (abstinence), it doesn't mean you're an unaffectionate prude. It simply means that you're electing not to have sexual intercourse at this particular time in your life.

More than 25 types of STIs have been identified, and virtually all of them are effectively treated if detected early. However, if they're ignored, some STIs can progress to the point where they result in infection and possibly infertility (Cates, Herndon, Schulz, & Darroch, 2004). Pain during or after urination or unusual discharge from the penis or vaginal areas are often the early signs of an STI. However, sometimes the symptoms can be subtle and undetectable; if you have any doubt, play it safe and check it out immediately by visiting the Health Center on your campus. Any advice or treatment you receive there will remain confidential. If you happen to contract a form of STI, immediately inform anyone you've had sex with, so that he or she may receive early treatment before the disease progresses. This isn't just the polite thing to do: it's the right (ethical) thing to do.

Summary and Conclusion

Research findings and advice from professionals indicate that physical wellness is most effectively promoted if we adopt the following strategies with respect to our bodies:

- **Pay more attention to nutrition.** In particular, we should increase consumption of natural fruits, vegetables, legumes, whole grains, fish, and water and decrease consumption of processed, fatty, and fried foods. Although the expression "you are what you eat" may be a bit of an exaggeration, it contains a kernel of truth because the food we consume does influence our health, our emotions, and our performance.

- **Become more physically active.** To counteract the sedentary lifestyle created by life in modern society and to attain total fitness, we should engage in a balanced blend of exercises that build stamina, strength, and flexibility.
- **Don't cheat on sleep.** Humans typically do not get enough sleep to perform at their highest levels. College students, in particular, need to get more sleep and develop more regular (consistent) sleeping habits.
- **Drink alcohol responsibly or not at all.** We should avoid excessive consumption of alcohol or other mind-altering substances that can threaten our physical health, impair our mental judgment, and increase our tendency to engage in dangerous, risk-taking behavior.
- **Minimize the risk of contracting sexually transmitted infections.** College students have basically three options for doing so: using latex condoms during sex, limiting the number of sexual partners they have, or choosing not to be sexually active.

In the introduction to this book, research was cited about the advantages of the college experience and college degree. Among the many benefits experienced by college graduates are health and wellness benefits: they live healthier, longer lives. This suggests that students manage to learn something about physical wellness and how to promote it by the time they graduate from college. The strategies discussed in this chapter can be implemented immediately to promote optimal health and peak performance throughout your college experience and beyond.

Learning More through the World Wide Web

Internet-Based Resources for Further Information on Health and Wellness

For additional information related to the ideas discussed in this chapter, we recommend the following Web sites:

Nutrition:

www.eatright.org

Fitness:

www.fitness.gov/resource-center/

Sleep:

www.sleepfoundation.org

Alcohol and Drugs:

www.nida.nih.gov

Sexual Harassment, Assault, and Abuse

www.princeton.edu/uhs/healthy-living/hot-topics/sexual-harassment-assault/

Chapter 12 Exercises

12.1 Wellness Self-Assessment and Self-Improvement

For each aspect of wellness listed here, rate yourself in terms of how close you are to doing what you should be doing (1 = furthest from the ideal, 5 = closest to the ideal).

	Nowhere Close to What I Should Be Doing	Not Bad but Should Be Better	Right Where I Should Be
Nutrition			
Exercise			
Sleep			
Alcohol and Drugs			

For each area where there's a gap between where you are now and where you should be, identify the best action you could take to reduce or eliminate this gap.

12.2 Nutritional Self-Assessment and Self-Improvement

1. Go to p. 330 and review the MyPlate chart in Figure 12.3.

2. For each of the five food groups listed below, record the amount recommended for you to consume daily, and next to it, estimate the amount you consume on a daily basis.

Basic Food Type	Amount Recommended	Amount Consumed
Fruits		
Vegetables		
Grains		
Protein Foods		
Dairy		

3. For any food group for which you're consuming less than the recommended amounts, click on that group at www.choosemyplate.gov/food-groups/ and find foods you would be willing to consume to meet the recommended daily amount. Write down those items, and answer the following questions about each of them:

    a. How likely is it that you'll actually add this food item to your regular diet?

        very likely   possibly   very unlikely

    b. If you did not answer "very likely," what would prevent you from adding this food item to your regular diet?

Drinking to Death: College Partying Gone Wild

At least 50 college students nationwide die each year as a result of drinking incidents on or near campus. During a one-month period in fall 1997, three college students died as a result of binge drinking at college parties. One was an 18-year-old first-year student at a private university who collapsed after drinking a mixture of beer and rum, fell into a coma at his fraternity house, and died three days later. He had a blood-alcohol level of more than .40, which is about equal to gulping down 20 shots of liquor in one hour.

The second incident involved a student from a public university in the South who died of alcohol poisoning (overdose). The third student died at another public university in the Northeast United States where, after an evening of partying and heavy drinking, he accidentally fell off a building in the middle of the night and fell through the roof of a greenhouse. Some colleges in the Northeast now have student volunteers roaming the campus on cold winter nights to make sure that no students freeze to death after passing out from an intense bout of binge drinking.

Listed below are some strategies that have been suggested by politicians to stop or reduce the problem of dangerous binge drinking:

1. A state governor announced that he was going to launch a series of radio ads designed to discourage underage drinking.

2. A senator filed bills to toughen penalties for those who violate underage drinking laws, such as producing and using fake identification cards.

3. A group of city council members was going to look into stiffening penalties for liquor stores that deliver directly to fraternity houses.

Reflection and Discussion Questions

1. Rank the effectiveness of these three strategies for stopping or reducing the problem of binge drinking mentioned in the last paragraph (1 = the most effective strategy, 3 = the least effective).

2. Comparing your highest-ranked and lowest-ranked choices:

   a. Why did you rank the first one as most effective?

   b. Why did you rank the last one as least effective?

3. What other strategies do you think would be effective for stopping or reducing dangerous binge drinking among college students?